Also by Hadley Freeman

*House of Glass: The Story and Secrets of a
Twentieth-Century Jewish Family*

Hadley Freeman

Good Girls

A STORY AND STUDY OF ANOREXIA

Simon & Schuster

NEW YORK   LONDON   TORONTO   SYDNEY   NEW DELHI

Certain names and identifying details have been changed.

Simon & Schuster
1230 Avenue of the Americas
New York, NY 10020

First Simon & Schuster hardcover edition April 2023

SIMON & SCHUSTER and colophon are registered trademarks
of Simon & Schuster, Inc.

For information about special discounts for bulk purchases, please contact Simon &
Schuster Special Sales at 1-866-506-1949 or business@simonandschuster.com.

The Simon & Schuster Speakers Bureau can bring authors to your live event. For more
information or to book an event, contact the Simon & Schuster Speakers Bureau at
1-866-248-3049 or visit our website at www.simonspeakers.com.

Manufactured in the United States of America

10   9   8   7   6   5   4   3   2   1

Library of Congress Cataloging-in-Publication Data is available.

ISBN 978-1-9821-8983-9
ISBN 978-1-9821-8985-3 (ebook)

For my cousin Catie Lazarus, whom I will always miss

When you're trying hard to be your best
Could you be a little less?

—Madonna, "What It Feels Like for a Girl"

Stay with me, the world is dark and wild,
Stay a child while you can be a child.

—Stephen Sondheim, *Into the Woods*

Contents

Introduction

Diary entry, December 3, 1995:

I just spent three years of my life in mental hospitals. So why am I crazier than I was before????

From the ages of fourteen to seventeen, I lived in various psychiatric wards, all close enough to my home in London so my parents could bring my homework on the weekends but not so close that I could actually attend school, which I wasn't allowed to do anyway. This would have been unimaginable to me—and my parents—when I was thirteen, when my biggest concerns were how well I had done on my French test and whether I should quit violin lessons to focus on my GCSEs. But shortly after my fourteenth birthday, I very suddenly stopped eating, that most basic of human activities that even infants can do. (I also soon after stopped passing any waste due to the whole not-eating thing, so I guess I had regressed to the fetal stage by that point. A zygote. Atoms. Pure nothing.) When I was checked into the first hospital, my body was cannibalizing my muscles and heart for nutrition. I had developed, the doctor said, anorexia nervosa. He was right about that, but pretty much nothing else he told me about anorexia turned out to be correct: why I had it, what it felt like, or what life would be like when I was in so-called recovery. Even the name was wrong: anorexia nervosa, nervous loss of appetite.

1

I didn't feel nervous—anxious, depressed, manic and hope-less, yes, but not nervous—and I never lost my appetite (if only! That would have made matters much easier). It was all a constant, ever-reverberating shock, even though, on so many levels, I was an archetypal anorexic, so you'd have thought someone might have foreseen how all this would go for me and warn me. But I guess they hadn't, because they didn't.

I thought everything would be fine once I left hospital, and certainly once I reached the weight my doctor had set for me as a target, because that's what the treatment focused on. ("Just get up to your weight, dear, things will feel differ-ent then." Wrong again.) Every story people told me about anorexia ended, posttreatment, with the promise of happily ever after: "My neighbor's sister's lawyer's best friend's daugh-ter had anorexia. Admitted to St. George's for a bit and now she's at Cambridge!" Send the girls away, feed 'em up, and then they come home, right as rain. So why, posttreatment, was I spending my days alone in my bedroom, obsessively wash-ing my hands to the point that the skin around the knuckles broke? After three years of fearing food, I now feared my own skin and spent hours a day washing until I bled, and I bled everywhere: on my clothes, on rugs, and, of course, all over my diary, leaving bloody trails on the pages that have now faded to brown streaks: I WUZ HERE. And when I finished writing, I went to the sink to wash my hands again, because who knew what I might have picked up from touching the pages? My horizons were so narrow, so closed. Where was the wide expanse of my promised happily ever after?

For the next twenty years, I had two full-time jobs: being a functioning anorexic and being a functioning but extremely obsessive adult. This was very tiring, not least because I also, eventually, got a third full-time job, which was working as a journalist at a newspaper, although at least I got a salary and vacation time with that job, which was a lot more than I got from the other two. For a long time, I told no one about my past, because I worried they'd see the madness I tried so hard to hide. But anorexia leaves scars, from the illness itself and the treatment of it, that left me traumatized, institutionalized and in a state of deeply arrested development.

Anorexia is probably the most widely discussed of the mental illnesses, because the media and public will always be fascinated by extremely thin girls and young women. It is also one of the least understood. People think it's about wanting to be thin. They think it's just a matter of refeeding the patient. And they think it's a modern illness that is simply a response to modern preoccupations. Wrong, wrong and wrong. The term *anorexia nervosa* was coined in the nineteenth century, but the phenomenon of adolescent girls refusing to eat has existed for more than a millennium. Yet for a long time, no one was sure if girls who starved themselves were suffering from a disease or if it was extreme holiness or—to use the more modern expression of the same idea—perfectionism taken too far. Despite the inherent condescension in such assumptions, anorexia has the highest mortality rate of all psychiatric illnesses, and doctors still can't predict which patients will recover and which won't. My GP had told my mother to prepare for my death. I didn't die, but I didn't recover for a long time. I was in a gray fog that no one could explain to me, and so I didn't understand it.

In the United Kingdom, fewer than 1 percent of girls and women develop anorexia, and this has remained steady for decades.[1] Yet rates are going up among children under the age of twelve,[2] and during the Covid-19 pandemic there was a rise in hospital referrals.[3] I find this both devastating and enraging, because girls and women should not still be suffering like this. And it is, by and very large, girls and women, because one statistic does not change: 90 percent of anorexics are female.

Today's girls are struggling. They are doing well academically, but beneath the successful surface, there is frantic paddling. A 2019 *Lancet* study said that girls' rates of self-harm had tripled since 2000.[4] A 2022 study of 15,000 secondary school pupils found that girls are twice as likely to suffer mental health problems as boys by the age of eighteen, and they are also likely to try to hide them.[5] Girls as young as eleven are 30 percent more likely to experience mental health problems than boys.[6] It also found that 80 percent of schoolgirls have a fixation on "unhealthy perfectionism and extreme self-control"; only two years earlier, before the Covid pandemic, the figure was 20 percent. Extreme self-control and self-denial are how so many girls express anxiety, and anorexia is an extension of that all-too-common female tendency.

This epidemic of extreme anxiety among girls, often expressed through perfectionism, is now such a universally recognized problem that two of the most successful movies aimed at girls ever made, both by Disney, featured it as a major plotline. In *Frozen*, Elsa—the perfect but unreachable princess whose unhappiness hurts everyone around her, especially her family—sings at the beginning of her famous song, "Let It Go": "Don't let them in, don't let them see / Be the good girl you always have to be / Conceal, don't feel, don't let them know." In *Encanto*, Isabela—the perfect daughter, the golden child—sings in her song "What Else Can I Do?": "I make perfect, practiced poses / So much hides behind my smile . . . / What could I do if I just knew it didn't need to be perfect?" Snow White and Cinderella never expressed such frustrations. By the end of both songs, the characters have progressed, promising "That perfect girl is gone" (Elsa) and "I'm so sick of pretty, I want something true" (Isabela). They realize their perfectionism was stifling their strength and talents. But neither film asks whether their anxiety came from an external source or was internally generated, and neither offers advice to their largely young and female audiences about how they, too, can stop caring so much about being perfect (building a magic ice palace, as Elsa does, or creating magical cacti, as Isabela does, are options for a very select few). Also, both of these characters are beautiful, thin and in possession of magical powers, somewhat undermining the films' message that girls don't have to be perfect to be enough.

Elsa and Isabela knew they were perfect and felt trapped by it. I longed to be perfect and was trapped by this ambition, paralyzed with shame over my flaws. Not eating, I thought, would help me achieve my aim, or at least excuse all my gross imperfections, although no one else around me agreed. But by the time I left hospital for the last time in the mid-1990s, they had come round to my way of thinking. The trend crudely known as "heroin chic" was taking off in the fashion industry at this point, when models so thin they looked like drug addicts were considered the epitome of elegance. This was followed by the "size zero" craze in the celebrity world in the 2000s, when famous women boasted about being a nonexistent clothing size (there has never been a more perfect expression of that feminine desire for self-erasure than "size zero"). Newspapers were full of editorials fretting about how this would surely spark an epidemic of anorexia, but as I read them, I recognized nothing of my own experience. These people were talking about drizzle when I had drowned. All the factors that have been blamed over the years—religion, models, social media—play a part in anorexia, because they are part of the culture in which those girls lived and live, and so they give an external shape to their internal unhappiness. So they are contributory factors, but they are not the cause, and root causes never change much. Anorexia is, in my experience, an astonishingly consistent disease in its message and expression, even if too many people willfully refuse to understand it.

As I said, I avoided talking about this for a long time, and I avoided writing this book for longer: there is so much else going on in the world, was I really going to sit here, staring at my belly button? Also, I was scared, still, of revealing how unhinged I was, during and for a long time after the illness. Was I really willing to cough up my blood in public?

It's been twenty-five years since I left hospital for the last time, and I am now at an age when many of my friends are parents to teenagers. Every so often, I get a quiet message from one of them, saying they're so sorry to bother me, but, see, their daughter has stopped eating and they know that I, well . . . But of course, my experience was so long ago, I probably barely remember it and I mustn't reply to this if it's a bother *at all.* The messages are anxiously polite, the pain within them palpable.

I remember everything about being ill. Of course I do. It was the most formative experience of my life. I remember promising to eat the toast my mother gave me for breakfast and then shredding it behind me on the way to the bus stop, like Hansel and Gretel leaving their trail of crumbs; I remember the expression on the doctor's face when he weighed me every week; the view through the windows of all my different hospital rooms. I kept diaries, because I was lonely and I needed to talk to someone who understood, and so I talked to myself.

That's what I remember perhaps most of all: the loneliness. I genuinely didn't understand what was happening to me, nor, it often seemed, did anyone else. So I eventually decided to write this book in the hope it might make some people feel a bit less lonely, to tell them things I wish I'd known at the time, and also to tell them that the present does not have to be a life sentence: things can get unimaginably better. Life can be enjoyed, rather than merely endured. I also wrote it for those who love them in order to give them hope, but also to brace them for the reality that there is rarely a neat "job's done" ending when it comes to mental illness. And I wrote it for anyone who wants to understand, because I think people do want to understand, and how can they unless those of us who have had it are willing to speak up and say that it really isn't about the food? It's about trying to say something without having to speak; it's about fear of sexualization and fear of womanhood; it's about sadness and anger and the belief you're not allowed to be sad and angry because you're supposed to be perfect; and it's about feeling completely overwhelmed by the world so you create a new, smaller world with one easy-to-understand rule: don't eat.

Also, I wrote this book for me, because there were still some things I didn't understand about anorexia: What makes some girls susceptible to anorexia when others can resist it, even when raised in the same environment, surrounded by the same cultural influences? Have treatments changed since I was in hospital, and has medical understanding of the disorder improved since I was in hospital, when it was rudimentary at best? I had heard that hospital programs for anorexics are now more individualized than they were in my day, when we were all given the same food and expected to gain weight at exactly the same rate. Why had things changed? What do doc-

7

tors think now about how I was treated? And most of all, why did I recover and so many others I knew didn't? To answer those questions, I combined the two halves of my life—the anorexic half and the journalist half—and interviewed not just the brilliant psychiatrist who finally got me into recovery, Professor Janet Treasure, but also over a dozen doctors working in eating disorders, adolescent psychiatry, neurology and autism health care. I tracked down some of the women I was in hospital with thirty years ago to find out how their lives had panned out and how they feel about their experience now, and I spoke with girls and young women suffering from the illness today to learn about their experiences. I read through medical and psychiatric studies into the illness and its comorbidities, and also various landmark cases that have changed the treatment of anorexia, one of which, I learned during my research, was inspired by a young woman I was very close to in hospital. And finally, I went back to the last hospital where I was treated to see how things had changed there, and how they hadn't. Personal experience is important, especially when talking about mental illness. But it also has its limits. I learned an enormous amount from experts while working on this book, so much so that I can now say the door to this part of my life, which stayed open in my mind for decades due to lingering questions, has finally closed.

This is not an encyclopedia of anorexia. It is, as the title says, a story about it, a story of girls who become restricting anorexics, which is the most common subtype of anorexia, and it means the person loses weight by restricting their food intake and, often, exercising. The other less common subtype is anorexia with bingeing and purging (the eating disorder term for vomiting), and what differentiates that from bulimia is that the patient is extremely underweight, which is a symptom of anorexia, whereas bulimics are generally at a relatively average weight. Anorexia can overlap with bulimia, and I've known anorexics who later develop bulimia, but I haven't written about bulimia here, because the physical and therefore mental effects of it are very different from those of anorexia, even though the two disorders are often grouped together. I think of them as cousins: there is some shared DNA, and they're often at the same places at the same time, but the differences are soon apparent.

Nor have I written about male anorexia. I shared wards with several male anorexics during my treatment, and they were, like most anorexia patients, kind, gentle and sad. But male anorexia, while certainly sharing some roots with the far more common female version, differs enormously in many aspects, not least in public attitudes toward it. This book is rooted in my own experience, and my experience was so typical of many anorexics' experience that I decided to focus on that, rather than trying to cover all ground.

There are things in this book with which some readers will disagree. Some may dislike my interpretations of anorexia, and that's to be expected: mental illness is extremely personal. Some will object to my occasional use of the term "an anorexic" rather than the now-preferred "a patient with anorexia." I've thought about this a lot, and of course I can see the merit in the latter, as it emphasizes that the person is not simply the illness, that they have an identity beyond it. This is hugely important for patients to remember, especially during recovery and especially for young people, who have always sought out prefabricated identities—from goth to jock—as they grow up, to explore who they are independent from their parents. But I also think there is value in the term "an anorexic," because it was only when I understood that the anorexia came from within me—as opposed to its being an external force, like a virus I had caught from somewhere—that I began to take control over my recovery. Alcoholics have understood this for a long time, which is why AA meetings begin with the famous introduction "I'm so-and-so, and I'm an alcoholic," and anorexia and addiction share certain traits. Also, when I was in the absolute grip of anorexia, I really was just an anorexic: there was nothing else in my life, the anorexia controlled every second of every day, every uttered word from my mouth, every fleeting thought in my head. I was no longer myself, and anyone who has had anorexia or known someone with it will have seen that transformation themselves. So I've used the term in this book when I believe it reflected my experience.

People blame anorexia on outside influences, because it shields them from acknowledging the internal confusion, guilt, shame, sadness, fear and rage that girls and women feel, and also the social strictures that prevent them—still—from articulating those feelings. So they turn them further inward, punishing themselves and all those who love them. Where that fear and rage often come from is what this book is about.

Chapter 1

The Trigger

May–August 1992

It was a warm spring day in London when I lost myself entirely and my mind and body became possessed by a stranger. It was the transformation of a minute, a shuddering loss of innocence, a single comment and the way I saw the world changed forever. This is probably of little consolation to any parents reading this who have watched their daughter go through a similar mutation, but if you found this shift bewildering, I promise it was far more so for her.

It happened in May 1992, just after my fourteenth birthday. Summer was starting to click in, and the whole school had that looseness and lightness that come when it gets warm enough to leave your blazer at home and the prospect of the long vacation becomes tangible. Despite the fine weather, we were told we were having PE inside, in the gym. As PE developments went, this was good news, because while throwing a ball around the gym wasn't my preferred pastime, it was definitely preferable to running up and down the hockey pitch. Some kids grow up playing football on the weekends, having swimming lessons in the summer, taking to exercise as naturally as splashing in puddles. This kid was not those kids. Teachers often described me with the twee word *bookish*, but really, I was just lazy and happiest inside, ideally sitting, with a book or watching a movie. I wasn't fussed, just as long as it required absolutely no exertion of energy. My parents were the same, so I grew up thinking of exercise as something other people did, like going to church or bungee jumping, and PE was my most dreaded school lesson, because while I could train myself to memorize historical dates and French irregular verbs, I couldn't do much about the fact that I ran like an asthmatic chicken. But I loved my PE kit: the white Aertex, the stiff gray gym skirt, the knee-high socks. The formality pleased me, especially compared to the sloppy T-shirt-and-blue-cotton-shorts combo I'd worn for gym at my school in New York.

I had moved to London with my parents and younger sister, Nell, when I was eleven, and although I vaguely missed the friends and very specifically the dog we'd left behind, I loved being in London. I liked the old-fashioned starchiness of my new school, with its Victorian building and rigid rules that let everyone know what was expected of them. I clung to rules like rungs on a ladder: they were reassuring, grounding, and they told me what I was supposed to do and, most important, if I was doing it well. Also, I liked who I was in London. At my school in Manhattan, I'd felt like a nobody: I wasn't one of the superrich kids, which back at my school was synonymous with being one of the popular kids, and I obviously wasn't one of the sporty kids, who automatically gained admittance to the cool clique. I knew I wasn't especially pretty, and despite what my parents said, I also knew I wasn't all that smart, because I was always in the middle stream for math. I pictured myself as an absence, not one thing or another, just average and definitely not special.

I also felt like I was being pushed into a world where I

didn't understand the rules. The summer before we moved, a bunch of my friends at camp were caught kissing boys behind our cabin with their T-shirts off. I didn't even know why a girl would take her T-shirt off with a boy, but I knew it was very wrong to do so, because they all got into big trouble. I'd started going to after-school ballroom dancing lessons in New York, which was something kids from my part of Manhattan did, maintaining an Upper East Side fantasy that we all still lived in an Edith Wharton novel. At the last dance, a boy put his hand on my bottom. Again, I couldn't understand why a boy would want to touch my bottom, but I knew I didn't like it. But I also knew that admitting I didn't like it—like admitting I didn't know why a boy would want to see my chest—would make people laugh at me. So I said nothing, to him, to anyone.

In London, all of these issues vanished. I was still terrible at sports—although that seemed to matter less to kids in the United Kingdom than it did in the United States—and being placed, again, in the middle stream for math caused the usual anguish. But at last, I had an identity: I was the American girl. Sure, the other girls in my class had more defined identities, it seemed to me—this one was good at tennis, that one was bilingual—but I'd take American. When you feel like an absence, you grab on to any identity that might give you shape, even if just to yourself. And far from feeling excluded, I found being an American outsider worked in my favor because I didn't yet understand the English social codes, so I sailed with happy oblivion past the inferiorities I'd struggled with in New York, English class snobbery being far more subtle than American flashiness. Being an outsider also meant that I wasn't part of any London social scene, and so for the first year or two I wasn't invited to the dances attended by the various schoolkids in West London, and my bottom remained safely untouched.

But that could last only so long. A few months before that afternoon in the gym, a girl in my class invited me to her birthday party held in her local sports club. Initially things seemed fine: boys and girls gazing suspiciously at one another from across the room, just as God intended. But when the adults left and someone turned the lights out, the room turned into a Hieronymus Bosch painting. Girls I'd been talking to mere minutes before disappeared under the snacks table with boys to do . . . what? I had no idea. But I didn't like it. I left the party and walked until I found a public phone box, called my mother and told her to come pick me up. A few weeks later, we were learning about reproduction in biology class, much to my classmates' amusement.

"This is the symbol for the male," our teacher, Mr. Templeton, said, drawing a circle and an upward-pointing arrow. "You can probably guess why." Everyone around me fell into hysterics, but I was bewildered. An arrow? What? Pretending I hadn't been able to hear, I asked the girl next to me why people were laughing, hoping she would explain the joke. Soon after that, a friend told me she had a boyfriend. I retorted that I had a secret older sister, a response that had the misfortune of being unimpressive, irrelevant and untrue. I was starting to do things—lying, light shoplifting—that I couldn't explain even to myself. The grown-up world was pressing in, monsters making the door bulge inward while I frantically tried to push them back.

It was the end of PE, thank God; no more trying to climb up a rope or not get hit by a ball or whatever important life skill we'd learned that day, and so we all sat in a circle around Miss Hall, as we did at the end of every PE class. Today, I happened to be sitting next to Lizzie Cooper, whom I didn't know that well, but whose identity in our class was that she was the thinnest. Our class was divided between the curvy girls who needed bras and the skinny girls who still wore undershirts. I was pleased to be part of the latter group for reasons that weren't entirely about aesthetics but also weren't not about aesthetics. I stretched my legs out in front of me. I liked the way they looked coming out of my loose PE skirt, and I loved my knee-high socks. I looked, I thought, like an ink drawing in an Enid Blyton book, rangy and scrappy. Next to Lizzie's bony limbs, though, my legs looked like matronly trunks, her thighs narrower than my calves. I'd never thought about Lizzie's skinniness before, but when I asked, "Is it hard to buy clothes when you're so small?" I felt a small ache. Imagine being so special that they don't even make clothes in your size.

"Yeah," she said. "I wish I was normal like you."

A black tunnel yawned open inside me, and I tumbled down it, Alice into Nowhereland. "Normal." Not "slim," not "thin"—"normal." Normal was average. Normal was boring. Normal was nothing. I looked down: when had my thighs become so much bigger than my knees? I leaned forward so I could inspect matters close up. My inner thighs, instead of going straight down like they should, ballooned outward, like drumsticks. The Snickers bar I'd had at lunch sat in my stomach like a bruise. And speaking of my stomach, was the waistband of my PE skirt . . . pinching? Were those . . . fat rolls? I thought of images I'd seen on the news of obese kids walking around on beaches, their flesh overlapping on itself like folds of cream. How had I been able to sit all day in school with these rolls on my tummy? How had I been able to concentrate at all?

I had been eating more recently, I had noticed that: stuffing down slabs of cheese and bowls of cereal when I came home from school. "I don't know how you can eat so much!" a friend of my mother's said as I ate two bowls of Frosties while watching *Neighbours*. I shrugged, but the comment had clearly lingered because it now banged around my brain. I was hungrier these days, and my parents said it was because I was growing. My mother had often told me I could eat anything and stay slim, because I was lucky. My mother, I now realized, had lied. When I think of that moment in PE, I think not of myself but of a china doll sitting on a bookshelf, protected and perfect, and suddenly, who knows why—maybe age, maybe atmospheric pressures, maybe just an internal weakness—a crack scores across her face. Just like that.

Doctors call it the "precipitant," or trigger: the moment that sets off the anorexia. I knew some girls whose illness was sparked by what most people would see as an obvious trigger: a father commenting that his daughter looks "a bit plump" in a family photo, a teenager wanting to be the same clothing size as her friend. But I know many others who were triggered by something far less predictable: one woman I met in hospital was worried about germs after a bout of food poisoning. Another stopped eating after her mother died and someone told her she needed to look after her father, which she took to mean she should stop looking after herself; by the time her father brought her into hospital, she was so ill she could no longer walk. I was told I looked normal. Anything would have triggered us, because the anorexia was a bomb inside us, just waiting for the right time, the single flame, the trigger.

And after the trigger, the fall. For some, it creeps up slowly as a cat. They become fussy eaters one year, get into jogging the next, dabbling with weight loss on and off during their

teenage years before the eventual collapse at university. But
my fall was instantaneous and vertiginous. Utterly ignorant as
to how diets or the body work, I cut out whole food groups.
Then meals. I constructed a world built on my own rules,
and I'd never obeyed any more faithfully in my life. Within a
month, I went from being a cheerful fourteen-year-old who
told my parents everything and would sing songs from MGM
musicals while Rollerblading in the garden to being a furious unreachable adolescent who every night, in front of the
mirror in my mother's bathroom, would stand naked, staring
and glaring. Initially I focused on my tummy, because that
was the part of the body that I knew denoted fatness, but I
would learn soon enough there were plenty more. I did jaw
exercises, as Oprah Winfrey advocated, to tighten any possible double chin. I joined a Bums & Tums class at my local
gym and was the youngest attendee by at least three decades. I
lifted weights—gotta tone those bat wings on your fourteen-
year-old arms! I jumped up and down in aerobics classes and
ran on the treadmill, so much movement to stay in exactly the
same place. The girl who used to fake injuries to get out of PE
was now doing hundreds of jumping jacks—and sit-ups and
push-ups and leg lifts and squats—every day. Such a shame it
was in the summer vacation, otherwise I might have gotten
my first good mark in PE. We had to burn the fat, the aerobics teachers shouted. Joan of Arc heard voices and dressed as
a man, and for that she was tied to a stake to burn her body
away. I also heard a new voice inside me, and I had adopted
baggy clothes, but I only had to go to a high-impact step class
for the burning. From that perspective, I had a pretty great
deal.

Being a woman seemed like an unceasing battle against
one's body, and I thought I was gaming the system by start-

ing early. If I do it now, my thinking went, at least I won't have a bum or a tum or a chin or any of these other womanly body parts that need erasing. Exercise was such a natural next step for me after starving because it was part of the same masochism: What can be more self-punishing than exercising obsessively when you hate exercise? Oh, you think you're suffering now, body, because I haven't fed you for two days? Just wait to see how you feel after a thousand jumping jacks. I couldn't escape my own thoughts: Am I taking in calories when I chew on my lips? Or walking past a supermarket? I crossed the road in front of Sainsbury's, just to make sure, and I decided lips were okay but lip balm definitely not, so my mouth became raw and scabby. Life took on an intense and claustrophobic hue, and it just so happened that my school had given us an especially intense reading list that summer: *The Bell Jar*, *The French Lieutenant's Woman*, *The Life and Loves of a She-Devil*. I don't blame John Fowles for my anorexia, but he did make an effective soundtrack for it.

In July, I was sent home early from the school French exchange because the host family felt they couldn't be responsible for me. "*Si je ne mange pas, je vais mourir*," I said grandly to my poor exchange host, who shrugged back, confused. I said I just wanted to be thin, but I also, it seemed, wanted to terrify people. I succeeded. In August I ruined our family vacation to the South of France, my mother crying in her hotel room while I did sit-ups in mine. My sister furiously refused to speak to me and my father took extra helpings at the buffet, trying to eat for me. I'd now entered that dizzying stage of starvation when all the senses become sharper and keen. Thirty years on, I can still remember the smell of the hotel kitchen that I had to walk past when I went down to the pool to do laps, the thick smell of food going claggy in the hot

Mediterranean wind, my nose desperately snuffling away at it, the scent repelling and enthralling me. In photos from that vacation, I am not yet skeletal, but the skin is pinching around my face, outlining where my jaw meets my cheekbone; when I smiled, my eyes stayed hollow, sockets in a skull.

"I want to be thin," "I feel fat": those became my mantras that summer. But I had as much understanding of the body as you'd expect of an emotionally immature fourteen-year-old. My parents didn't even own a set of scales. All I had to go by was how I looked in front of my mother's mirror: How much did my tummy stick out, how chunky did my legs look, how could I bear to sit with myself, me and all that flesh? As guides went, they were imperfect.

These days, thinness is a symbol of aspiration, sexiness and wealth, and this has made many people believe anorexia is about wanting to look like a model or celebrity. Less frequently noted is that skinniness has also long been a symbol of stoic strength, silent distress and internal rage, especially among women, as those women from centuries past, Catherine of Siena, Rose of Lima and Orsola Giuliani, aka Saint Veronica, whose refusal of food resulted in their being deified, knew well.[1] Some[2] argue that those ancient saints should not be discussed alongside modern anorexics, because it is impossible to compare fifteenth-century women with twenty-first-century ones, which is true. But it is also true that the phenomenon of women starving themselves has endured for millennia, and even if they were not classed as suffering from the same syndrome, they all learned that a woman not eating is an effective way for her to seize control when she feels otherwise powerless. It has always been a very visible way of communicating that something is not right when you feel unable to vocalize those words. It's a way of asking for help, although I'm sure that will sound ironic to any parents enduring daily battles with their furiously stubborn child. But if they didn't want you to know they're unhappy, they wouldn't be expressing it so publicly, rejecting food at the family table, losing weight in front of everybody. They would be quietly self-harming or secretly taking drugs. They would have chosen a language more private. "Feeling fat has become a code language for feeling insecure, unimportant, scared or anxious. With anorexia, one's underlying feelings are more extreme, often representing deep wounds that are encoded in body language," Hilde Bruch wrote in her seminal 1978 book about anorexia, *The Golden Cage*, which helped to broaden awareness in the medical community that anorexia was not just an extreme diet. Although that belief certainly persisted among the media and wider public. In 1981, only two years before she died, Karen Carpenter was interviewed on the BBC. Her illness was painfully obvious: chin sharp as a point, knee bones pointy and palpable within her trousers. Sue Lawley asked her if she had been suffering from "the slimmer's disease, anorexia." "No," Carpenter replied, rolling her eyes at her brother.

When *The Karen Carpenter Story*, a biopic of Carpenter's short life, was first aired on US TV in 1989, the media reaction was polite and positive, accompanied by wide-eyed explainers of what anorexia nervosa is ("a severe dieting disorder," according to one review[3]). When Netflix's fictionalized film about anorexia, *To the Bone*, was released in 2017, it sparked a wave of outrage at its potentially "triggering" nature.[4] I became ill in 1992, just before the transitional moment when the illness shifted from being seen by outsiders as "dieting gone wrong" to a serious mental health problem with an identifiable and external cause. The wan and wasted look became fashionable in the mid-1990s, at which point politicians and the media suddenly grew very exercised about what they saw as the triggering influence of the fashion industry on the minds of the young. But that was still to come. In 1992, Carpenter had died nine years earlier, her poor wasted heart finally giving out at the age of just thirty-three. People were slowly—very slowly—beginning to accept that maybe it wasn't just dieting that had killed her. But what had?

Lots of culturally sanctioned messages are beamed out around us, telling us how to have a happy life: Get rich! Be popular! And famous! Drink alcohol! Have lots of sex! But not too much! Get married! And have children! But never age! Yet for reasons that I didn't understand until many years later, from that moment in the school gym when I was told that I was normal, tall antennae sprouted out of my head that sought out only messages telling me to make myself as small as possible, and I found many. Once I had thought of the newsagent as the place where I bought *Smash Hits* and Snickers bars. Now all I saw there was the row of diet and fitness magazines. It was like discovering a secret world that had been there all along but I'd been too blithe to notice it until now. How had I been so stupid as to not understand that the only point to life was to be thin?

People often get distracted by the trigger when it comes to anorexia. It seems so inexplicable, this decision to starve yourself, so of course they want to know why, and because there's always a simple trigger—anxiety about exams, say, or a gauche comment, or a fascination with a fashion model—that seems to be the answer. Bish bosh, mystery solved. If it wasn't so belittling, I would find it almost quaint how many people still don't understand that the cause is very different from the trigger. Have these people ever seen an anorexic? Do they honestly think all that masochism is powered simply by *Vogue* magazine or TikTok? Can they really not see what is standing right there in front of them, polite flesh stripped away so all that's left is anger, misery and fear?

"People make the mistake of thinking of anorexia as a behavioral disorder, one to do with skipping meals and exercising obsessively. But those behaviors have become very common in our society among women who aren't actually anorexic," Professor Hubert Lacey, director of the Eating Disorders Service at St. George's Hospital in London, tells me. "Anorexia nervosa has a pathognomonic psychopathology, which is that the sufferers have a very deep-rooted fear—a phobia, even—of looking, in a sense, well." In other words, anorexia is not a desire to be thin—it's a desire to look ill.

Anorexics have a mental illness, but they are not stupid. They know that healthily thin—slim—people eat more than two apples a day, weigh more than seventy pounds, don't exercise for six hours at a time. That's because they don't want to be slim; they want to waste away. This is one of the big differences between anorexia and bulimia, as women with bulimia generally want to be slim; women with anorexia want to look skeletal. Both are forms of self-hatred and self-punishment, but their expression is very different. So when anorexics say that very common but seemingly nonsensical anorexic statement that they see themselves, even at their most frail, as fat, they're telling the truth: they see themselves as fat because they're fatter than they want to be.

Anorexics themselves also confuse the cause and the trigger, because when the illness clamps around their brain, they will fixate on anything that confirms their rationale: skinny celebrities on TV, diet magazines in newsagents, detox suggestions on Goop. They tend to be able to say very easily what their trigger was, because it is on the surface, shallow and specific—unlike the actual cause of the illness, which is deep-rooted, hidden and complex. But when an anorexic says, "I don't want to be fat, I want to be thin," they are saying, "I want to be other than what I am, and what I am is unhappy. I want to be someone else." And once you understand that, you understand that the trigger is not the point, because when a person is that unhappy, anything can be a trigger.

Trigger warnings didn't become popular until the 2000s, first on American university campuses and originally to warn readers about potentially upsetting content in books in an effort to avoid exacerbating the trauma suffered by female victims of sexual violence. So in 1992 there certainly weren't warnings in women's magazines that an article about diets was "potentially triggering," as is often the case today, and if for some reason a story about eating disorders was featured on the TV news, it wasn't prefaced with the comment that "some viewers may find this upsetting."

None of these would have made the slightest difference to me. Discussions about trigger warnings these days tend to collapse into arguments about whether the public is being sensibly protected or unduly coddled. A more useful question is whether they help anyone significantly (and studies have shown they do not[5]). But I have a bigger objection to them when it comes to anorexia, which is that focusing on potential triggers of anorexia is a grasp for control over the illness, and that control doesn't exist.

One of my favorite movies is *When Harry Met Sally*, and one line in it flashed like a live wire for me the first time I saw it, shortly before I became really ill. It was not "I'll have what she's having" or "Men and women can't be friends" but a decidedly less celebrated one. It comes when Harry is talking to Sally about running into his ex-wife: "Her legs looked heavy, really. She must be retaining water."

It's a funny line, Harry trying to cover up his heartbreak by denigrating his ex in the most banal way. But all I heard was that even men like Harry judge women on their appearance, and here was yet another body part I needed to worry about. (Also: Water is fattening. Who knew?) Years later, when I'd been out of hospital for more than a decade, the Streets' album *A Grand Don't Come for Free* was released, and my favorite song on it was the final one, "Empty Cans." But the last lines made me wistful:

My jeans feel a bit tight, think I washed them too high
I was gonna be late, so I picked up my pace to run.

Imagine, I thought. Imagine being so at ease with the space you take up in the world that your jeans pinching into your waist—your tummy!—doesn't immediately send you down a spiral of self-disgust but rather makes you casually think of your washing machine.

Parents don't like to hear this kind of talk, and I understand that. They want guarantees about how to protect their child, to be told that if they ban this or don't let them see that, then everything will be fine. But when you're vulnerable, the whole world is a trigger. After all, millions of other people can look at photos of models or be told they look "normal" without becoming anorexic, so the issue isn't the trigger but the triggered. An upsetting comment is upsetting only if you find it so. A friend who works in TV once asked me if I thought a program he was making about diets would "upset" people with eating disorders, to which the answer was, of course. But so will songs by the Streets and Nora Ephron jokes. Of course people should stop equating thinness with achievement, because it makes a lot of people—anorexic and not—unhappy. But you cannot remodel the world to protect those who are constantly looking for justifications to hurt themselves.

Many years after that PE lesson, I came home from work to find my flat flooded. The rugs were sodden, the sofa already stained, the skirting boards a mulchy mess. The plumber told me it had happened because someone upstairs had left their tap dripping, which had somehow cracked a blocked pipe and then flooded through my ceiling. Tearfully, I asked how a small drip could cause such damage, and he showed me the broken pipe. It was totally corroded, years of rust gnawing away at metal, grit and grime pushing down on the cracks. The drip had been a tiny thing, but the damage was already there, years and years and years of it, and if it hadn't been that drip, it would have been another, because that's how the pipe reacted to the accumulation. Other pipes can endure such drips, no problem. But occasionally, one pipe reacts differently, and no one really knows why. But they sure have a lot of theories.

Chapter 2

The Theories

An incomplete list of reasons doctors, therapists and outsiders have given over the years for why I became anorexic.
Because:

I was born by caesarean
I was the firstborn
My mother worked before I was born
My mother didn't work after I was born
My father worked too much
My parents gave me too much
My parents didn't give me enough
My parents were too strict
My parents were too indulgent
My parents cared too much about my academic
    achievements
My parents didn't care enough about my academic
    achievements
I was too close in age to my sister
I didn't have any brothers
I grew up in Manhattan
I moved to London
I went to private schools

I went to an all-girls school
I was too smart for my school
I was not smart enough for my school
My school was too rigid
My school was too flexible
I did ballet as a child
I was vegetarian
I was overly verbal
I couldn't express myself
I spent too much time on my own
I had an imbalance in the part of my brain that regulates
 appetite
I had an imbalance in the part of my brain that regulates
 mood
I had an imbalance in the part of my brain that regulates
 self-perception
I had a hormonal imbalance
I was just unbalanced
I was exposed to toxins as a baby
I read too much
I watched too many movies
I put too much pressure on myself
I wanted to skip school
I was on the autism spectrum
I was too mature for my age
I was painfully immature
I am Jewish
I had inherited trauma from the Holocaust
I felt survivor's guilt about the Holocaust
I wanted attention
I wanted to disappear
I was bullied

I wanted to be beautiful
I wanted to be ugly
I was a narcissist
I was abused as a child
I was sexually abused at summer camp
I was depressed
I was bipolar
I was obsessed with sex
I had an aversion to sex
I was gay
I wanted to be a boy
I wanted to be Kate Moss
I was part of the zeitgeist
I was privileged
I was bored
I was strong
I was fragile
I was precocious
I had mother issues
I had father issues
I was a spoiled brat
I was a masochist
I was a sadist
I wanted to die
I wanted to stay a child
I wanted independence
I was just going through a phase
I was a darling
I was a demon
I was a lamb

How do you solve a problem like an unhappy teenage girl?

Chapter 3

Childhood

New York and London, 1984–1992

When I was six years old, I learned a painful lesson: I could not do the splits. I would soon learn a worse one. My best friend, Abigail, could stretch out her legs at a 180-degree angle with such ease that I believed I could, too. I was wrong. I hovered far above the floor, legs in a V shape, like a wobbly compass, and burst into tears.

"Oh, Hadley, what's wrong?" my teacher Miss Moss said to me.

"I wish I was Abigail, I hate me!" I sobbed.

Miss Moss's eyes filled with tears: "Oh, don't say that! You shouldn't ever say that!" she said.

This was interesting. I'd never before had an effect like this on an adult. I could make my mother cross by teasing my little sister, sure. But I'd never seen an adult cry, let alone been the cause of it. I tentatively tested my new powers.

"I do. I hate Hadley," I said with more fierceness than I felt.

"Oh, sweetheart!" she said.

"I hate me."

"No!"

Poor Miss Moss. She was probably, at most, twenty-four, and had gone into teaching because she loved little children, and I was exactly the kind of little child such teachers loved: well behaved and always desirous of adult approval. Doing things well, I'd quickly grasped, brought me praise, but suddenly there was a glitch in the system. What if your determination to do well upset the grown-ups around you? I looked at Miss Moss's sweet, sad face, baffled as to how her Little Miss Sunshine had turned into a raging storm cloud, and the lesson I learned was this: never tell people how you really feel, because it will destroy them.

The recurring dream, the one in which I tried to speak and no sound came out of my mouth, wouldn't come for another decade. I dreamed that several times a year, sometimes several times a week, from my early teens to my midthirties. But my memories of my school years are a patchwork of moments when I felt like the Little Mermaid, walking but voiceless. It never occurred to me that when girls who claimed they were my best friend were mean to me, I could tell them to stop. I believed it was obligatory to like someone if they said they liked me. "Evan likes you," a friend told me at summer camp when I was twelve, and I gasped with delight, even though I had no idea who Evan was. "He's the one who has a poster over his bed of a woman in a bikini lying on top of a car," she said, and I clapped my hands with joy. I'd have done the same if she'd told me, "He's a serial killer with at least three secret families stashed around town." After all, I wouldn't have wanted to hurt his feelings.

My parents told me every day how clever I was, how special I was, but they were my parents, so they didn't count. Nor did teachers (whom, post Miss Moss, I no longer saw as infallible), nor did my friends (whom I only occasionally liked). So I sought approval from everyone else. In conversations, I would exhaust myself by trying to figure out what the other person wanted me to say, as opposed to saying what I actually thought, to the point that I had no idea what I thought about anything. It was an approach to life that worked for me, mostly. I wasn't ever cool, but I was popular, because I was friends with everyone. I didn't have a boyfriend at camp, but that was because I would run away from them when they got too close, petrified that they would expect something from me that I didn't know how to give. But I have decades-old letters from kids with names like Josh, Seth and Zack, asking if I would be coming back to camp next year. And who could blame them? I was compliant, cheerful and utterly incapable of expressing my real feelings. Aside from being terrified of sex, I was dream girlfriend material.

But something about this amenable persona didn't work for me. Sometimes a mad, bad and sad feeling would rise up in my chest and I'd found a secret way of soothing it, and it involved my going into the school toilet on my own. A teacher noticed this and she followed me one day—I guess I'd been doing it a lot—and she caught me in the cubicle, my small and frantic hand between my legs. "Nice girls don't do that!" she gasped, and she took me to the school nurse and told her to examine me for "a rash down there." Now I'd learned something else: pleasure is shameful.

These were not terrible things that happened to me. After all, most girls pick up these messages at some point; their feelings are of secondary importance to those of others, and their sexuality should be denied (which is very different from telling them they should simulate sexiness for others, which they are told to do all the time). All needs, wants and appetites must be suppressed: this is the most basic tenet of femininity, and no girl can evade being schooled in that, often by female relatives, sometimes by friends, always by TV shows and movies. The biggest rom-com when I was growing up was *Pretty Woman*, a film so tied up in femininity that the female protagonist had literally no desires of her own. What did she like to eat? Whatever the man ordered for her. What were her clothing tastes? Whatever he liked. Did she want to have sex? If he paid for it, sure. Masculinity is all about being active: doing, achieving, overpowering. Femininity is passivity: you are observed, you are judged, you are chosen. And the closer a girl gets to womanhood, the more femininity can feel like her doom. She is reminded of this every time a boy or man looks at her changing body and observes it, judges it, chooses it.

People don't talk about femininity when they wring their hands over why eating disorders are so disproportionately a female problem. Instead they focus on diet culture and models, and that's because people tend to get distracted by the "eating" part and forget the broader "disorder" side of the equation. There are definitely cultural reasons why 90 percent of anorexics are female. Yes, thin, for women, is always in, and this trend is itself rooted in femininity, because thinness is proof of a woman's lack of appetite and it reassures onlookers of her physical frailty. Some girls take messages about femininity and spit them out in disgust, some swallow them easily, and for others, they cause hiccups. Because I was such a little conformist, I didn't understand that I could reject these absurd ideas, and so instead of understanding there was something wrong with the expectations of how girls are supposed to be, I assumed that there was something wrong with me. The incidents with Miss Moss and then in the school toilet burned into my brain so that they became an inextricable part of me. Religious people talk of souls, scientists prefer DNA, others use words such as *identity* and *essence*. But I think the thing that makes us truly who we are is the part of our brain that chooses which experiences will pierce us the most deeply.

I never told my parents about those incidents. I couldn't even articulate them (don't tell anyone how you really feel!). I didn't know what I was doing in the toilet cubicle or why my teacher had cried. I knew nothing bad had happened to me—it's not like I'd been kidnapped, like the kids I read about on the backs of milk cartons—but I knew I'd been bad. Soon after the toilet incident, I developed OCD tics: if I spun one way, I had to spin back in the opposite direction or I'd be twisted; if I stepped on a crack in the pavement with one foot, I had to step on a crack with the other foot or I'd be unbalanced. I struggled to fall asleep at night because I kept going to the toilet, terrified I would wet my bed in my sleep. But how could I tell my parents any of this when they gave me everything?

What kind of girl becomes anorexic? People love to define the type. I had a run of therapists who were especially interested in birth order: firstborns become anorexic because they soak up their parents' anxieties; middle children and twins become anorexic because they're trying to carve out their own identity; no, it's the youngest children who are most at risk because they're trying to stay their parents' little baby. Many of these kinds of theories, I noticed, conveniently covered all situations: children who grow up in a home with no rules become anorexic because they're looking for structure; children who grow up with too many rules become anorexic because they equate structure with safety. One psychiatrist told me I'd developed anorexia because I had been born by C-section, "so you always try to look for the easy way out," he said. I was fifteen years old, under seventy pounds, manic with hunger, and I looked at him and thought, "You think this is easy? Let's see you try it, pal."

One particular theory about anorexia has been held for millennia: "The medieval anorexic . . . is a happy and obedient child of well-to-do, perhaps even noble, parents, and always beloved. At first her devout parents encourage her spiritual impulses. Quickly, however, the conventional nature of their religiosity becomes apparent [and she] rejects not only their worldliness but also the accepted path of an established convent, . . . Toward others, the holy girl is docile and uncomplaining, even servile, and yet in her spiritual world her accomplishments are magnificent. . . . To obliterate every human feeling of pain, fatigue, sexual desire and hunger is to be the master of oneself," Rudolph M. Bell writes,[1] describing the starving girls whose self-denial would be worshipped as evidence of saintliness. Several centuries later, the description had hardly altered: the physician Samuel Fenwick wrote in 1880 that "fasting girls" were "much more common in the wealthier of society than among those who have to procure their bread by daily labor."[2] According to Hilde Bruch, this still held true almost a century later: "Most anorexic girls come from upper-middle-class and upper-class homes. Their mothers were usually conscientious and devoted. . . . [Her parents insist] that the miserable, angry and desperate patient had been the best, brightest, sweetest, most obedient and most cooperative child ever. . . . There is no doubt that these children were well-cared for physically, materially and educationally," she wrote in 1978.[3] In other words, anorexia is a self-indulgence limited to the daughters of the wealthy.

This template was set with the first recorded case of female self-starvation, which afflicted not merely a wealthy girl but a princess. She is now known as Saint Wilgefortis, a derivation of *virgo fortis*, or "strong virgin," and according to the legend, she lived some time between 700 and 1000 A.D.[4]

Her father, the king of Portugal, decided she should marry the king of Sicily. But Wilgefortis was determined to remain a virgin and was so appalled by the prospect of marriage that she stopped eating and hair grew all over her body and face, as often happens with anorexics. Because of this, she is often represented in religious iconography with a beard. The king of Sicily then withdrew his proposal, and Wilgefortis's outraged father had her crucified. When a posthumous cult grew around her, worshippers offered votive offerings of bowls of oats. Poor Wilgefortis. Even in death, people continue to nag at her to eat.

Princesses still get anorexia. Princess Victoria of Sweden, who is about the same age as me, had anorexia at almost exactly the same time as me and, also like me, made a full recovery and is now married with children. Probably the highest-profile sufferer of chronic anorexia is the billionaire heiress Allegra Versace, daughter of Donatella, whose late uncle, the designer Gianni, used to call her "my princess." Even beyond princesses, the popular image of an anorexic today has hardly changed since medieval times: she is upper middle class, white and privately educated. This is why anorexia tends to get much more coverage in the media than, say, schizophrenia, as the former is easier to illustrate with photos of thin, pretty girls. The downside is that it is more likely to be dismissed as a silly rich girl's problem, like tennis elbow or daddy issues. "Whenever I issue out a press release about anorexia, I'll generally get a lot of media interest in it, and I'll have to extract a promise from the reporters that they won't use an inappropriate photo with it," says Professor Gerome Breen, a psychiatric geneticist at King's College London. In other words, one that plays on the stereotype that anorexia is a rich white girl's disease.

It is true that anorexics are largely white, although no one really knows why. Maybe it's cultural, some doctors say; maybe it's genetics, others suggest. The truism that the more westernized a country is, the higher the rates of eating disorders, is correct only in regard to bulimia.[5] Rates of bulimia tend to track with a country's development and modernization, and it is very much on the rise among black and Asian communities in Western countries. Anorexia's global rates have remained steadier, and it is seen in all cultures,[6] but the sufferers are mainly Caucasian. During my years in hospital, I met only one patient who was Black. "We've had some BAME patients, and a few with Indian backgrounds and a couple of Chinese patients, but they're still in the minority," Sarah McGovern, the manager of an eating disorders ward, tells me; a minority, yet they do exist. But when families, schools and health care professionals assume anorexia is a problem that affects only a certain type of girl, they then miss it in those who don't fit that mold. "The BAME girls and women who come in as inpatients battle with the stigma that this is a white and middle-class illness and it's difficult for them," says McGovern. "They'll say, 'In our family, we eat and we don't look at magazines or models or want to be really skinny, so it's not the done thing.'" Perhaps because of the stigma, studies have found that Caucasians with eating disorders are much more likely to seek out treatment than those from different backgrounds,[7] so a confirmation bias is established with doctors expecting eating disorders only in white patients.[8]

So the stereotype about girls with anorexia being white and wealthy is broadly correct in regard to the former—but it's wrong about the latter. "The majority of our patients are white, but they are definitely not all upper-middle class," says McGovern.

"There is no social class bias now in anorexia, possibly because our cultures have changed," says Professor Hubert Lacey.

Maybe anorexia was once a privilege afforded only to princesses. Or maybe princesses were the only girls who were deified for it, while the anorexic peasants quietly died, unnoticed and unheralded, just as upper-middle-class families can pay for their daughters to access private mental health services, while the rest languish and sometimes perish on waiting lists, unknown and unseen. One study of thirteen-to-eighteen-year-old girls found that patterns of disordered eating were more common among those from lower socioeconomic groups than those from higher ones.[9] "The patients in here definitely aren't just from well-off families. It's no different from any other mental health ward. But I've noticed that some of the other wards get lots of vouchers and donations from big companies, and that's great, but we don't. I don't think they think about our ward, and I wonder if they think it's full of rich girls and Daddy can buy them what they want," says McGovern.

The cliché about anorexia and privately educated white girls isn't the full story. But that is very different from saying it's the wrong story. After all, few embody that story more fully than me.

My father grew up in a lower-middle-class family, but by the time I was born, he was a successful investment banker, determined to give his children more than he'd had as a child. So I was privately educated from the age of three, and my New York school was filled with girls who shared their surnames with art foundations and nationally celebrated writers; in London I went to school with the daughters of minor British celebrities and MPs. I wasn't Ivanka Trump—who went to school around the corner from our apartment in New York—

but I lived a life unimaginable to most people. But unlike Ivanka, my parents raised me to know how fortunate we were. So how could I complain?

Separating how you grew up from who you become is like trying to extract the eggs from the cake: that's the stuff that binds it all together. For a while, I assumed that my background had sparked my illness: I had been given *too much*, you see, and that made me feel undeserving (there's nothing like developing anorexia in adolescence to make you realize, in retrospect as an adult, that parents really can't win). This was easy to believe when I was in, first, a private hospital, and the other girls were like me and had names such as Tabitha and India. That theory looked less certain when I went into the NHS system and lived alongside girls who'd grown up in foster care, teenagers from deprived rural backgrounds, women who had been homeless. The "poor little rich girl" shtick is predicated on the idea that rich kids get toys but not love from their parents, and that was not the case with me.

As far back as the 1980s there was a theory that anorexia might be a female twist on autism. "Initially there was a lot of skepticism around this, but recent studies are showing that among patients who have chronic anorexia, who don't respond to treatment, as many as thirty to thirty-five percent have not full-blown autism but autism spectrum disorder," says Dr. Agnes Ayton, chair of the Faculty of Eating Disorders at the Royal College of Psychiatrists. It's easy to see a connection between autism and anorexia: the rigidity, the obsessiveness, the lack of realistic self-perspective, the retreat from the world. "It's mainly males who are diagnosed with autism, and it's mainly females who are diagnosed with eating disorders. But females are very good at masking their autistic symptoms. They mimic, they repeat social rules, they can hide autistic features behind a facade. But then adolescence comes along, and this can get trickier as social interactions become more complicated, which may then lead to anorexia," says Professor Kate Tchanturia, professor of psychology in eating disorders at King's College London and the author of *Supporting Autistic People with Eating Disorders*.

Other doctors say that symptoms of starvation can be mistaken for symptoms of autism. "There may be personality traits that get amplified with anorexia, including autistic ones. But if someone is operating at limited capacity because they starved themselves, interpreting their symptoms has to be done with caution," says Professor Gerome Breen. "Historically, as has been the case with pretty much all medical and psychiatric diagnoses, women have been inaccurately diagnosed, and the diagnostic criteria for autism spectrum disorder [ASD] is very much geared toward males. So there's a popular theory that girls have been getting undiagnosed. But it is hard to separate out the kids who are distressed and are exhibiting ASD symptoms as part of their distress and ones who haven't been diagnosed properly and are living a distressing life as a result of being neurodiverse," says Anna Hutchinson, a clinical psychologist who has worked in eating disorder and gender dysphoria health care. In Breen's view, anorexia is a lot closer to obsessive-compulsive disorder than it is to autism.

Breen studies genetic factors in anorexia and says there are "very definite links between anorexia and metabolic factors, hormones that control appetite, insulin and so on. It seems obvious that anorexia has been seen through a sexist lens quite a lot, so there's been a dismissal of observations about metabolic defects in patients." In other words, doctors have been so fixed on the idea of silly girls and their silly body obsessions that they've overlooked a possible physiological factor.

According to Breen, people with anorexia generally have a high metabolic rate and low blood sugar: "It's like the reverse of type 2 diabetes. So there is probably an interplay between the metabolic and psychological processes, in the sense that losing weight might be rewarding for them or evoke a greater magnitude of response than it would in someone with a less robust metabolism."

Professor Janet Treasure, the director of the Eating Disorders Research Unit and a professor of adult psychiatry at the Institute of Psychiatry, Psychology and Neuroscience at King's College London, was the last psychiatrist who treated me. She was always calm and cheerful, even when dealing with a ward of angry and truculent girls and women, and despite her being a globally renowned expert on eating disorders, I never felt intimidated by her because she had the warm, thoughtful manner of a kind librarian. She still does: I hadn't seen her in twenty-five years, but when I sent her an email to ask if she would talk to me for my research, she said yes immediately, and soon we were talking by video chat (we were still in lockdown at that point). I asked if there was greater understanding of what causes anorexia today than when I was ill.

"Maybe one of the biggest things is finding that there is an overlap with metabolic and psychological features, which varies over the whole eating disorder spectrum, but it shows that they are a form of psychosomatic illness. In other words, you need genetic soil and environmental triggers," she said.

Some studies have found that people with eating disorders have specific neurobiological differences in the brain from the rest of the population.[10] For example, multiple studies have found that people with a tendency toward anorexia have high levels of serotonin in the brain, which leads to greater anxiety and obsessiveness.[11] Starvation causes the serotonin levels to drop, bringing a sense of calm,[12] although the brain then tries to compensate by increasing the amount of serotonin.[13] This means the person has to starve further to regain the calm—the eating disorder equivalent of having to increase one's drug intake to achieve one's high. Similarly, other studies have suggested that anorexia stems from a surplus of dopamine in the brain,[14] which would explain the high levels of anxiety, hyperactivity and the ability to forsake pleasurable things such as, most obviously, food.[15]

There are lots of takes on anorexia that are far from displeasing to anorexics themselves. One is that anorexia is suffered only by the brilliant. "A lot of our patients are very intelligent, but they turn that intelligence against themselves," says Sarah McGovern. As a celebrated international genius, I humbly endorse this theory.

"Thin girls get anorexia" is another popular one, and one that few anorexics will refute. If you're naturally thin to begin with, you're likely to have a relatively fast metabolism, which will speed up the weight loss. But, like many of these theories, it also has a counter. "The biggest risk factors for the development of eating disorders are being female, body image dissatisfaction and dieting behavior, and these behaviors are most common in those who are at higher weight," says Dr. Dasha Nicholls, head of the child and adolescent mental health research team in Imperial College London's Division of Psychiatry. "So you have an overweight child who adopts overly zealous dieting behavior, develops anorexia nervosa and then as anorexia resolves, develops bulimia."

After talking to enough eating disorders specialists, you realize that even now, after all this time, after all those girls and women have sickened and died, no one actually has any definite answers about who develops anorexia and why. But I do know some things for certain: I am not autistic, and while I was always slim, I was never strikingly so ("normal"). I wouldn't say that not eating made me feel calm, exactly. Mainly it made me feel tired, cold and miserable. But it did distract me from my constant anxiety, which I guess was the point, and certainly when I was ill, it was a lot more calming not to eat than to eat. So it mainly felt like a form of OCD, in that not obeying that seemingly nonsensical urge was unimaginable. But when I try to understand why I developed such acute anorexia nervosa, I increasingly think less about my demographics and genetics and more about my personality. Because if my background made me a typical anorexic, then my personality was pretty much conceived in a laboratory for it.

"Clinical observation has long suggested a link between personality and eating disorders. Research has consistently linked anorexia (particularly when the patient does not also have bulimic symptoms) to personality traits such as introversion, conformity, perfectionism, rigidity, and obsessive-compulsive features," Drew Westen and Jennifer Harnden-Fischer write in the *American Journal of Psychiatry*, as if reading off a checklist description of me.[16]

Clearly some demographics and environments encourage those traits more than others, and perhaps this is where the social class and ethnicity factors come into play. In New York, I went to one of the most academic all-girls schools in the city, and I always felt the sting of not being smart enough there. Probably a lot of the other students did, too, and they found their ways to cope. My tactic, between the ages of eight and ten, was to make my handwriting as small as possible. My teachers would get a little exasperated that they couldn't read my homework, but they praised me for the tidiness of the assignment. No one seemed to think it odd that a child was trying to shrink herself into invisibility.

Private all-girls schools still have a bad reputation when it comes to anorexia. A 2016 study found that girls who go to schools with more girls than boys and who have highly educated parents are more likely to develop anorexia,[17] and private girls' schools tend to tick both of those boxes. But looking back on my own education, I wonder if other factors about the schools play a part, too. The private girls' schools I've known took great pride in telling their students that they could be anything, and given the girls' privilege, the schools were not wrong. But being told you can be "anything" can sound—to those of an anxious bent—like you'd better be something, and something really special, to justify all you've been given, and that can feel terrifying. There was a strong emphasis on conformity, potentially making some students fear a life without rules and structure, and it was implied in the teaching that there is always A Right Answer, instilling in some students a terror of making mistakes or straying from the rigid norm. Private schools shelter students from the realities of the outside world, and for a long time the outside world felt to me unknowable, unimaginable and intimidating. Anorexia was in some ways like a security blanket for me because it allowed me to hide from the world, it provided structure and rules, and there was always one simple right answer: don't eat.

Even before the anorexia, I was a perfectionist, I was an overthinker, and then there was the OCD. These are all expressions of anxiety, and I was definitely an anxious kid. After Miss Moss, I was terrified of hurting other people's feelings and would come home weeping when I thought I'd inadvertently upset one of my classmates. (My mother would then call the classmate's mother to apologize, and invariably neither the mother nor the classmate knew what I was talking about.) My mother called me "tenderhearted" because things that bounced off other kids would completely floor me. After reading Hans Christian Andersen's faintly sadistic "The Little Mermaid," in which the mermaid fails to bag the prince and so dies and turns into froth on the tide, I hated going to the beach, devastated by all the dead mermaids (i.e., sea-foam). Films that were slightly melancholic—*Mary Poppins* (Mary leaves at the end!), *The Purple Rose of Cairo* (Mia Farrow doesn't run off with Jeff Daniels!)—weren't even allowed to stay in the house, and my mother had to take the videocassettes to the local charity shop. Concepts such as "compartmentalizing" and "maintaining perspective" were as foreign to me as Mandarin; when I worried about something, that was all my mind could focus on, so that I no longer knew what was real or not—like those magic dot pictures when you stare hard at a black circle on the page and then when you look away, your eyes are dazzled by optical illusions. It got so bad that when I was eight my mother took me to the child psychiatrist Dr. David Shaffer. "I have a space inside of me that I think will always be sad," I told him. He told my parents that he couldn't take me on as a patient, but he was impressed by my ability to describe my feelings. I could describe them but not control them, and learning that the one thing that relieved my anxiety, my private rubbing in the toilet cubicle, was verboten did not lessen the problem.

This oversensitivity was the reason I became vegetarian at the age of four. I asked my mother where meat came from, and when she told me, I announced that I was no longer eating meat or fish, and she respected that. How on earth could I justify an animal or fish dying for me? This was in the 1980s when vegetarianism was very much not the norm, and certainly not among small children, and there was always a bit of a fuss when I went to someone else's house for a playdate. Oh dear, what would Hadley eat? the mothers would fret. Surely chicken nuggets or fish fingers are okay? They were not. My people-pleasing instincts competed with my sensitivity, and when it came to food, the latter won. I liked that my fussy eating earned me attention from my classmates ("You don't even eat cheeseburgers?!") and admiration mixed with exasperation from their parents ("Such thoughtfulness in a child! But I wish she'd eat meat loaf").

"Anorexics are normally highly articulate, highly intelligent and highly gifted. But they are like a child looking for their own vegetable patch, their own identity," says Dr. Georges Kaye, who looked after me when I was ill and is still my GP today. On those playdates, my tricky eating was my identity.

Vegetarianism is not an eating disorder, but studies have shown that people who have an eating disorder are exponentially more likely to have tried vegetarianism than those who don't.[18] Yes, it can be a healthy way to eat, but it's also a legitimized way of excluding food. I quickly became accustomed to cutting major food groups out of my diet, and I thought of food as something less associated with pleasure and more with anxiety and revulsion. The idea of eating something that had once been part of a cow was genuinely repulsive to me, and I couldn't understand why others didn't see that, nor, conversely, why I did when so many others didn't. Vegetarianism was almost certainly my gateway drug into anorexia, because it was the first manifestation of my association between food and self-identity and control. Yet if my mother had forbidden it and made me eat a burger, that would only have heightened my feelings of disgust about food. So maybe nothing could have been done differently.

Out of all the mental illnesses, anorexia is most commonly discussed as if it's sparked by an external source, whether it's anxiety about exams or anxiety about Jodie Kidd's thighs. In fact, the opposite is the case. "It's fairly well established that personality disorders, depression and schizophrenia can develop from trauma. But anorexia has the lowest relationship with trauma," says Gerome Breen. Of the many anorexics I've met in my life, one was abused by her brother and another accidentally killed her twin in a car crash. But in the vast, vast main, nothing massively terrible had happened to any of us. It was just an accretion of small, normal-awful life experiences that we had metabolized differently from most people.

"A lot of our patients have past trauma, but it might be something that isn't obviously traumatic. I think people assume if you haven't been sexually or physically assaulted, then you haven't suffered a trauma, but it can be something seemingly smaller, especially things like bullying at school, and the patient can feel embarrassed at the impact it's had on their life, so they have never talked about it. So much of anorexia is about suppressed conversations," says McGovern.

Physical frailty, I'd learned, was a great way to say something that I'd otherwise suppressed. One night at summer camp when I was twelve, I woke up, needing to use the loo. The toilets were outside, which was very much the worst thing about camp, worse even than having to do sports every day, and so I crept out of the cabin in my nightgown and walked across the wet grass. It had been raining overnight, so when I was done and walking back down the outhouse's slippery steps, I skidded, smashed my back on the steps and landed flat on the grass. I couldn't move, and I also couldn't summon up enough breath to call for help. So I lay there for what was probably at most an hour, waiting for the sun to come up and someone to find me.

Anyway, I was fine. I'd banged my back up a bit and the wind had been knocked out of me, but that was all. This was America, though, and the camp feared litigation from my parents, so I was instructed to sleep in the infirmary—which had an indoor toilet!—for a week and to do no sports for the rest of the summer. This was a revelation. Being sick— properly ill or physically maimed, not merely faking a sore throat—got me out of things I didn't want to do, and no one could blame me for it, because I hadn't asked for it, so it wasn't my fault. So began the era of faking sprained wrists and blatantly nonexistent menstrual cramps to get out of PE. (Really, it's remarkable that I only developed anorexia later and not Munchausen's syndrome.) It wasn't that I deliberately set out to make myself ill to get out of things—not exactly. It was more that I didn't know how to say I didn't want to do something and so I found ways to avoid it without saying it so I wouldn't look ungrateful. It wasn't my fault, in other words. So maybe that psychiatrist was right. Maybe I did look for the easy way out, although I'd put it differently: I looked for the difficult way out.

According to Professor Treasure, anorexia is a mix of things: "There's genetic predisposition, a bit of brain disorder, some metabolic factors. Then there are things that interact with development and time, such as people being perfectionist, high-achieving, having a few social problems."

I asked her whether I had been a typical anorexic. She hesitates. "I don't think you were very atypical," she says and laughs.

So that was the girl at age fourteen: privileged, anxious, a people pleaser with some light OCD; obsessive, food focused and unable to express unhappiness without hiding behind the crutch of illness. All those pins, so beautifully lined up. And

47

now here comes the bowling ball of puberty to blow them all to bits.

I was—no one will be wildly surprised to learn—a late developer, physically and emotionally. At fourteen, I still didn't even need deodorant, and periods felt about as relevant to my life as pensions. But these things were clearly more imminent than I liked to acknowledge, and the proof of that is that I developed anorexia.

"The hormonal changes in puberty have a role in triggering anorexia, but it's not that the hormones suddenly switch on and you develop an eating disorder," says Dr. Dasha Nicholls. "There are intervening mechanisms in the process. The social and emotional challenges of adolescence are also factors. Even emotionally intelligent kids find adolescence confusing because the subtleties and nastiness of adolescent interaction are a minefield, and if you struggle to understand what's going on socially, you'll become unstuck. The other big issue is the changing body shape that comes in adolescence and the fear that stems from that."

In a survey of a thousand anorexic patients at St. George's Hospital, Professor Lacey says, "Not one had started the illness after eighteen, so it is an adolescent condition. It might not have become a problem until later, but it definitely kicked off then." Several doctors I spoke to suggested that perhaps one reason anorexia is being diagnosed in increasingly younger girls is because puberty is starting for girls at an increasingly younger age.[19]

The world, once so steady and predictable, was warping and my feet couldn't get a purchase on it. My body felt similarly out of control, soft where it had once been hard, dangerous where it had once been safe. Is it any wonder that I tried to control the one thing I could, to reverse time the only way I knew how? Sometimes I think it's a miracle only 1 percent of adolescent girls develop anorexia. How do the rest stay afloat when the waves rise so suddenly and so high?

From this perspective, my becoming anorexic seems inevitable. How did no one see that train barreling down the track, heading straight into my bedroom? But there is another perspective to this story that is just as true.

The months leading up to my fourteenth birthday were very happy ones. We had been living in London for three years, and it had snowed that February, properly snowed, and at last a London winter felt like the kind I used to have in New York. My sister and I took our new dog, whom I adored, to the park and debated whether we preferred Luke Perry or Jason Priestley while we made angels in the snow. I had a best friend, Esther, whom I was extremely close to in the way only two thirteen-year-old girls can be when they feel that obsession with each other that verges on being true love, and we would spend all day at school together and then all evening on the phone. I'd also recently made a new group of friends who lived near me, and we took the bus together to and from school, loudly singing at the back (East 17's "Stay Another Day," Paula Abdul's "Rush Rush"), annoying everyone else but amusing ourselves enormously. This was as naughty as I got, and it was thrilling. I was also starting to develop my own interests, seeking out things that neither my parents nor teachers knew or cared about. I became obsessed with the Channel 4 improv show *Whose Line Is It Anyway?* and stayed up late all by myself every Friday night to see if it would be Tony Slattery or Mike McShane or Josie Lawrence who won that week. I took out a subscription to the film magazine *Empire*, which I studied like the cool kids studied the *NME*, and the journalists who wrote for it were as exciting to me as the celebrities they interviewed. I was allowed to go to the cinema by myself, so every free afternoon I went to the local Odeon, taking in cultural classics of the '90s: *Green Card, My Girl* and *Robin Hood: Prince of Thieves*. (I gasped when I realized Mike McShane was playing Friar Tuck. My two great cultural loves—*Whose Line Is It Anyway?* and '90s mainstream cinema—colliding in one cassock.) I then compared my thoughts about the films with those of the critics in *Empire*, changed mine to theirs and told myself I had always thought that. I developed crushes on safely asexual celebrities—Keanu Reeves, River Phoenix, Jordan Knight—and kissed my posters of them every night. I was just a kid, a completely average kid, singing on the bus, struggling with trigonometry. My favorite food was pasta. My special breakfast was pancakes. My favorite book was *Jane Eyre*. My favorite singer was Madonna. My biggest worry in life was that I might be moved down a set in French. I could not have been more ordinary. Everything seemed fine. Everything was great! I was starting to graduate from New Kids on the Block to Nirvana. I was so close to crossing that threshold from childhood to adolescence. But one afternoon in PE, I stumbled. Then my lovely little world shattered, and none of it made any sense at all.

Chapter 4

The Splitting

September 1992

"Looks like we have a problem here, don't we?" my English teacher, Miss Clover, said to me on the first day of the autumn term, pointedly looking me up and down. I felt simultaneously irritated (I *don't* have a problem, Miss Clover!) and thrilled (yay, Miss Clover thinks I have a problem!). I had lost more than one-third of my body weight in one summer, but no one else at school seemed to notice, or at least they didn't say anything about it to me, which was both a relief (Phew, they can't tell) and annoying (Can't they tell?). Not even my best friend, Esther, said anything. She must have noticed, though, because before, we had gone to the candy store every lunchtime to buy chocolate bars, which we'd eat together at our desks. Now I only stared wide-eyed as she ate hers, and as soon as she finished, I begged her to get another so I could continue watching her eat, all the while insisting I wasn't hungry. But I certainly knew something was wrong. One lunchtime, I went to the school library and asked for a book about anorexia, a word I'd never said before and felt funny in my mouth, an oversize marble sitting on my tongue. Lord only knows what the librarian thought, but she handed me *Catherine: The Story of a Young Girl Who Died of Anorexia*

Nervosa, written by Maureen Dunbar about her daughter. I read it quietly in the corner of the library, this biography of a girl who developed anorexia at fifteen and died at twenty-two, and I felt both terrified (Is this me?) and excited (This is me!).

An internal splitting happened when I became anorexic. Whereas previously I had always been me, only me, entirely within my body, there was now an ill me, who was inside my head and reveled in what I was doing to myself, and a well me, standing to the side, observing, fascinated, shocked, scared. The longer the illness went on, the more the well me disappeared, like a crack of light getting smaller as a door shuts. It was such a seismic self-splitting that when I look back on the summer of 1992 I think I can almost hear it. That lunchtime in June when I surprised myself by announcing to my friends that I wouldn't join them for pizza because I wasn't hungry, even though I absolutely was: Crack! That warm evening when I walked with my parents to our local Italian restaurant, and I asked my mother whether pasta was fattening: Shatter! That lazy August day when I went out to buy a book for school and instead bought a calorie counter: Smash!

"Everyone who is born holds dual citizenship, in the kingdom of the well and in the kingdom of the sick," Susan Sontag wrote in *Illness as Metaphor*. I now straddled the two countries, still able to speak the language of the former but adhering to the customs of the latter. After we came back from our summer vacation in France and before school started, my mother took me to see our GP, Dr. Kaye, for help. Even aside from my body size, he could see there was a problem. "It was the detachment. It was like there was another soul or being inside of you, as though you had come in with a twin, and you couldn't see how it related to you. There was a profound sense of disconnection, like something had been sundered from you, and it was something one couldn't negotiate with," he later told me. When another doctor asked me to draw how I felt, I drew the outline of a person with a smaller person inside, but I wasn't sure whether I was the bigger figure controlled by an internal alien or the smaller one trapped inside a monster.

I was so tired, all the time, but also constantly doing jumping jacks in my bedroom, so much so that I made our house shake down to its foundations, literalizing the metaphor of what I was doing to my family. The sit-ups were even more of a problem. My spine protruded from my back like the fin of a fish, and when it rubbed against the floor, the flesh around it broke and bled. I knew my mom would cry if I asked her to bandage it up, so instead I wore black T-shirts beneath my school uniform, so as not to bleed through my blouse. Obviously none of this stopped me from doing daily sit-ups, the skin breaking a little more with every one. When I'd done my set amount and it was too painful to do bonus ones, I'd switch to leg lifts or squats or more jumping jacks. "The more exercise you do, the faster your metabolism will become, and the more you can eat but still lose weight!" the diet magazines promised, so I exercised constantly and doubled my chances by eating nothing. But sometimes I was in situations where it was harder to exercise, such as at school, or pretending to eat dinner with my parents but actually dropping it on the floor for the dog (my keen collaborator). So I'd jiggle my legs, bounce on my feet, flex and unflex my fingers, a frantic bird in perpetual motion. There was never any peace, just a constant hum of guilt that I should be burning calories. I couldn't bear to think of all the time I'd wasted in my life being sedentary when I should have always been burning.

My hair, never luxuriant anyway, fell out in clumps—mainly from the top and front of my head, making it especially noticeable. This is a common effect of sudden weight loss, and the few hairs that somehow clung on in there dangled around the sides, stringy, nutrient deprived, entirely unlovely. But I didn't notice—I focused only on fatness, not my face—until a woman stopped me on the street and asked if I had cancer. But I didn't care. If the price of being thin was looking like death, so be it. Bald and furry death: while my scalp became increasingly naked, my arms, stomach and back grew a soft, downy pelt. It was as if some internal mechanism inside had become scrambled and my body no longer knew where I was supposed to grow hair. If I had become anorexic to look more beautiful, to look like Kate Moss, as many people would suggest to me in later years, I can't say I achieved my aim, unless Kate Moss was a bleeding, balding, twitching, furry mess.

Whatever joy I'd once felt had drained away, going from Oz's colors to Kansas's black and white. The world shrunk to the size of a pinhole, and in my memories from that period there is no peripheral vision at all, just a crazed myopic focus on the tiny view in front of me, as if it took all my energy to take that one step forward. What exactly was my end game here? "I just need to be thin enough so I can eat what I want without getting fat," I'd think. But I never asked myself what "thin enough" would be because my brain was too busy reveling in erotic fantasies of the foods I would eat at that magical-if-unspecified weight: Toffee Crisps, toasted crumpets, pancakes with maple syrup. See, I needed to be superskinny in order to eat how I wanted but not get fat—there was logic here, okay? I collected recipes ripped out of newspaper supplements, and I lovingly stuck them in my notebooks and read them in bed like pornography, wide-eyed and turned on. The world was filled with encouragements to eat and warnings against it, and I was fascinated by both. I replaced my Keanu Reeves posters with articles about food ("How much sugar does your favorite fruit have? You'll be surprised!"). At night, once everyone was asleep, I would sneak down and, by the light of the fridge, I would—not binge eat, no. That thought never even occurred to me, in the way jumping out of a plane without a parachute doesn't cross most people's minds. Instead, I would binge on smells, holding to my nose tubs of ice cream and packets of cheese, inhaling lasciviously. Feel the anticipation, taste buds! Oh, no, it's all gone back in the fridge, another disappointing night for you. I did that every night for weeks, until my brain decided I was deriving too much pleasure from it and the black serpent inside whispered that there were calories in the food particles I was inhaling, and then I never did it again.

"Where's my little girl who used to run through the house singing songs?" my mother asked tearfully. "She's gone," I snarled back. But I hated seeing my parents upset, fighting with them at every mealtime. It made me feel guilty but helpless. Didn't they understand I had no choice? I had no idea what was happening to me, and in the early days of that summer of 1992, I confided a little to my mother, desperate. One evening she announced with obviously faux casualness that we were all going out to my favorite restaurant, the one reserved for my birthday and other special occasions. My mother sat next to me, and while my father and sister pretended everything was normal and talked between themselves, my mother told me that of course she understood my anxieties about food—she'd had some herself when she wasn't much older than me. But I needed to understand how food works, she said, and one plate of pasta would not make me fat—it just wouldn't. And especially not now, when I was growing. It would just make me taller, and wouldn't that be great? I looked at her, and I wanted to please her so badly and to make this a nice evening for my family, rather than ruining another one. Also, I was hungry. God, I was so hungry. And so I ordered my favorite dish, and before I knew it, I'd eaten almost all of it, and when I stopped to take a breath and saw the empty bowl, I screamed inside. My family smiled happily at me, and my parents looked at each other with a "There, all sorted" look on their faces. They were happy, and that was better than them being angry with me. But later, as I lay in bed, unable to even touch my stomach, I loathed myself with a depth I didn't know I possessed, and I realized I could cope with my family's anger better than my own. We went back to that restaurant the following week, and this time I refused to eat anything, because there was no way I was going to repeat the torment of last week. My sister pointedly ignored me, my dad stared at the table and my mother got tearful. "I guess you didn't enjoy it as much as I thought," she said. That's when I realized she didn't understand me anymore: How could she fail to realize that enjoyment was beside the point when it came to eating? I had lost my footing on a bridge, but I hadn't wanted to fall, not at first, so I'd grabbed her hand and she'd gripped me as I was suspended over the ravine. But in the time between those two trips to the restaurant—only a week, really—I slipped out of her grasp and vanished into the darkness. It wasn't her fault. Once the momentum had started, the fall was inevitable.

I came up with all kinds of tricks to stop myself from eating, from imagining the most repulsive thoughts possible (someone sneezed on this cake, there's snot all over it, it's dripping with snot) to telling myself that what I was feeling wasn't hunger, it was just how humans always feel. I thought I'd come up with these myself, but anorexics had been thinking such thoughts forever.[1] So although these ideas seemed to come to me unbidden, it was the thick black snake, now tightly coiled around my brain, who put them there.

Women's bodies suddenly fascinated me. Fascinated and repelled. I stared at the ones in tight clothing: the waistband digging, the sleeves gripping. How could they bear it? It was the slim women in loose clothes whom I liked the most: their legs lost within their trousers, their sleeves floating around their arms. That's what I wanted, for my body to touch nothing, for it to feel nonexistent. Size zero.

At school, I went from being friends with everyone to being friends with no one. I couldn't think of anything to talk about other than food and exercise and weight, and it turned out my classmates had limited interest in those subjects. When they talked about other things—pop music, *Neighbours* and *Home and Away*—their voices faded away, the world disappearing as I fantasized about what they would eat for lunch that day in the school canteen (Mashed potatoes? Cauliflower cheese? *Crumble??*). I was addicted to starvation, and like all addicts, I could think of nothing but my fix.

"How about if we see a psychiatrist who will make you feel better, darling? What do you think?" my mother asked. I thought, I need to do my sit-ups now. I thought, And my jumping jacks. I thought, I can't think about this, I'm busy thinking about food. I thought, I'm so tired and miserable and I don't think I can keep going. I thought, I can't feel worse than I do now. I thought, I want someone to help me, please, can somebody please help me? So I said yes. My brain was too dazzled with deprivation to understand that when my mother said the doctor would make me "better," it meant "fatter."

• • •

Our eyes met across a crowded room. We knew at once that we'd been waiting for each other. If we hadn't been in a psychiatric hospital, it could have been the start of a love story. His name was Dr. R., and he was the head of the eating disorders unit at Hospital One, a well-known private hospital. He was over six and a half feet tall, which I came to like, because it made me feel even smaller. During the drive to Hospital One, I had both hoped and dreaded that it would look like a gothic prison, with bars on the windows and screams coming from within. Instead, it looked like a stuffy stately home, and inside it felt like a chintzy hotel, full of beige wall-to-wall carpets and giant vases filled with dried ferns. The waiting room was upstairs, and there was a disappointing lack of lunatics in straitjackets. Everyone looked genteel, normal, and they all kept their heads bent down, determinedly not making eye contact with anyone, looking instead at old copies of *Hello!* magazine. When the clock struck on the hour, the door swung open and a troupe of men marched in, and from the sudden fizz of excitement it was clear that they were the doctors—the in-house celebrities! our saviors! the great white knights!—coming in to check with their receptionists who their next patients were. I noticed Dr. R. right away because of his height, and his eyes scanned the room, looking for possible contenders. As soon as he lighted on me, sitting with my mother, he knew, and from the way he looked at me, I knew then, too.

In all the many novels, movies and jokes about therapy, I've yet to come across one that reflects how hard it is to find a good doctor. In movies, you just see Woody Allen lying on a sofa complaining that Annie Hall doesn't have sex with him often enough or Robin Williams giving Matt Damon some life lessons on love. The therapist is always the calm fount of knowledge, the restorer of equilibrium. But finding a decent therapist is like searching for a romantic partner, and you have to go on a lot of bad dates before you get there. I didn't know that then, though, so I took one look at all the medical certificates on the wall in Dr. R.'s office and unthinkingly fell into his care, which is like agreeing to marry someone because you like his hair.

Our appointment was half an hour, which seemed a little short, but what did I know, and I noticed he didn't take any notes, which also seemed odd, but he had the medical certificates and I did not. I told him that I thought I might be anorexic because I'd read the book about Catherine Dunbar and it sounded like me.

"Oh, I treated her!" he said, suddenly perking up.

I thought, "But didn't she die?" But he seemed so pleased with his celebrity connection I guessed I must be missing the point.

I tried to describe how I felt and how my brain no longer seemed to work right, but he seemed interested only when I got on his scales and he looked at the numbers. I was forty-two pounds underweight. He summoned my mother in.

"Well, she's anorexic," he said in a "we all know this already" tone of voice, which was probably true but still felt a little blunt, especially when my mother then burst into tears. He said my weight was dangerously low but if I was able to stick to a meal plan he'd treat me as an outpatient. If not, in forty-eight hours I'd be brought into hospital, where I'd be fed six times a day and have to eat everything I was given. I could see my heart thumping in terror through my blouse. Did being scared burn calories? Something else for my brain to obsess over.

"What's the meal plan?" I asked, almost laughing at the words in my mouth.

"To start, you have to eat a biscuit as a morning and afternoon snack, so have one when you get home," he said.

"Okay, fine!" said my mother with forced cheer, and I could tell what she was thinking: "A cookie! That's fine, Hadley always loved cookies. We just needed a doctor to tell us what to do. I'll buy some Oreos on the way home, and then everything will be fine." She smiled through her tears at me and I smiled back, but when Dr. R. and I then looked at each other, I knew we both knew that this was not going to play out like that.

When I was about eleven, I heard the word *schizophrenic* for the first time. My parents took my sister and me to a van Gogh exhibition, and the tour guide said he'd probably suffered from schizophrenia.

"What's that?" I asked.

"It's a mental illness where someone thinks they can hear voices in their head," my father said.

That didn't seem like it should be a big deal. Annoying, sure, but if you know they're just voices in your head, why don't you just ignore them? I wondered. Well, when I became anorexic, I found out.

Anorexia is not schizophrenia (although 1 to 4 percent of schizophrenics also suffer from anorexia[2]). But I said to Dr. R. in that first appointment that I felt like I was schizophrenic, because it was as though some other voice was in my brain and it was doing all my thinking for me. I no longer thought the way I used to, I said.

Starvation changes the brain. It's known as cerebral atrophy—or "starved brain"—and when a person is severely anorexic, their brain ostensibly shrinks, with a reduction in volume of white and gray matter. This is particularly evident in the hippocampus, the part of the brain that looks after your memory, learning and visuospatial processes and possibly also regulates food intake.[3] Because of this, anorexics often suffer from memory and learning deficits, and because starvation is (to say the least) stressful, they have increased levels of the stress hormone cortisol and therefore lower levels of serotonin. Obviously, starving yourself is pretty depressing, but it's more than that: it changes your brain chemistry so that you become more depressed, more emotional and more confused in your thoughts. The knock-on effect aggravates the cause. In other words, anorexia starts as a psychological problem, becomes a physical one, and the physical problem then exacerbates the psychological one and vice versa. As Professor Treasure put it to me, "Not eating damages the organ needed for change." How do you untangle a knot when it's inextricably inter-woven?

The quilt on the guest room bed was gingham, blue and white, and I used to lie on it for hours playing Nintendo. But then I stopped caring about what I enjoyed and cared only about what would make me thin, and so spending all day playing Super Mario Bros. had been swapped for all-day exercising. It was a struggle, but I'd managed to find a hobby that was an even bigger waste of time than video games. The guest room was downstairs, next to the kitchen, and my mother took me in there for privacy, away from my little sister, so I could eat the fate-deciding cookie. We sat on the bed, and she held the Oreo toward me.

No way.

Eat it, or you'll have to eat hospital food six times a day!

I know, but I can't.

I can't.

I can't.

"I can't," I said to my mother, and it really did feel as

though there was some inverted magnetic force between my mouth and the cookie, repelling us away from each other. But the force was my own fear of myself: fear of how anxious I'd feel if I ate and how much I'd then hate myself. God, just the thought of the minutes after eating—the horror at what I'd done, the terror that I could do nothing about it now, the frantic pacing for hours afterward, feeling the fat sprouting on my body, my inner thighs rubbing against each other, my bulging tummy pressing against the waistband. It was unbearable, this hypothetical future. It was unthinkable! And therefore, the food was inedible. So much of anorexia is powered by this fear of the future—the next meal, adulthood—and a lack of faith in oneself to be able to cope with it.

For the second time that day, my mother cried in front of me, and I couldn't help her. That cookie would not be eaten. But as had become the way with me, there was also something else going on: I wanted to go to hospital. I definitely didn't want to eat six times a day, but I needed to get away from my family. I couldn't bear seeing their sadness anymore. I needed someone else to take charge, because the strain was wearing me out. At home, I was in control of me, which was like having an army sergeant in my head constantly shouting at me to exercise more and eat nothing. Could that voice be swapped for that of the tall doctor? As I looked at my mother crying on the gingham bed, I was willing to try. I pictured the hospital where Madeline had her appendix out in Ludwig Bemelmans's books, which was so lovely that all of Madeline's friends wished they were in hospital, too. A white room with a comfortable bed where I could lie all day on my own, unbothered save for a nurse bringing in occasional bowls of broth. "A crack on the ceiling had the habit / of sometimes looking like a rabbit / Outside were birds, trees, and sky—/ and so ten days passed quickly by." Just a little break, I told myself. This would be fine.

And when we arrived at the hospital, it seemed to be. My parents and I were taken to the eating disorders wing, which was a small carpeted corridor of five rooms, all looking into the nurses' station—or, to be more accurate, the nurses' station was looking into all the rooms. I had my own room, and it was lovely, with a bed, a desk, even a sink. This was a private hospital, and for decades afterward I worried how much this had cost my parents. Thousands? Millions? It wasn't until I started to write this book that I dared to ask them and the answer was: nothing. I had been on my father's work health insurance. Still a privilege, of course, but also yet more years of pointless guilt and anxiety.

As I considered its ditzy floral curtains and blandly cheerful pastel color scheme, I felt like my parents were checking me into a hotel, but then I noticed that the chair in the corner had a toilet seat instead of a cushion and a bowl hanging down beneath it. A nurse took me into the bathroom and searched me to make sure I hadn't brought in any laxatives or razor blades to cut myself, neither of which I'd ever considered before. She tutted when she saw my gouged-up back and tenderly cleaned it and bandaged it for me. I relaxed a little. She brought me back into the room, where everyone else was waiting for me.

Dr. R. sat on the window seat—window seat! this was better than my room at home!—and told me to sit opposite him on the bed. I jiggled my leg so much it made the bed bounce. After all, this was cutting into my exercise time.

"You will live here for twelve weeks," he told me.

So far, so good.

"To make sure you are not making yourself sick, you will not be allowed to use the toilet, but instead you will use the commode in your room, and everything you put down your sink goes into a bucket underneath. The nurses will check and empty both twice a day," he said.

Gross, but whatever—as with the laxatives and razor blades, vomiting had never occurred to me as an option. I'd been in hospital for less than hour, and already I'd learned so much.

"You will be on bed rest, which means at all times you are either lying in your bed or sitting in a chair, and your door will be kept open so nurses can check you're not exercising."

That's what you think, Doc.

"You will start on half portions for a week."

Great.

"And then full portions after that, and all your meals will be in your room and supervised by a nurse."

We'll see about that.

"And you will stay here until you weigh . . ." and then he said a number.

Suddenly, the room, window seat and all, disappeared. All I could see were calves bulging out over my school shoes. Chunky upper arms stretching out the seams of my school sweater. Fat rolls spilling out over my school skirt's waistband. Multiple chins rippling over the collar of my school blouse.

For the first time in months there was no split reaction inside, because when the doctor said that number, the ill part of me ballooned and eclipsed entirely the dwindling vestiges of my well self. I collapsed on the floor, hysterical, crying, pleading with my parents—take me home, I'll eat all the cookies in the packet, I promise, please please please, don't leave me here, please, I don't need this, the doctor will make me fatter than I ever was, fatter than I should be, please take me home, please, I'll do anything, please—and I felt only one thing: absolute hot terror.

Chapter 5

Hospital One (First Time)

September–December 1992

The world is big—terrifyingly so, it seemed to me—so from an early age I looked for ways to make it smaller. Being vegetarian helped, because it limited my options every time we went out to eat, especially in the 1980s and '90s. I generally had only two dishes to choose from on the menu or, if I was lucky, just one. For the same reason, I was always comfortable in institutions. Schools, summer camps, synagogues: they contracted the world's parameters, the general population reduced to a few familiar faces, the expansiveness of life boiled down to the petty dramas of who's off sick today and has someone stolen my chair. Some people find that limiting. Presumably those are the same people who dream of being Indiana Jones, tearing through the jungle. But I always fancied him more when he was Dr. Jones, teaching in a dusty university, wearing his spectacles, safely inside and behind a desk, where human beings belong.

One therapist I later saw as an adult told me that a fear of freedom is common among firstborns because their parents are so anxious when they have their first baby, and the child picks up from them the idea that the outside world is full of danger. (By the third child, the parents are so exhausted that they let the baby play with knives.) I don't think my parents were abnormally fearful for me, but I do remember feeling, from a very young age, overwhelmed by the world. I hated to make decisions, because I worried I would make the wrong one, and I became wild with homesickness if I was away from home for too long, like a fish wrenched from the water.

Anorexia remains the most effective means I ever found to shrink the world. No longer did I wake up and think, "Oh god, it's the French test today, should I have toast or cereal for breakfast, perhaps I should wear my new scarf today, I wonder if Sarah is still cross with me for not sitting with her at lunch yesterday, will Amy invite me to her birthday party next week?" Instead, I just had one thought:

Don't eat.

That's it.

Don't eat!

The world swapped for a message—a walk-on part in the war exchanged for a lead role in a cage. There is no fuzziness with anorexia, no nuance; you always know if you're doing it well (not eating) or badly (eating). It could be a brochure for a meditation retreat: "Make life simple for yourself: don't eat. Then all other cares will fall away."

So being locked up in a psychiatric hospital suited me pretty well. Like the vast majority of eating disorders units at that time, the system there was both intensely hierarchical and laughably patriarchal: the male consultant was the king, the invariably female nurses reported to him and we, the female patients, were the lowly peasants who did as we were told by the big man and his female minions. Thank goodness a man is here to tell these silly girls how to live, Dr. R. always seemed to me to be thinking when he arrived on the ward, breezily striding through as if he was just squeezing us in on an especially busy day, while we could only languish and wait for his arrival. But I didn't mind. My concerns were now limited to wondering which nurse would be on duty that day and had I been good enough to be allowed to use a normal toilet, and I very quickly became comfortable with that. Regimented days, everyone strictly supervised: aside from the occasional police van pulling up outside to drop off another patient and someone watching me whenever I had a shower, it felt a lot like camp. It was just the food that was the problem.

I have no memory of what they tried to give me for dinner on my first night, but it clearly didn't go well, because I was too hysterical to write about it in my diary that night. Breakfast the next day, however, was faithfully recorded: "½ a mini box of Cornflakes with SEMI-SKIM milk, orange juice, ½ a piece of toast WITH BUTTER ARE THEY KIDDING???" The nurse told me I had to eat it. I refused. And so the games commenced.

As mental illnesses go, anorexia does not have a great reputation, personality-wise. Alcoholics are generally portrayed in films as the life of the party (until they become very much not), and people with bipolar disorder are shown having their good days (and their very, very bad ones). But there are no fun moments with an anorexic. They're either quiet and miserable or—well, the common euphemism is "difficult," but what this really means is manipulative, raging, stubborn and entirely untrustworthy. It's true that anorexics lie. They lie all the time: about whether they've eaten that day, if they've put on weight and how much they've exercised. If they didn't, people would make them eat more, so what choice do they have? But it's more than mere mendacity. Anyone who has had the misfortune of looking after an anorexic—and specifically, trying to make an anorexic eat—will have encountered that fierce fire within them. When it was in me, I was Sigourney Weaver in *Ghostbusters*, possessed by an ancient demigod: "There is no Dana, there is only Zuul," Weaver growls at Bill Murray when he tries to take her on a date. There is no Hadley here, there is only anorexia, and then I'd roar at everyone to leave me alone.

It's not an internal demigod you encounter when arguing with an anorexic—it's strength of will, and one that comes wrapped in a palpable sense that anorexics know they are stronger than you, they are smarter than you and they will beat you at this game. Partly this comes from their own experience: they've proven they can starve themselves, so they feel they can master anything. But it also comes from something else.

Anorexia is a very isolating illness, socially and mentally. You lose your friends, because it's scary to be around an anorexic, and you don't want to be around anyone anyway, not when there are jumping jacks to do and recipe books to read, plus there's the constant risk that your friends might notice that you're not eating, therefore it's best to stay away. So you learn to live in your head. I talked to myself all the time when I was anorexic, silently and aloud. Who else would understand the sweet victory of squeezing in extra sit-ups that weren't even on my self-written schedule? Who else would share my rage when there was *dressing* on my salad when I *specifically* asked for it to be plain? Who else could I fret to when the waiter assured me he'd given me a Diet Coke but it definitely tasted like a normal one? I trusted no one, so I was my own ally, me and me against the world, and we needed no one else. Other people increasingly felt faded and unknowable. I had no understanding anymore of how they lived or thought, and I knew they felt the same about me, and therefore their opinions about me were irrelevant. If I could ignore my own starving body, why on earth would I listen to them? They think they can control me, I inwardly marveled that first night in hospital. They clearly don't know who they're dealing with, I replied.

The standoff lasted two days. They can't make me eat, I thought. I was wrong about that. Force-feeding—pumping glucose and fats straight into a patient's body through a tube—has long been viewed with reluctance by doctors, mainly for ethical reasons but also for others. William Gull, the nineteenth-century physician who gave anorexia nervosa its name, was said to scorn force-feeding, because he liked to think that his "moral authority would always prevail [over the patient's]." (The history of eating disorders is littered with men who were extremely comfortable with their power over female patients.) Nonetheless, it was fairly common practice up to the 1980s, and it is still used in extreme cases, no matter how much moral authority the doctor may possess. I arrived just at the time when eating disorders units were increasingly turning toward a more therapeutic approach, rather than relying on the brutally physical, and so the tube wasn't the first resort. But it swung over me, a hangman's noose.

I was not allowed to shut my door, because Dr. R. knew that given half an inch of privacy, I would jog in place for a mile. (Although I soon discovered that, from the far corner of the room, I could spot people coming down the corridor before they saw me, and I did frantic jumping jacks there whenever the ward was quiet, leaping back into bed at the glimpse of a shadow.) My limb jiggling became so frantic it probably registered on the Richter scale, although I had to be quick to move away from the nurses' outstretched hands when they attempted to still me. Even worse were the gentle and— it seemed to me—half-mocking raps on the door the nurses made when they came in, bringing yet more trays of food, as though I had the power to refuse them entry. Knock knock. Who's there? A nurse with a million calories for you to eat. Go away. No. Great joke!

First there was gentle cajoling. Then came the bargaining: just eat, then we'll leave you alone, they said. But they didn't understand there was no bargaining with me, because eating anything would mean eating more than I would if I wasn't in hospital, so that wasn't fair. Also, how would I ever forgive myself? Come on, you've been here two days, this is silly, you have to eat. No, no, no. You'll have to have a tube up your nose—is that what you want? Want? Since when did what I want come into it? Anyway, it wasn't up to me, it was my parents' decision, because I was a minor, and they already said they'd do anything to save my life. I imagined it: the nurses pinning my arms down to get the tube inside me, gagging as the plastic went down my throat. (Does plastic have calories? Annoyingly, the nurses had taken away my calorie counter so I couldn't check.) A constant calorific injection while I expanded like Violet Beauregarde in *Charlie and the Chocolate Factory*, turning into a giant blueberry. They'd have to roll me down to the juicing room. But, but, but. Maybe the tube would be for the best, because I'd finally have no control. No, no, but I'd have no control! I was a mouse, cornered, and I became—I knew it, I could feel it—hysterical, a whirling ball of anguish, fear and desperation, and I hated these stupid fucking nurses and this stupid fucking doctor. The stupid fucking doctor decided I needed some stupid fucking treatment. He suggested electroconvulsive therapy to my parents, aka ECT, aka electric volts shot through my brain aka the treatment that traumatized Sylvia Plath so badly she wrote about it in *The Bell Jar*, which I'd read only the previous month. But again he needed permission from my parents, and they, thankfully, said no to that—tubes up the nose were one thing, but electrical lobotomies were pushing it a bit. So instead, he got out his prescription pad and I was given a dose of Prozac and lithium to, respectively, cheer me up and calm me down. But I wasn't depressed and I wasn't bipolar, which is what those medications are for. I just didn't want to eat. Perhaps because I didn't need them, the medicines didn't have the doctor's desired effect on me. Instead, for the first time in my life, I had a grand mal seizure. As I fell forward and the room went black around me, I had the brief sensation of my wish being granted: I had left hospital.

That seizure took root in my brain and blossomed to become a lifetime of regular fits. Was it sparked by the medicines? I will never know. Certainly lithium is safe to prescribe to bipolar children (although—in case I haven't made this sufficiently clear—I wasn't bipolar). Prozac is a different story, and doctors have since said that giving antidepressants to children and adolescents does "more harm than good." (Also, as I might have mentioned, I wasn't depressed.) But I wasn't just a child, I was extremely underweight, and that has just as much of an effect on brain chemistry as age. "Lithium has a long list of side effects, as has Prozac, and any medication will have an exaggerated effect, not just in its treatment, but in its side effects on people who have so little reserves from being underweight. That lack of reserve lays people with anorexia open to so many adverse effects, such as risk of death from a simple viral infection to side effects from drugs," says Dr. Penny Neild, co-lead of the Adult Eating Disorders Program for London. Partly for this reason, there are no approved pharmacological treatments for anorexia. "The NICE guidelines are very clear: we don't have any specific medication for anorexia," says Dr.

Agnes Ayton. "But the rate of comorbidities is really high. It could be up to seventy percent across the age range, and you can treat those with medication." Comorbidities are other mental illnesses that can exist alongside the anorexia, such as depression, OCD and so on. But it's very hard to separate them from the symptoms of starvation. And some anorexics are just anorexic, and unfortunately for doctors of a certain bent, that can't be magicked away with medication.

The upside to that seizure (and the thirty-plus years of seizures that followed) was that I scared myself so badly that I accepted I would have to put on weight in hospital. There was clearly no getting around that. But I had a plan that I thought was ingeniously original but has been considered by pretty much every anorexic who has been an inpatient: I would gain the weight as fast as possible, so as to leave hospital, and then lose it all again and then some more as a special "fuck you" to the doctor. I hugged this plot close to me throughout my entire stay, and it soothed me as I watched my tummy balloon outward, my thighs widen toward each other, my upper arms expand so I could no longer circle them with my thumb and forefinger. (Do they jiggle? Burn them!) I didn't even complain when I had to drink two high-calorie shakes a day. Give me four! Seven! Why would I care about any of it when I knew it was all temporary? Just as my real self had become lost behind my anorexic self, now my anorexic self had to be temporarily parked behind this scheming self, the one that was gobbling down crumbles and cakes. But the anorexic part still gasped out occasionally. "I am SO fat now. Fat literally HANGS off me," I wrote in my diary during my third week in hospital. And then added in the next sentence: "I have to get my back bandaged up again. At least I'm still skeletal somewhere."

Now that I had accepted the situation, thanks to the secret

addendum of my brilliant plan, I could relax into the reassuring rigidity of Hospital One's schedule. Like most eating disorders wards then, Hospital One operated on a simple reward/punishment system: for every bit of weight you gain, you earn special privileges, such as being allowed to leave your room, come off twenty-four-hour supervision, make a telephone call, use the toilet, go to group therapy, have visitors and so on. And if you lose weight, you lose your privileges. I already saw weight as a commodity, one from which I gained by losing, and now it became an entire economy that I traded in: How much can I get for this pound? What do I owe you, Doctor, for that visit with my parents? My weight became something entirely separate from me, just this amorphous thing that I could barter with, and while that kind of dissociation helped me to put it on, it certainly didn't normalize it. Instead, it encouraged my belief that this weight was something I'd shed—like an itchy scarf or a bad dream—as soon as I left hospital.

We were all given the same food to eat, the same schedules to follow, and no exceptions were made for anyone or anything. You were allowed to be vegetarian, but personal preferences were completely ignored. Don't like mushrooms? Or marmalade? Tough. You had to fit yourself into their mold, and any dislikes were assumed to be the anorexia and were therefore ignored. I'd always hated eggs but was made to choke down omelettes and quiches, which did little for improving my feelings about food. But that wasn't the point here. The focus was entirely on weight gain, and therapy was kept to a minimal afterthought. The official reason was that there was no point in bothering with someone's mind when their body was so destroyed, and there is some merit in that. But the main reason was that therapy is just too time consuming. Psychological treatment can take years, so inpatient treatment was really just about feeding up those in mortal danger, shoving them back out into the world and starting the therapy then, in the vague hope that they would somehow maintain their weight on their own, which is a little like dropping someone onto a high wire and assuming they'll figure out how to balance.

"That punitive approach was based on false concepts," says Dr. Agnes Ayton. "If there are specific risks [from a patient's being at an extremely low weight], it is explained to the patient why they are not allowed to do certain things. So now, instead of a punitive approach, treatment has become much more patient focused. We look at the individuals, rather than doing a one-size-fits-all approach: we look at their age, their history, and we involve them more in the treatment."

Christopher Fairburn, emeritus professor of psychiatry at Oxford University, has been helping to evolve modern treatment for eating disorders for almost half a century. Since he began working with people with eating disorders in the 1970s, he and his team have developed a therapeutic approach called cognitive behavioral therapy enhanced (CBTE) which, like traditional cognitive behavioral therapy (CBT), helps patients to break destructive thought patterns. But the "enhanced" part comes from tailoring the treatment to each patient's needs, as opposed to offering a blanket approach. In 2015, NHS England and the chief medical officer recommended that CBTE be offered to all patients with eating disorders, and it is now used around the world, from New Zealand to the United States.

"You need to engage the person, even if they're hostile or resistant. You need to engage them, understand their perspective, ask what they want to change about themselves and then devise an eating plan based on that, and this works with inpatients and outpatients," says Professor Fairburn. "Some people see anorexia as a brain disorder or a biological disorder, and they wring their hands and choose a drug treatment or simply refeed people. Or there's the family-based approach, which has a lot of evidence to support it, especially for teenagers who have been ill for a year or two. Then you teach the parents to act like nurses and regain control over their child. But this approach is anathema to me, because I believe that eating disorders are about control, and when someone is struggling with control, the control can get displaced onto their eating. The family approach doesn't acknowledge that and takes away the person's control, rather than enhancing it. With CBTE, we focus on helping people to have a healthy level of control over their eating and for it not to be the be-all and end-all but something you manage in the background. When parents take control, it stays center stage."

The high incidence of autistic traits among anorexics means that many eating disorders wards have become more aware of their sensitivities to certain noises, colors and tastes. There has also been an awareness that far from crushing the anorexia, the punitive approach enabled it in some cases.

"Some patients would prefer eating food they don't like, because that would ensure they don't associate food with enjoyment, and it was a way to punish themselves," says eating disorders ward nurse Sarah McGovern. "So we now have more individualized meal plans for people, and we encourage them to think about which foods they really don't like and which are just fear foods. Because everyone has some things they don't like; that's normal. This, then, helps them to think about which foods they do enjoy, and that's a big step for a lot of them."

Some wards even allow patients to continue their anorexic behaviors, such as exercising and vomiting. "For some, it's just too overwhelming to stop exercising and purging entirely, and it doesn't work to force them to do so. If someone used to purge five or six times a day, if they're on toilet supervision [i.e., chaperoned to the toilet], then they'll stop. But once you take away that supervision, they'll just start again. We use a graded approach, which a lot of patients find more sustainable. So with purging, we'll say, 'How about if you try not to do it after breakfast and we'll see how that goes?' Or we'll say, 'How about if you wait another five minutes in the lounge before you go and purge? And how about another five minutes?' And with exercising, we'll say, 'How about if you reduce your step count by a thousand steps? Or five hundred steps?' It's difficult finding the pace that someone feels comfortable to cut down, but you have to work with them. It's about finding a balance between us taking all the responsibility and them gradually taking it back," says McGovern.

In 1992, we were a long way from this kind of treatment. Instead, we were barnyard animals being fattened for the kill, adhering strictly to the punitive method. We were woken every morning at seven, and if you were a suicide risk or an obsessive exerciser like me, you were on twenty-four-hour supervision and accompanied to the bathroom by a nurse, who would make sure you didn't do jumping jacks during your shower (although they couldn't see your bottom half so wouldn't know if you sneaked in some leg lifts). We were watched, fed, reprimanded, cajoled and consoled by the nurses. If the ward was our world and the doctors our gods, the nurses were our queens. They were all from Northern Ireland or the Caribbean, and I quickly memorized their schedules so I'd know who was working when, especially Marie (Belfast) and Jocelyn

(Antigua), whom I liked best because they were stern but kind, understanding but no fools. They were certainly smarter and more empathetic than Dr. R. They never accused me unfairly of hiding food, but they always caught me when I tried. Anorexics tend to think of themselves as smarter than anyone else, because when it comes to their anorexia, they've been able to outsmart everyone. That can be reassuring, but it's also exhausting and lonely. So to find someone who outsmarts you is a relief, because you can hand over the responsibility, and it's no longer all on you. It's not your fault anymore.

The day was punctuated—as Dr. R. had promised—by three three-course meals and three snacks, which were supervised by the nurses and eaten either in our rooms or—in the case of the snacks—the TV lounge. Somehow the TV always seemed to be showing *This Morning*, and thirty years on, every time I hear that show's theme music, I taste the gaggingly sweet, throat-clogging high-calorie shakes they gave us with our morning and afternoon snacks. The days were reassuringly predictable, mentally unchallenging, comfortably numbing.

We were on the same floor as the addiction ward, so in the evenings we watched TV with drying-out alcoholics and heroin addicts in withdrawal, who occasionally had seizures on the sofa. My classmates, talking about their geography coursework and whose birthday party it was that weekend, felt very, very far away. In an astonishingly short amount of time, I stopped thinking about them at all, those girls who had once seemed like the whole world to me. I didn't even think about my best friend, Esther, who called a few times, but she kept saying she didn't understand why I was in hospital, which I resentfully took to mean that she didn't think I was very thin but later understood that she was asking me why on earth I was doing this to myself, to us. Initially, some friends came to visit, allowing me to live out my Madeline fantasy as they looked shyly at me lying in my bed: "In they walked and then said, 'Ahhh,' / when they saw the toys and candy / and the dollhouse from Papa. / But the biggest surprise by far— / on *her stomach / was a scar!*" I preened at my new identity—the sick one!—but they seemed less impressed by it than I'd expected, and soon they had better things to do on the weekend than take a forty-five-minute train journey to a psychiatric hospital. I stopped thinking about what classes they were in at what time, stopped caring if they remembered me at all, and my fickle mental landscape was entirely repopulated with my fellow inpatients. It was as though I'd slipped through a grate on the street and at first I watched the people hurrying above me, living their normal lives, wishing I hadn't taken my own normal life for granted. But soon enough they faded into the background, and I forgot they were there at all.

One of the first patients I became aware of was Lesley, who was childlike and cheerful, and she lived downstairs with the schizophrenics, but as the hospital's longest-term resident, she was allowed to wander where she pleased. It was rumored she had been living there for more than sixty years, paid for by her family, who didn't want to deal with her, and one day she would die there. She was a link back to the era when families would dump mentally challenged relatives into asylums, because certainly Lesley never seemed to have any visitors. Instead, she filled her days doing her rounds around the hospital, saying hello to all the nurses by name, visiting the kitchen staff in the canteen, asking them what was on the menu that day, seemingly happy in her shrunken world.

Back on my floor there was a very handsome, very posh twenty-four-year-old cocaine and heroin addict named Chris. When he mentioned that he lived off Kensington High Street,

I excitedly said that was just around the corner from where I lived, and he greeted this coincidence with the bored lack of surprise of a man who only ever encountered people who lived in Kensington and to have really stunned him I'd have had to say I lived in Peckham. But I thought about our neighborly status a lot: Had I seen his dealer going to his flat on my way to school? Had I walked my dog past it when he was inside, getting high? Before I went into hospital, I thought there was only one kind of drug—just "drugs"—and all the names I'd heard in movies—weed, crack, coke—were different nicknames for it. Now I was learning about dealers and overdoses. It was a different kind of education from the one I had been expecting in my first year of GCSEs. Chris had the easy entitlement of the extremely privileged and the hollowed-out sadness of one who knew he had already failed at life. He had been dumped by his girlfriend—his very cruel girlfriend, I decided—and I listened to him talk about that for hours in the TV lounge. Occasionally he would look up from his lap and gaze around at the rest of us, at the nurses, at Lesley, at me, this skinny, near-bald child who hung on his words, and no doubt wondered why he was here when he should have been in Courchevel or Mauritius, taking cocaine with his girlfriend. There was something about him that intrigued me, and looking back now, I see it was his weakness. I was only fourteen and barely seventy pounds, so there was no hormonal activity going on. But clearly this was a formative meeting for me, because I spent most of my twenties and early thirties dating versions of that man.

The only other patient from the addicts section who talked to me was a boy named Joe. He was sixteen and closer to my age than anyone else else in hospital. I could never figure out why he was with the addicts because, according to him, the reason he was in hospital was he had tried to kill himself. He went to a school very near mine, and he was the first person I met who read poetry for pleasure. He had dark hair and round wire-rimmed glasses, Adrian Mole but a lot less funny, and he raged against the stupidity of everyone in the world, especially his parents, who never visited him. He seemed to like hanging out with me, even though I had limited under-standing of his anger and would tell him to please lighten up, which, in retrospect, was not an especially helpful thing to say to a teenager who had recently tried to hang himself. He left after two months, and we didn't stay in touch. But four years later, on my first day at university, when I thought I had left all the badness and madness behind and could start life anew, someone tapped me on the shoulder, and I turned around and there was Joe. We hung out a little at first, keeping each other's secrets. But he was thrown out after a few months for, I heard, fighting with his tutors, and I never saw him again.

Living in hospital is what I imagine working on film sets must be like, in that you make these very quick, incredibly intense connections with people who are living alongside you. And then suddenly they're gone, and you're expected just to continue, as though you hadn't given so much of yourself to someone who has disappeared.

My fellow anorexics lived alongside me on the eating dis-orders corridor. Selena, Alison and Kelly: my neighbors, my new best friends, my sisters, my mother figures. Later I would meet anorexics who were competitive about who weighed the least, who would hide their food and make others feel bad for not doing the same, who were bullies when they were well and bullies when they were ill. But these girls were gentle and kind—like nurses to me, although they needed nursing themselves. They were all five to ten years older than me and had been there for a while by the time I arrived, but they never treated me like the intrusive new girl, the silly baby. We became a little crew. This was, for all of them, their second or third admission, and they helped me to acclimatize to the unfamiliarity of the hospital. They even showed me where the weekly menus were kept in the nurses' station, and the four of us used to huddle around them daily, staring furiously at the details of our upcoming meals, as if we could erase the words with the power of our eyes. After having been isolated in my own thoughts for so long, it was amazing to find other people who thought like me. This was by far the best thing about hospital: the pure relief of being with people who understood me.

After I put on six pounds, I was granted the privilege of being allowed to sit on the bench outside the hospital for a few minutes by myself. I almost never sat, because I read in a diet magazine that it burned too few calories (never sit when you can stand, never lie down when you can sit). So I stood by the bench, closed my eyes and felt the breeze on my face for the first time in weeks. All of the eating disorders rooms faced out onto that bench, so when I came back inside, Alison said to me, in front of Kelly and Selena, "I was just looking out of my window, and I thought, 'What's that stick doing next to the bench?' And then I realized, 'Oh, that's Hadley!'" Then she smiled at me. Whenever my mother compared me to a stick, she meant it in a bad way and she would cry. But Alison had meant it as a compliment, and she knew I'd take it as such and that I'd want the others to hear her say that. I beamed. It was wonderful, this unexpected bond with the other patients when I'd felt so alone before. It seemed so miraculous that it felt, a little, like falling in love.

Selena was the most obviously ill, with a face so thin it looked like a skull. She had been tube fed, and when I found that out, I felt—for the first and far from last time—a twinge of anxiety that I hadn't been ill enough, because I hadn't had the tube. (One of the downsides to finding kindred souls in hospital is that you now have people to measure yourself against.) Selena was in her mid-twenties, although she looked three times that age. Anorexia can be an attempt by the sufferer to return to girlhood, but after you cross a certain point on the scale, you go the other way and resemble an old woman. The emotional damage in her was as visible as the physical. Her life had been shattered by multiple horrific family tragedies, and she was so lost in her own sadness that she was the most remote to me. But somehow she could occasionally see through the fog of her own misery to reach out when I was crying because a nurse had made me eat more of my meal than I thought was reasonable. I saw her cry only once, and that was when she returned from a much-longed-for weekend at home with her mom. The hospital scales showed that she'd lost a kilo, meaning she wouldn't be given such a weekend again. As she cried, she let me hug her in the corridor, and I felt her, for a moment, relax into me. Then she suddenly stopped and, as if she'd remembered an urgent appointment, hurried to her room and shut the door. I still occasionally look for her online, scrolling through social media sites and Google. In my more optimistic moments, I imagine her living happily offline, enjoying the kind of life she never had when she was young.

Kelly felt like someone who, in other circumstances, could have been my babysitter. She was nineteen, soft spoken and a people pleaser, always concerned not to offend or upset anyone. She managed to keep the anorexia that lived in her on a tight leash: she didn't want to eat, but any negative emotions she felt about herself were never allowed to surface. She went home after I'd been there for a month, and the last I heard about her from the nurses was that she had lost weight again and her parents were trying to find another inpatient facility for her.

Alison was in her early twenties and my mother hen. She hugged me and let me cry on her, even though she was at least as ill as me. She never told me anything about herself but encouraged me to talk about my life, my past, and she felt like an especially friendly teacher and I cleaved to her. I was never intimidated by her, despite being ten years younger than her, because her obvious vulnerabilities closed that age gap. She was so terrified of making decisions that even choosing what to watch on TV would take her several hours. She had been in for so long that she was allowed to eat her meals unsupervised as long as she kept the door open. One evening, I finished my supper before her, and as I walked toward the TV lounge, I passed her room and glanced in to wave at her. But she didn't see me, because she was scraping some of the food on her plate into a plastic shopping bag hidden in a drawer.

Two months into my stay, another patient arrived: Amanda, who was nineteen. She had been in before, and I guessed she was extra difficult, because the nurses put her in the room directly opposite their station, meaning that they could always watch her. Like Selena, she seemed unhappy in a way I knew I was too young to fathom, and even though she was only five years older than me, I felt like a toddler next to her, because she radiated a quiet sadness, which I retrospectively understand was depression. Despite that, and despite my occasional gaucheness with her, such as walking into her room while she was eating because I wanted to talk, she was always kind to me, and neither of us, I later learned, ever forgot each other.

All of us were patients of Dr. R., although you wouldn't necessarily have known that as an outsider, because he hardly saw us. He appeared on the ward once a week and would talk privately to, on average, just one of us, leaving the rest to wonder what they'd done wrong. He never, ever took notes. I was too young to understand then that I was expected to have a crush on Dr. R. This was the dynamic he enjoyed most with his patients, and I noticed how he grew a little taller when he saw Selena and Kelly waiting for him in their doorways, hoping he would talk to them for twenty minutes, ten, just five. I, on the other hand, saw him as a strange old man who had a disproportionate amount of control over my life, and he clearly liked me about as much as I liked him. Once he walked into my room when I was doing sit-ups and he shrugged at me. At the time, I thought maybe this was a sign of respect, that he knew me well enough by now to not hold me to the nurses' petty rules. But now I think he probably didn't care. Once I'd hoped that he would enlighten me as to why I was the way I was and that his brilliance and charisma would over-whelm my anorexia so that I'd no longer have the black snake's voice in my head. Instead I'd have his, rich and booming. But his voice was a bored monotone, and he was neither brilliant nor charismatic. "I tell him what I know he wants to hear, and he seems happy with that, because he's an idiot," I wrote in my diary two months into my stay. In his eyes, I was just another anorexic, ticking all the boxes, a stat, a cliché, a paycheck. Our exchanges were cursory, our curiosity about each other non-existent, although that is more forgivable on my side, because I wasn't charging him money to be his psychiatrist.

Some weeks he didn't come to the ward at all, and the four of us would all look out of our windows on Friday evenings toward the staff car park, see him get into his car—we all knew which was his car, of course; we saw it arrive every morning—and watch him drive off, back to his happy family home, while we stared down the long tunnel of the weekend in hospital. It killed us a little inside, every time. He had forgotten us. Did that mean that, like Lesley, we would live in this shrunken world forever?

Chapter 6

Alison's Story

Alison was the patient I relied on the most in Hospital One, the one who felt closest to a mother figure, by which I mean I dumped all of my anxieties on her and she never burdened me with hers. This was exactly what both of us wanted: I was a narcissistic, immature teenager who only wanted to talk about myself, and she was a self-effacing young woman who wanted to be invisible. I was devastated when she left, six weeks into my stay at Hospital One, and I deeply resented the woman who was admitted into what I stubbornly thought of as Alison's room (Jessica, a late twentysomething who smoked constantly and abused laxatives, which both fascinated and repelled me. For years afterward, I associated the smell of cigarettes with laxatives and excrement).

I missed Alison, but it never occurred to me to stay in touch with her, because I thought of her as the adult and me as the child and it would be weird if I wrote to her, like writing to a teacher. But I never forgot her, and when I made the decision to write this book, it felt time to try to track her down to see how things had worked out for her. When I at last found her, we arranged by text to meet on a weekday afternoon at a bar in central London. I think we both wondered if, after thirty years, we'd recognize each other or have anything to say to each other. But when we spotted each other on the street, we said simultaneously, "You look exactly the same!" And she really did. It wasn't until we sat down and ordered a bottle of sparkling water to share that I understood why she looked so unchanged to me.

Alison was now fifty-two and the mother of two boys. I assumed she'd come from her home to meet me, but no. She had come from an eating disorders center, where she was now a day patient after relapsing recently.

"When I relapsed, I felt such shame around my age, being so old. But a doctor said it is quite common for former anorexics to relapse when they're older, when the hormones are changing. I think a lot of older women don't seek help, so people don't know about them, they just think they're skinny older women," she said. She then stopped and apologized for talking so much about herself, even though she knew that we'd met up so I could ask her about her life for this book. Repeatedly, she tried to change the subject by asking about me: How many kids did I have? How old were they? It took effort on my part not to revert to my narcissistic fourteen-year-old self and spend our whole time together talking about me. How much of this shy self-effacement was Alison and how much of it was the anorexia, and did the former encourage the latter, or vice versa? After thirty years of struggling with the illness, Alison found that knot impossible to untangle.

She had always been an anxious child. "Very shy, always hiding behind my big sister, a people pleaser, a perfectionist— all the classic traits," she said with a small smile.

All of these traits became more pronounced after her parents separated when she was four. Like many children of divorce, Alison thought that she needed to please the parent who had left so he wouldn't leave her, as he had left her mom.

"I believed that I was a disappointment to my dad and I worried that I was the cause of him leaving, which contributed to my lack of confidence. I thought the only way to impress him was academically, so when I didn't do as well in my A levels as predicted, I felt I'd really let him down. I was so desperate to prove something to him and put so much pressure on myself," she said.

At the same time that she was trying to show her father how capable and grown up she was, she felt terrified of leaving her mom behind at home. Torn between two impulses— adulthood and childhood—she started to lose weight, and in 1990, when she was twenty, she was admitted to Hospital One for the first time.

"In total, I was in Hospital One nine or ten times, sometimes just for a weekend when I was really struggling with depression, sometimes for six months. I ended up having ECT during my last admission. But when I look back now, I don't know if I really needed it. It's such an extreme thing, and I was really underweight then, so how do we know if it was depression or anxiety?" she said.

For a long time, I felt guilty that my memories of Hospital One were generally happy ones. How could I look back on being in a psychiatric hospital with fondness? But I did. I remembered Alison, Selena, Kelly and me lying around the TV room or walking down the road with them to rent a video and the feeling that we were a little team, always looking out for one another. When Alison tells me she feels the same, I experience the same sensation I had when she told me I resembled a stick: at last, here is someone who understands. I'm not a freak after all.

"It was a laugh in hospital, which sounds bad, but it was, wasn't it? In hospital, I felt like I had the permission to eat that I couldn't give myself, and also there were boundaries and feelings of safety that I craved and at times lacked at home as a child," she said.

Because I was ill when I was still at school, it felt a little as though I were playing with fake money: I wasn't losing real time by being in hospital, only time I'd otherwise spend at school, and I could catch up later. Being ill as an adult seemed to me back then to be a more serious statement of intent: no amount of extra homework could help you catch up on your years out of the workplace. I asked Alison what she had been doing in her twenties in between hospital stays.

"Nothing. I just lived with my parents—who got back together in my teens—and did a bit of voluntary work. But around my thirtieth birthday, something clicked and I think I finally felt fed up with my life revolving around gaining weight in hospital and losing it at home. Then my grandad died and I didn't want him to be looking down at me and thinking 'Oh, God, she got worse because of me,' because I knew he'd be devastated. Also, my sister had a baby and I'd wanted children since I was nine, and I fell in love with her kids. So I kept a pretty low weight, but it was enough to keep me out of hospital. My sister set me up on a blind date with this guy, and although I knew that he didn't have a great track record, I was desperate to be loved and didn't feel worthy of anyone better. We got married, but within a year we separated," she said.

By now, Alison was working as a teaching assistant in a primary school, and it's so easy to imagine her doing that, with her gentle manner and soft voice. After her divorce, she met her current husband, Michael, and soon after became pregnant.

"I didn't want anyone to say that I had made the baby small or whatever, so I stopped restricting. But I did still do things like measure my arms and my legs because I wanted to make sure that while I was putting on weight for the baby, I wasn't putting weight just on me, if that makes sense. I was still seeing Dr. R. then, and he was worried about what would happen after, because a lot of anorexics struggle after having the baby. But I was just so excited—all I had ever wanted was to be a mom. I'm such an organized person, so I had everything ready at home for him, the socks all folded. We knew we were having a boy, and we were calling him Charlie, and I kept saying 'Everything's here except for the baby!' The night I started to go into labor, Michael said he'd try to get a few hours' sleep, but I was too excited to close my eyes. I couldn't wait for him to arrive! You just don't imagine anything will go wrong, do you?"

Alison had a complicated delivery. "And then the baby had a heart attack. And then he died," and when she saw the shocked look on my face, she said, "Sorry, I thought I could talk about this without crying, but I guess not."

The hospital advised her not to have a postmortem, telling her the baby "had suffered enough," and in shock, Alison and Michael agreed. She was certain that it had been her fault, that she'd somehow ruined her body and destroyed her baby, and she went to a private gynecologist for confirmation. Instead, he told her that he didn't believe there had been anything wrong with Charlie, and if she'd had a C-section, he believed, the baby would have lived.

Alison pushed the trauma down and, desperate to be a mom, she and Michael soon went on to have two more boys: Josh, followed by Joe.

"I still saw Dr. R. for a while afterward, but I don't think he recognized the grief. So even though everything on the surface seemed lovely—living in Surrey with a nice husband and two kids—underneath I had to paddle desperately to stay afloat, and I was becoming really OCD. Everything in the playroom had to be just so, all color coordinated, everything in their boxes; if someone put something in the wrong place, I wouldn't say anything, but afterward I would fix it. I was fine with the boys messing it up, as long as I could tidy it up when they went to bed. But if someone had said, 'You have to leave the mess for a week,' I wouldn't have been able to do it," she said.

After the birth of her younger son, Alison felt strong enough to ask questions about Charlie's death, and eventually there was an inquest that suggested that the problem had been with the birth and not the baby.

"For Michael and the rest of my family, it felt like closure, because they felt they could blame someone. But for me it was the start of a nightmare because then I knew he should have lived, and that was the hardest to deal with. From that point on, I started a slow descent. It's just really hard, when you've lived with anorexia for so long, to know how to cope when things in life don't go right or, when you're feeling so low, to not chase those feelings of high you get when you lose weight," she said.

By now, we'd been talking for more than two hours, and it felt—as it always did with Alison—like talking to a big sister I'd never had, someone who'd been through so many of the same experiences as me, whose mental processes made as much sense to me as my own. Because how would I react if one of my babies died needlessly? How could I possibly justify eating when they were dead? And how could I cope with the sadness? Better to starve and not think about it at all. Of course she'd lost weight. I saw it as clearly as I see my own reflection in the mirror.

"I didn't want my children to be affected [by my anorexia],

but I just couldn't cope. But even at my age, you can recover, and recovery looks different for everyone. I remember them saying in hospital that an anorexic is a bulimic's dream and a bulimic is an anorexic's nightmare, and I know what they mean, because anorexia is about control, and that's hard to give up," she said, and I laughed, because I remembered the group therapist saying that, too. The reason we both remembered it is because it had sounded to us like praise for anorexia, and after all these years, we still hugged that close in our memories.

I had to get home to my children, so we walked out of the bar and onto the street together. We talked about the impact our children had had on us and our attitudes toward anorexia.

"Despite loving Michael and my children more than anything in the world, even they couldn't stop me from relapsing, but they're the reason I want to recover—although there is a voice inside me saying, 'Yeah, but only to a certain weight,' and I really hate myself for that," she said.

Alison can see differences between how she was as a child and how her sons are. Just the other day, one of her sons had told her he was anxious about starting at a new school. "And I was so glad, actually. Not that he was feeling anxious, but that he felt able to tell me and not keep it inside, like I did as a child. I remember at school I used to get terrible tummy aches because I kept all my anxiety inside, and the school said, 'Oh, it's all just in her head,' instead of seeing it as a red flag."

I asked what her boys knew about her illness.

"I have tried to protect them from it as much as I can, but they obviously know now about me being ill. They really try to understand, but I know it's hard with an illness as illogical as anorexia," she said quietly, and I squeezed her hand, two mothers walking down the road together.

Chapter 7

Mothers and the Woman Problem

A lot of things changed in my family when we moved from New York to London: we went from living in an apartment to residing a house; we left one dog behind and got a new one; we all—to varying extents—switched from speaking American to English, referring to "jacket potatoes" instead of baked potatoes and "the cinema" instead of the movie theater, even to each other. But perhaps the most unexpected change was this: my mother ate a "chocolate bar" (candy bar). It was a Bounty, and she'd been waiting for it for a long time. "I haven't had one of these for over thirty years!" she said afterward, laughing. And it was true. I'd never even seen her eat dessert.

My mother was always very slim. Her younger sister, Libby, teased her about her "skinny WASPy" friends, but it would have been more surprising if my mother had had lots of overweight friends, because, as she herself says, she always had "a thing about weight." When the then governor of New Jersey, Chris Christie, who is overweight, briefly ran for president in 2015, my mother said she could never vote for someone "who looks so out of control." She is now in her seventies and she never weighs herself, but she has worn the same clothing size for the past four decades, and if her clothes start to feel tight, "that's how I know if I need to restrict," she says.

My mother developed anorexia in her first year at university. "I just didn't like the food, so I would eat only bagels in my room," she says. "Also, I loved it that my thighs didn't touch." Her periods stopped, and in photos from that era her legs go from thin to scrawny. Eventually, her parents sent her to a doctor who also happened to be a relative, so when he gave her a gynecological exam to ascertain why her periods had stopped, she wanted "to jump out the window." She was so horrified by the experience that she decided if she had to eat to prevent it happening again, she would. Eventually, she says, the anorexia "just lifted and my period came back, which actually I didn't mind." Some girls and women who dabble with anorexia can slough off the worst of the illness as quietly as a snake shedding its skin. The downside, however, is that they are less likely to get treatment than more acute anorexics like myself. Instead, the illness lingers alongside them like a faint shadow, unexamined and unacknowledged, sometimes for the rest of their lives. So my mother never had any therapy for eating issues. "We just didn't back then," she says. "But it follows me in a way. I am still aware of weight, but now it's cloaked in health." To this day, when my mother is upset or anxious, she loses weight. "I don't comfort eat, I comfort not eat," she says.

Until I started researching this book, I had never talked to my mother about her experience with anorexia. We had never even discussed her feelings about weight. I just didn't want her to feel that I blamed her for any of it, which I didn't and don't, especially because I knew she blamed herself. But what if anorexia wasn't something I learned from her but, as Professor Treasure and Professor Breen had suggested, something I inherited?

"A lot of people think that depression has a high rate of

inheritability, but eating disorders have a higher one," says Breen. "Depression and anxiety have a thirty to forty percent rate on inheritability, and with eating disorders it's sixty percent. Schizophrenia, autism, ADHD and bipolar disorder are higher still, at seventy to eighty percent. I'm not saying the environment—the culture, experiences and so on—are irrelevant in regard to why someone develops anorexia. I'm saying they might not be the most important factors."

Some families reach for alcohol in times of stress. Others tend toward violence. My family has a different coping mechanism. My father's mother almost never ate meals with the rest of us, leading to the family joke that she didn't have knees so she couldn't sit at the kitchen table. A close cousin on my mother's side had bulimia. A cousin on my father's side had anorexia. One of my mother's cousins had to leave university when she developed anorexia. And then there was my mother's immediate family: her older sister, Marty, was overweight, "which was considered a sin in my house, because of my mother's ideas about how girls should look and also her need for all of us kids to be socially popular," my mother says. When my mother was thin, her mother "loved it."

My maternal grandmother, Harriet, was extremely pretty, which is a strangely girlish word to use for a woman I mainly knew in her eighties, but that was the word for her: pretty. She had blue eyes and reddish blond wavy hair that she wore brushed back and "set," as she put it, styled and curled at the nape of her neck. She was clever and loved nineteenth-century English literature, which she wrote about for local journals. She was also extremely feminine, always properly dressed and with a sweetly flirtatious air around men. She did not like fatness. Of her three daughters, my mother—thin, cheerful, popular—was probably the closest to her ideal, and my aunts

Marty and Libby occasionally made comments about my mother being the favorite daughter. My grandmother's house was filled with photos from the greatest periods of her life: when she was a sought-after young lady in 1930s Ohio and her wedding to my grandfather, Simon, whom she adored. Walking through her home, I'd encounter multiple smiling images of her, turned three-quarters toward the camera, chin lifted, breath held, as she excitedly faced her future, which seemed to promise only happiness. In the end, her husband died relatively young and my grandmother was looked after by her children and sons-in-law. She was able to write eloquently about Charles Dickens but totally unable to look after herself, because she'd been raised to expect that a man would do that.

I went with my mother to visit Grandma Harriet at some point between my hospitalizations, and she was, as always, very kind and loving to me, never complaining when I insisted we go to the same café every day because they served food there that I had decided felt safe. As kids, my sister and I were both small and cute, so we were the kind of little girls my grandmother understood. This, I knew, was something that my beloved aunt Marty—who had been a different kind of little girl—had struggled with, in her childhood and afterward. (I never got to discuss any of this with Marty, because she sadly died from cancer in 2001.)

Despite my mother's resistance to chocolate, I did not grow up in an anorexic home. But maybe there was a dynamic within my family that taught me food was the medium through which women express unhappiness. How can you separate heritability—as in a genetically inherited trait—from learned behaviors within families? Is there something in my family's DNA that makes us cleave toward anorexia, or were we all just picking up cues from one another and copying accordingly?

"A strong family history of anorexia going back in time is much more indicative of a high genetic load as opposed to just an anorexigenic dynamic in the family," says Gerome Breen. That genetic load relates to metabolic factors, hormones that control appetite, nonpsychiatric phenotypes that relate to body size, and so on. In ten to twenty years, Breen says, the genetics will help doctors predict who might be at risk of anorexia and make interventions earlier. "It's like if you have cardiac disease in the family, you modulate your behavior to reduce your risk. It can be the same for anorexia," he says. But with cardiac disease, it's only the potential sufferers who have to change their behavior; with anorexia, the whole family has to break the chain together. That means no casual comments equating food with guilt; no lives still lived in the lingering shadow that then engulfs those around them; no suppressed conversations that feel too terrifying to broach so self-erasure becomes the easier option. Despite all the talk about the role fashion magazines and social media play in anorexia, the family is far more crucial, because it is a much bigger part of the anorexic's life than *Vogue* is. Often, a girl develops anorexia because something within the family has made her susceptible to those kinds of superficial cultural influences.

I am not blaming the families. Different girls react in different ways to the same dynamic—it's rare, for example, for two sisters to develop anorexia, despite nearly identical upbringings. So just because your daughter develops anorexia, it does not mean you've failed as a parent. I wish I could paint that in red across the sky. Parents are not omniscient but shaped by their own times, their own upbringings, and all we have are the tools we were given and the ones we've happened to acquire. I'm now a parent myself, and I get things wrong with my kids every day, because I'm just another flawed human, and hopefully, when they're older, my children won't blame me too much for that. But for a long time, mothers were very specifically blamed when their daughters developed anorexia. This is quite common with seemingly inexplicable mental illnesses. From the late 1940s to the 1970s, it was assumed that there was a "schizophrenogenic mother" who induced schizophrenia in her child. In the 1940s, the psychiatrist Leo Kanner claimed that children who developed autism were reacting to a lack of warmth from their mothers, known as "refrigerator mothers." Both theories have since been completely debunked, but stereotypes about the mothers of anorexic children remain as firmly fixed as those about anorexics themselves:

"The mothers had often been career women, who felt they had sacrificed their aspirations for the good of the family. They are submissive to their husbands in many details, and yet do not truly respect them. They are enormously preoccupied with physical appearance, admiring fitness and beauty, and expecting proper behavior and measurable achievement from their children. This description probably applies to many success-oriented middle-class families, but the traits appear more pronounced in families of anorexics," Hilde Bruch wrote.[1]

This does not describe my mother, especially regarding her relationship with my father, which was always close and demonstrative. But I have yet to meet a mother of a girl with anorexia who doesn't, on some level, blame herself for her child's illness. It does seem like an illness specifically designed to trigger maternal guilt: the first thing a mother does with her child is feed her, and now her child is rejecting that feeding. It can only feel extremely pointed. I took it up an extra notch when I was ill, telling my mother repeatedly that I didn't want to put on weight because I didn't want to look like her. But even anorexic girls who aren't quite as cruel as I was make the same implication: They are resisting becoming adult women, and who is the closest adult woman in their life? Their mother. Only a particularly strong-minded mother can resist making that connection.

One reason the theories about refrigerator mothers and schizophrenogenic mothers collapsed is because the parents finally took a stand against them. As the trend shifted in the late twentieth century away from long-term institutionalization and toward home care, the parents of schizophrenic and autistic people found that they were demonized for their children's illness and also were expected to be the long-term carers for them. Unsurprisingly, this led to an enormous amount of frustration, and in 1979 the parents of schizophrenic children formed the National Alliance on Mental Illness (NAMI), demanding better treatment for their children and more accountability from the psychiatrists who had unfairly damned them.[2] Something similar, but less dramatic, has been happening in treatment for anorexia for a while, with psychiatrists increasingly resisting simple causation and thus dumping the blame on mothers. And just as with young schizophrenic and autistic people, the parent who often ends up being the carer of their anorexic child is the mother.

"Whereas with most illnesses everyone comes together supportively, anorexia really splits families," says my GP, Dr. Kaye, who has treated multiple anorexics over his long career. "There is often one parent who says, 'She just wants attention,' another who says, 'She's ill, she needs me'; one who gets impatient, one who's always there; one who's a soft touch, one who says, 'She's playing you like a violin.' It's like with addiction in families, and it's divisive rather than cohesive."

I've met a lot of families dealing with anorexia during my time in hospital and out of it, and I have seen the occasional father become the primary carer. But in the vast main it is the mother who devotes herself to her sick daughter, while the father looks on from the sidelines, scared, impatient, helpless. I've met mothers who've quit work to look after their daughter; mothers who've divorced their husband because he's not sympathetic enough to their daughter's difficulties; mothers who've made it their mission to cure anorexia in general, starting up support groups and writing impassioned blogs and articles for newspapers. They make anorexia—and their daughter—their job. None of this is necessarily bad, and all of it is understandable. If my daughter was wasting away in hospital, would I still be able to do my job, go on vacation, live any kind of life that didn't revolve around trying to get her better? It's hard to imagine.

But if those around the sufferer collude in making her world just about anorexia, how will she know there is a life beyond it? And if the anorexia is an expression of the daughter's desire to stay close to her mother, what lesson does she learn when that illness achieves the desired effect? Alternatively, if the anorexia is an attempt by the daughter to have something of her own away from her mother, her mother is potentially defeating that point when she decides she will be her daughter's savior. She is not giving her child the autonomous identity that she was asking for when she developed anorexia in the first place. Being the mother of an anorexic is incredibly painful and extremely lonely, and it is totally understandable why so many mothers write about their experience. I know it provides comfort to other mothers going through that experience. Maybe it's because I am a writer, but I am very grateful that my mother never did that. A child with anorexia is different from one with cancer or a brain tumor, in that they developed the illness in reaction to something else—in my case, my difficulty in making the transition from childhood to adulthood. So as unfair as this undoubtedly is, if my mother had written about my anorexia, it would have felt as though she was colonizing my story, my life, when it was mine to tell.

My first psychiatrist, Dr. R., told my mother that her "entire focus" had to be on me while I was ill and trying to get me better. In contrast, my second psychiatrist, Professor Janet Treasure, was absolutely emphatic that our family life should not be subsumed by my anorexia, and she was right. My mother was very involved with me while I was anorexic, but my diary is also filled with exasperated comments about how she still went to her book group in the evenings or that she had gone on vacation with my father and sister again, leaving me behind in hospital. Her absence stung, but it undoubtedly helped me to recover. I wasn't being rewarded with her attention by being sick, and even at my most institutionalized, I couldn't ignore the existence of the Real World entirely, especially when that Real World was my family on vacation in Florida, while my shrunken world was a psychiatric ward in the suburbs of South London.

The difficulties many mothers experience when they watch their once needy toddlers become relatively independent teenagers are well known. Less discussed is that some teenagers are highly attuned to those difficulties. Children are very good at gleaning their parents' expectations of them, and often from a very young age. How could it be otherwise? Parents are a child's whole world, so of course they study them to better anticipate what they want. A sensitive child can be better at understanding what their parents want than the parents themselves are. By developing anorexia, a teenager on the verge of independence may feel she is restoring her mother's role. Instead of breaking away and leaving her mother behind, the anorexic regresses, relying on her mother to feed her, watch her and reassure her, as if she had returned to the toddler years all over again. How can the daughter then recover, when that would mean, ostensibly, firing her own mother? This feeling can be especially overwhelming if one of the motivations for the anorexia was the daughter's deep, loving and honest desire to stay close to her mother.

I mentioned that my grandmother was smart. Well, my mother is more so, smarter than her mother and smarter than me. She graduated magna cum laude, and her idea of a fun afternoon is to reread some Anthony Trollope, watch a documentary about Eleanor Roosevelt and then teach herself the history of illuminated manuscripts. She has a hugely curious mind, but she left her job when I was born because her boss didn't allow her to work part time. Being a stay-at-home mother was not uncommon among her class and her generation, but one of the cruelest truths about being motherhood is that the hands-on part of it lasts only a relatively short amount of time—twelve years, maybe thirteen. Then what do you do when you're in your early forties and your kids don't need or even want you around as much and you've been out of the workforce for over a decade? This is not an original question, but it has yet to be answered satisfactorily.

Since the end of the Second World War the trend has been for more women to enter the workplace, and today around three-quarters of mothers in the United Kingdom[3] and United States[4] work. But these sweeping upward trends hide many complexities. In the mid-1980s, when my mother was raising my sister and me, only 29 percent of married American women held full-time jobs and married women contributed only 18.6 percent of the total incomes of their families. Between 1960 and 1980, the incomes of working wives fell in relation to the incomes of their husbands, dropping from 40 percent to 38 percent.[5] Thus, in my mother's generation, there was an absurd situation in which the demographic of women most likely to receive higher education (i.e., upper and middle class) was also the least likely to then work, because they didn't have to and it made little economic sense. So when I think about my mother's anorexia and my grandmother's anxiety about fatness before her, I think less about genetics and more about these generations of women who were so bright and not able to channel it in satisfying ways. They were trapped by their biological sex, and so they attacked themselves.

My mother and I were and are extremely close, and my anorexia was partly a reflection of that. On the one hand, I was trying to break away from her in a way that I thought wouldn't hurt her (I'm sick, so it's not my fault!). And on the other, it was my panicky attempt to try to stay close to her as puberty started to sweep me away (I'm sick, look after me!). (Dual contradictory messages often lie behind anorexia, which is partly why it's such a slippery illness. One friend from hospital who had very anxious and overly protective parents recently said to me when I asked if she knew why she'd developed the illness, "I think on the one hand I was begging my parents to protect me from the outside world, which they'd convinced me was a scary place that I couldn't possibly cope with, and on the other I was saying to them, 'See? You can't protect me from everything. Back off.'") All my mother ever wanted for me was to be happy and healthy, so she'd have been horrified to think that I felt I needed to make myself ill to grow up but still be close to her, and certainly my little sister never picked up any such signals from her. But I don't think I was interpreting signals from her specifically, because my anorexia was not just an expression of my confused feelings about my relationship with my parents as I grew up. For me, anorexia was also a rejection of womanhood—not specifically of my mother but of the state of being an adult woman. Anorexia almost invariably begins before the age of eighteen, and many people have argued that this is because that's when a girl's body changes and her role in life is changing, too, and the two together can feel overwhelming. But this happens frequently throughout a woman's life: her body and life change during and after pregnancy, and they also change during menopause. But there is not an epidemic of anorexia among pregnant women, and that's because those women already *are* women. It comes on in adolescence because these girls—girls like me—haven't become women yet, and they don't want to.

We refuse to bleed, and we shrink our breasts back into our bony chests. Sex? No way. A lot of that is to do with fear. But it's also to do with straight-up anger. We look at the choices modern mothers have to make—they're called compromises, but we know they're sacrifices—and we want no part of it. Is the end point of all our hard work in school, all our perfectionist striving, simply domesticity? We're told the world has changed, but that just seems to mean that our mothers now have to work in jobs but also still do everything else they always did: cook and clean and wipe their children's noses and flatter their husband every day, all day. Women's professional labor has changed over the years, but not the emotional. Outside the home, we see what being a woman means: to be looked at, to accept less, to subsume our own intelligence to build up the egos of mediocre males, to accept invisibility at the age of forty. We see the impossible standards set for women: be smart, but not ambitious; look perfect, but don't be vain; don't age, but don't get plastic surgery; be slim, but don't be obsessed with diets; be smart, but not smarter than the men around you; be pleasing and have no needs of your own. And it looks appalling. We see the hypersexualization of women, the expectation that we are as prone as a blow-up doll, and we read the articles teaching us how to make our throats wider, our anuses pinker and our vaginas tighter. And it sounds horrific. The effects of the illness are antifeminist, in that it reduces women to a helpless, self-destructive, childlike state. But its intent is often inadvertently feminist, because it is a rejection of all this nonsense. We don't want to be sexy, we don't want to be pleasing, we don't want to have to say yes all the time. Instead, we're going to be ugly, we're going to be difficult and we're going to say no.

So maybe those self-denying medieval girls weren't saints; they just didn't want to get married at ten and starved themselves into a convent instead. They rejected the life laid out for them. They said no.

Saint Wilgefortis, that original anorexic, was explicitly rejecting the life forced on her when she refused to marry the man her father had chosen for her, preferring instead to stay a virgin. She rebelled the only way she could: she stopped eating. By the fourteenth century, she was worshipped as a saint who had "divested herself of female problems";[6] in Germany—where she was known as "Saint Kümmernis" (a derivation of *kommer*, or "liberated from care")—she was worshipped as one who had divested herself of female problems so thoroughly that she had fully changed sex. But in the main, she was viewed by her (largely female) worshippers as a woman who had evaded the problems that come from being a woman. In Portugal and Spain, she was the protectress of women who suffered problems in childbirth; in England, where she was known as Saint Uncumber, she was prayed to by women who wanted to rid themselves of their troublesome husbands. As Wilgefortis allegedly said while dying on the cross, she had "liberated" herself from "the passion that encumbrance all women." She had stopped her menstruation, her appetites, her needs. She was unencumbered.

Thirteen hundred years later, there are still many girls and women who wish to unencumber themselves of being a woman. "The ideal body is attainable only by plastic surgery. The ideal woman has the earning powers of a CEO, breasts like an inflatable doll, no hips at all and the tidy hairless labia of an unviolated six-year-old. The world gets harder and harder. There's no pleasing it. No wonder some girls want out," Hilary Mantel wrote in 2004 in an essay about anorexia and why some girls try to reject womanhood.[7]

Others are more perplexed by the number of girls who try to reject womanhood. "Why Do So Many Teenage Girls Want to Change Gender?"[8] was one of many similar headlines that ran in the spring of 2020. This referred to the widely covered news story that the number of children being referred to the NHS Gender Identity Development Service (GIDS), at the time the United Kingdom's only NHS clinic for adolescent gender dysphoria—a condition in which someone feels their biological sex does not reflect who they really are—had increased from 77 in 2009 to 2,590 in 2018–2019. But the real story was in the details: 74 percent of those referrals in 2019 were girls, whereas only a decade earlier, the majority of children coming to the clinic were boys.

According to GIDS' records from the period of 2019 to 2020, prepubescent boys and girls were referred to the clinic in equal numbers:[9]

Age seven: 13 girls and 16 boys
Age nine: 24 girls and 21 boys

Then at age eleven, when young people start to go through puberty, there is a notable shift:

Age eleven: 52 girls, 23 boys
Age twelve: 127 girls, 37 boys
Age thirteen: 270 girls, 45 boys
Age fourteen: 404 girls, 90 boys
Age fifteen: 470 girls, 152 boys
Age sixteen: 350 girls, 162 boys

Puberty is also when anorexia generally takes root, and it is when girls are especially susceptible to mental health problems. Doctors now see girls as young as eleven and even younger experiencing difficulties, including anorexia, possibly because puberty is kicking in earlier and earlier for female adolescents.[10] In the winter of 2021 I spoke to Anastassis Spiliadis, a psychotherapist who has worked in GIDS and eating disorders clinics, and he told me, "We are heading to a similar sex ratio in GIDS as in eating disorders clinics, which are ninety to ninety-five percent female in the adolescent cohort. That makes me think about female adolescence, and how that can be traumatic for some girls, and whether we are doing a good enough job to support young people and to help them connect with their bodies in a healthy way."

Just as doctors have long suggested a potential overlap between anorexia and autism, some are now noting a similar one between anorexia and gender dysphoria, as well as one between gender dysphoria and autism.[11] Anorexia, gender dysphoria and autism are, potentially, a three-ringed Venn diagram, with adolescent girls in the middle, sometimes dealing with one of these issues, sometimes more. In 2016, GIDS published a study looking at associated difficulties suffered by young people with gender dysphoria, such as self-harm and depression.[12] According to the study, 13.9 percent of gender dysphoric girls and 12.3 percent of gender dysphoric boys suffered from eating difficulties, the exact same percentages as those who had attempted suicide. Also, 10.5 percent of the gender dysphoric girls and 18.5 percent of the gender dysphoric boys had been diagnosed with autism spectrum conditions. In the United States, studies have found astonishingly high rates of disordered eating among young people with gender dysphoria. A 2015 study[13] found that transgender college students were more than four times as likely to have an eating disorder as female ones, and a 2013 study[14] found that transgender high school students were three times as likely to restrict their eating as nondysphoric ones.[15]

I asked Spiliadis about the comorbidity of eating disorders and gender dysphoria in young people. "There's a hypothesis where people think that the eating disorder is always simply a response to the gender dysphoria.[16] So if someone is dysphoric, they say the eating disorder is just a way to suppress the development of their bodies. But what I see clinically is things are a bit more complex than this," he says. "Both things can be part of puberty, rather than saying one causes the other in a simplistic way. I think of them both as being under the umbrella of female identity in adolescence, and I call them embodied experiences."

Eating disorders and gender dysphoria are disorders of the body: body obsession, body hatred, body alienation. They are both rooted in the belief that if you change you body, you will no longer hate yourself. Girls are represented so disproportionately in both disorders because they learn from an early age that how their body looks determines how onlookers define them; it speaks louder than their own voice when it comes to how others see them. Is it really such a surprise that so many of them learn to see their bodies as prisons to be rejected? Or that they believe that if they change their body, they will change their life, their destiny, their inner self?

"Apart from factors such as anxiety, there are many different ent pathways into anorexia that are also connected to gender. For some it might be misogyny, a fear of being sexualized by others, a feeling that they don't fit into the preexisting mold of womanhood. For others, such as those with high-functioning autistic traits, it might be a need to control things, and when puberty kicks in, and women go through drastic changes early in life, they might want to seize control of their body, consciously or unconsciously," says Spiliadis.

All of the girls I knew in hospital dressed in a way that would now be described as gender neutral: baggy sweatshirts, oversize tracksuit trousers, boys' jeans. There was the occasional long skirt, but nothing that gave any hint of our bodies beneath, because we all hated our bodies in a way that went beyond a mere desire for skinniness: we didn't want to look like women. One girl, Carla, said in group therapy that she had stopped eating after a relative described her as looking "womanly," and all of us shuddered at the word, imagining rounded hips, pendulous breasts, a drooping bottom. All those stores of fat! Was anything more evocative of need and greed than a womanly body? Another time, I heard a scream from the room next to mine that was so agonized I thought I was overhearing a failed suicide attempt. I ran in: it was Sarah, a self-harming twentysomething with anorexia, who had been admitted two months earlier. She was standing in the middle of her room, arms crossed over her chest, crying.

"I have to wear a bra again! A fucking bra!" she sobbed, looking at me for help, but I had none to give.

A nurse came rushing in.

"I know, darling, I know," she said, embracing Sarah and shooing me out of the room.

I walked out, sad for Sarah but quietly thrilled that my own chest was still so bony, neat and spare.

It's too simple to say that Carla, Sarah or any of us was gender dysphoric and people just didn't understand that in the 1990s; nor am I saying that all gender dysphoric girls today are anorexic. Girls and women can feel loathing for their body for many different reasons. I am not discussing the experience of transgender adults; this book is about unhappy adolescent girls, and, given the long tradition of girls expressing their unhappiness by rejecting their bodies and the disproportionate sudden rise of gender dysphoric girls alongside the simultaneously rocketing rate of adolescent female anxiety, many doctors I spoke to now believe there to be an increasing overlap.

Until relatively recently, the word "gender" was interchangeable with biological sex. In the past decade, it has come to mean something very different, thanks to the rise of gender theory, which argues that everyone has an internal gender identity that may be different from their biological sex but is just as important because it determines how they feel and how they express themselves outwardly.[17] Gender activists claim that this broadens the definition of what a woman and a man are, because these terms no longer refer to people's bodies but to their inner feelings. Gender critical feminists argue that it narrows it, because gender theory ties women to femininity and men to masculinity. For example, Mermaids, a UK charity for what it describes as gender-diverse children, has defined gender identity as being on a spectrum from "GI Joe to Barbie." After this was reported in the press, Mermaids issued a statement that didn't deny its use of stereotypes but insisted they had been "tongue-in-cheek."[18]

We live in a world with starkly delineated gender lines. As anyone who has been to a toy shop in the past decade knows, toys are very divided between girl toys and boy toys, and it is no coincidence that the rise of gender theory has happened alongside the increased gendering of toys. In the first half of the twentieth century, girls were encouraged to play with toy cleaning sets and boys with tin soldiers, preparing them for their respective lives of domesticity and aggression. By the 1970s, toy ads showed boys playing with toy fridges and girls with carpentry sets, reflecting the rise of feminism and working mothers. But by the mid-1990s, specifically gendered toys were again the norm, with princesses for girls and cars for boys, and so it remains today. In an article titled "Toys Are More Divided by Gender Now Than They Were 50 Years Ago," the academic Elizabeth Sweet wrote that this is due to "a cultural backlash toward feminism [that] began to gain momentum in the 1980s. In this context, the model outlined in *Men Are from Mars, Women Are from Venus*—which implied that women gravitated toward certain roles not because of oppression but because of some innate preference—took hold. This new tale of gender difference, which emphasizes freedom and choice, has been woven deeply into the fabric of contemporary childhood. The reformulated story does not fundamentally challenge gender stereotypes; it merely repackages them to make them more palatable in a 'post-feminist' era. Girls can be anything—as long as it's passive and beauty-focused."[19]

This is all clearly true, but it's hard not to suspect that as well as reflecting a backlash against feminism, the increased gendering of toys was motivated by simple avarice rather than ideology: by telling parents they have to buy different toys for their sons and daughters, toy companies potentially double their potential takings. A 2012 study showed that all the toys on the Disney Store website were marketed either "for girls" or "for boys."[20] Corporate forces have colored children's worlds pink and blue.

Being a girl isn't just about pretty toys these days. One high-profile gender activist wrote in 2019 that the "barest essentials [of] femaleness" are "an open mouth, an expectant asshole, blank, blank eyes."[21] In 2017, another defined her desire to transition to being a woman like this: "I just want to get fucked like a woman, which is what it's about. It's not about what hole it's going in, it's about getting fucked. And I think that comes from a very instinctual place."[22] These are very feminine ideas of women, in that they are about passivity, and they are both heavily influenced by modern internet pornography, which took root and exploded just as gender theory started to gain credibility. To some girls and women, this vision of womanhood—sexually prone, mutely receiving—may sound extremely exciting. To others, it will sound as appalling as having to burn all their ambitions on the altar of motherhood.

I was never gender dysphoric. But I do know something about how hard it is to be an adolescent girl, how fear and anxiety can mutate into loathing of the body, and how this can lead to a total detachment from the body so that it no longer feels part of you but something separate and treacherous that must be altered and controlled. I understand the deep self-loathing that leads to a desire to become someone else, someone who is no longer in competition with the other girls at school. And I know how much ideas about gender hurt me as a child ("Nice girls don't do that kind of thing!"). Many girls are terrified of becoming a woman, and it's not because they should all be boys. Rather, it's because of externally imposed restrictions placed on women that have always made them unhappy and still do. Some of these restrictions relate to women's biological sex (pregnancy, childbirth, menopause, etc.), and they're told to accept them as their lot. Others stem from beliefs about women's gender identity (beauty standards, sexual objectification, femininity, etc.), and women are told to enjoy them. When I was fourteen, they all looked like a trap to me and I didn't see how I fitted into any of them anyway. So, like so many others before me and many others after, I wanted out.

"Girls and women have always found ways to show their distress through their body and have used their bodies to restrict womanhood, whether that means sex or the demands of adulthood. Anorexia is very much about that, and gender dysphoria is an extension and elaboration of that, with the added bonus that you can totally reinvent yourself and be part of a tribe," Dr. Melissa Midgen tells me. Dr. Midgen is a child and adolescent psychotherapist who worked for several years at GIDS and now works with people with eating disorders. "It was becoming obvious from about 2014, in CAMHS [the United Kingdom's Child and Adolescent Mental Health Services], when suddenly all these distressed postpubescent girls were coming through and expressing their distress by saying they wanted to be boys. From 2015 in GIDS we'd look through referrals and it would be all 'female, fourteen; female, thirteen; female, fourteen' and then occasionally 'male, five.' These were kids who had experienced trauma, neglect, isolation, but it was seen as wrong to look at the context of the unhappiness. Instead, there was a belief that what was wrong with them was that their real gender identity wasn't being affirmed, and once that happened, everything would be solved. I wrote in my notes at the time, 'This could be the new anorexia,' because it feels like a permitted way to self-harm and make yourself disappear." In 2022, the journalist Sam Ashworth-Hayes showed, using a Google trends alert graph, that, prior to 2014, global online searches featuring the word "anorexia" easily exceeded those that mentioned "transgender." In November 2014, for the first time, the latter exceeded the former, and this has remained the case ever since, with interest in anorexia diminishing as interest in trans issues grows.[23]

In the United Kingdom, Dr. Hilary Cass, the former president of the Royal College of Paediatrics and Child Health, was commissioned by NHS England to conduct an independent review of services provided to children and young people struggling with their gender. This was known as the Cass Report, and in March 2022 Dr. Cass published her independent review about the quality of care for children with gender dysphoria in England. She criticized in particular GIDS' "affirmative approach" to gender dysphoric young people, which argues that a child's chosen gender should be affirmed—validated—by their doctors and those around them. This, Dr. Cass pointed out, does not allow therapists to explore with the young person whether other factors play a part in their distress, such as mental health issues or trauma, as generally happens in therapy for unhappy young people. This is called exploratory therapy.

The debate over whether gender dysphoric children should be treated with affirmative therapy or exploratory therapy reflects disagreement among many professionals about whether gender dysphoria should be seen as akin to homosexuality and therefore treated with an affirmative approach or as something closer to eating disorders and therefore requiring the exploratory approach. After all, you would not say to a patient with anorexia, "Yes, being five stone [seventy pounds] is your true identity. Embrace it!" But equally, you wouldn't say to a fourteen-year-old who is telling you he's gay, "Maybe you'll grow out of it."

As is often the case when it comes to mental health treatments, there isn't a one-size-fits-all solution. Stonewall said in response to Dr. Cass's interim report, "It's paramount that children and young people have access to timely, high-quality health care and the right pathway for treatment will be different for every individual." (Mermaids, by contrast, issued a statement saying it supports the affirmative approach, "which simply means supporting a young person's understanding of who they are.") But an exploratory approach is clearly needed to understand why adolescent girls have been so disproportionately represented at GIDS.

"There has been a culture of self-loathing among teenage girls for a very long time," says Stella O'Malley, a psychotherapist who has worked extensively with adolescents. "First there was anorexia, which was a way of manifesting self-loathing as well as repressing sexuality and womanhood. Then it moved on to bulimia, then self-harm, now it's gender dysphoria. There's a golden thread between all these conditions: punishment to the body, sexual repression, self-loathing and a rejection of self. These kids feel all wrong, and they want to be someone different. Anorexic and gender dysphoric kids were always good kids. They were the ones who did the chores at home and were compulsively compliant. They never caused any problems—until this."

Like Dr. Midgen, the clinical psychologist Dr. Anna Hutchinson worked for several years at GIDS before leaving in 2017 to focus more widely on adolescents and adults with embodied distress. When I ask about a potential overlap between anorexia and gender dysphoria, she says, "What you have are miserable kids, and they often talk about not wanting to grow up. We see a lot of kids who are both gender dysphoric and have an eating disorder, and it's interesting to think about which came first. If you lose weight, you lose your breasts, and that's great if you're gender dysphoric. If you're gender dysphoric and are put on puberty blockers, that's great if you're anorexic because you don't develop a woman's body. So there are a lot of overlaps."

Gender dysphoria differs from anorexia in one important aspect: anorexia is deemed, rightly, to be an illness that requires treatment. Gender dysphoria is not and is often defined as an expression of the person's authentic self. Gender theorists believe that it is advisable to give gender dysphoric kids puberty blockers for the sake of their mental health, even though blockers cause a loss of bone density,[24] may affect their sexual function in adulthood and have unknown long-term psychological effects.[25] In July 2022, Dr. Cass published further recommendations about the treatment of young people with gender dysphoria, and she was excoriating about the overuse of puberty blockers, pointing out that the rationale for using them relied on data relating to boys who displayed signs of gender dysphoria. No one knew the short-, medium- or long-term effect they had on teenagers, including, Dr. Cass wrote, "the predominant referral group of birth-registered girls."

"Children are not short adults—but they have autonomy as well, and they can know their gender," Dr. Diane Ehrensaft, director of mental health at the University of California, San Francisco Child and Adolescent Gender Center, told the *New York Times* in 2022.[26] Other clinicians I spoke to disagreed and asked why doctors are—in this area alone—encouraging unhappy, confused adolescents to diagnose themselves. Medically altering a dysphoric adolescent's body—whether through blockers or surgery—is, Stella O'Malley said, "like giving liposuction to anorexics." Dr. Midgen added: "We don't say to anorexics, 'We will affirm your starvation because you have found your true self, and to do anything else would be a contravention of your human rights.'"

I ask Stella O'Malley why we can't just tell young people that men can be feminine and women can be masculine.

"Think of it this way," she says. "It's very easy for us to say to gender dysphoric kids, 'Women don't have to be feminine.' But that would have been like telling you when you were ill that women don't have to be thin. You'd have thought, 'Okay, sure. But I want to be.'"

And she's right, I would have.

Today's world is still very much set up for the slim and the conventionally pretty, and anyone who diverges from that template has an extra hurdle to scale socially, professionally, mentally. The older generation always hopes things will improve for their daughters as people become more progressive, more tolerant, more open-minded. But some things never change, and conventional female beauty is still fetishized to the point that it can feel like the expected norm, as just a glance at Instagram will prove. Anorexia and gender dysphoria are both reflections of that, because they take the feeling of not fitting into a template to the extreme. But whereas rates of anorexia have remained relatively steady for the past few decades, the number of adolescent girls being diagnosed as gender dysphoric has escalated. When asked in a Radio 4 interview why so many girls were suddenly presenting as gender dysphoric, Dr. Elizabeth van Horn, consultant psychiatrist at GIDS, replied simply that she did "not know."[27]

In July 2022, it was announced that GIDS would shut by spring 2023 after Dr. Hilary Cass deemed it neither a "safe or viable long-term option." Instead, young people with gender dysphoria will be able to be treated at smaller regional places where staff should, Dr. Cass wrote in her recommendation to NHS chiefs, "maintain a broad clinical perspective . . . in order to embed the care of children and young people with gender-related distress within a broader child and adolescent health context." Her report stresses that a child or young person with gender dysphoria is very different from a transgender adult, and they need to be treated differently. In October 2022, England's NHS issued new guidelines for the treatment of young people with gender dysphoria. Taking its lead from Dr. Cass's recommendation, it states that staff should "embed the care of children and young people with gender uncertainty within a broader child adolescent health context." In other words, the exploratory approach should be used, not the affirmative one.

Perhaps gender dysphoria is being diagnosed more in girls and young women because it's being recognized more by young people and medical professionals. But some who have worked with GIDS have other theories. Dr. Hutchinson and Dr. Midgen have written that "there are multiple, interweaving factors bearing down on girls and young women that have collided at this particular time causing a distress seemingly related to gender and their sex. These factors comprise both the external world (i.e. the social, political and cultural sphere) and the internal (i.e. the emotional, psychological and subjective). The external and internal interact and feed each other." Girls, they add, "have long recruited their bodies as ways of expressing misery and self-hatred. . . . For some, the terror of female adulthood is overwhelming."[28] They cite, as external factors, the internet, in particular Instagram and online pornography, both of which, in their own ways, make some girls feel that they just don't fit in as females. This is a feeling many anorexics can relate to, the sense that your body is making promises to the outside world that you can't keep.

"We're just seeing the first generation that's grown up online, grown up with online porn. Porn when I was growing up was pictures in magazines of women with big breasts, but now it's women being choked, BDSM. Common sense says these things will have an effect," says Dr. Hutchinson.

When I was anorexic, I didn't want to be a woman, but neither did I want to be a man, which—it was obvious to me even then—came with its own terrifying kind of baggage (sex, yes, but also sports, which was possibly even worse). I wanted to be suspended in time, a permanent child, skinny and scrappy, because that was how I felt safe, and so that's how I stayed in my mind. The first time I had a seizure at home, my parents called an ambulance, and as I came around they asked how old I was to check my mental state. "I'm seven," I replied. I was fifteen. This still happens. I had a seizure at a friend's house recently, and when I woke up, I insisted that I was twelve years old. So that's my inner identity, not gender dysphoric but age dysphoric, which is another way of resisting womanhood, by clinging to childhood. Old fears cut deep. It partly explains the anorexia, but it doesn't justify the starvation.

Research on the overlaps between gender dysphoria and anorexia is still very nascent. But, as with autism and anorexia, it seems clear that there is not one answer. Sometimes the dysphoria is an extension of the anorexia, and sometimes it is not. Sometimes the symptoms will fade during recovery, and sometimes they won't. Sometimes it's an expression of unhappiness, like anorexia, and sometimes it's something else. But there is one truth that has never changed, and that is that female adolescence is very complicated. Society has always idealized young girls' bodies, so it's easy to forget how ugly and filled with shame so many young girls feel and how desperate they are to escape themselves.

I asked my mother recently why she had eaten the Bounty bar when we moved to London. After thirty years, why break the habit of self-denial?

"When we moved to London, it felt like being in a movie. All rules were gone, so it didn't feel real," she says.

I understand that. Many years later, after I left hospital for the last time and really needed to maintain my weight, I changed my name for a year, because that was the only way I could bear to eat. Sometimes you need to pretend to be someone else for a bit in order to accept yourself.

Chapter 8

Anorexia Speak

Three months was pretty much the standard amount of time for an anorexic's inpatient stay at Hospital One, so in late November 1992 I was told I would soon be going home. I thought about the supermarkets near our house and what I would buy there (the aisles of crisps, the smell of baking bread, the fridges full of cheese—my heart banged in my chest). And I thought about going back to school and everyone staring at me, and I felt like I was going to pass out. What I did not think about, and what my parents did not think about, was that when I came home, they were going to have to learn a whole new language to talk to me. They were going to have to learn Anorexia Speak.

Most people know that anorexics see the world differently from others, but it is less understood that they hear the world differently, too. They don't just have anorexia goggles on but also anorexia hearing aids, an electronic device implanted within a sufferer's ear which retranslates everything they hear into Anorexia Speak. The words "You're looking good!" become "You're obese and must never eat again!" Families who are dealing with anorexia have to learn this language to communicate with their once sane relation to at least minimize the risk of her turning into the kid from *The Exorcist* midway through the conversation. Depending on the patient and the extent of the illness, this may be an unavoidable scenario, but there were certain comments that would set me off instantly. This is how the Anorexia Speak worked in my head:

"Boys like girls with curves on them."—If you ever eat anything, you will be mauled by thuggish boys with giant paws for hands.

"Don't you get hungry?"—You are so strong and special, and I envy your strength and specialness.

"Don't you want to be healthy again?"—Don't you want to be fat again?

"Have you tried swimming? I find that really improves my appetite."—You need to do more exercise.

"I don't know how you have the energy to do so much exercise."—You are extremely impressive, and also I am watching everything you do, so you'd better keep doing it or I will comment on your laziness.

"I understand what you're going through, I worry about my weight, too."—Everyone thinks like you, they're just not strong enough to follow it through.

"It's your body, and you need to take care of it."—So continue to starve yourself so you can make your body perfect.

"Look, if you're feeling anxious, just have a bowl of steamed vegetables for dinner. Don't force yourself to do things."—You have my full permission to never eat again.

"Look, just eat a nice roast dinner, you'll feel much better."—I am a complete idiot, and you should not listen to a word I say.

"Look, just forget about those fashion magazines. I know

you want to look like a model, but it's not important!"—I think you're a complete idiot, and I have not listened to a word you said.

"This is the time of your life when you can eat what you want. Just wait until you're middle-aged, and then you'll really have to think about dieting!"—All women wish they were as strong as you, and they're only telling you to eat so that you get fat like them.

"Wow, you're so skinny."—So you must never put on a single ounce because you look just how you want.

"You are making your parents so unhappy."—You are a bad person and deserve this joyless life.

"You look like a skeleton."—And if you put on any weight I will notice and comment on it.

"You look well."—You are so morbidly obese it is astonishing you are able to move without a forklift.

"You look like a concentration camp victim."—No one can be mean to you or expect anything of you, just as you wanted.

"You're going to end up sectioned and being tube fed. Is that what you want?"—You're not *really* anorexic until you're sectioned and being tube fed, so keep working on that.

"You've got to get some weight on you."—I will make you fat.

"You are doing so well."—You're fat.

"You will get through this."—You are fat.

"You are"—Fat.

"You look"—Fat.

"You"—Fat.

Nonpractitioners of Anorexia Speak said stuff like this to me all the time, even in hospital. From the temporary nurse who told me I looked "good and healthy now" (paralytically obese) to the recovering alcoholic who told me his daughter was thinner than me ("She just has those naturally skinny legs"). Not even my safe place was safe.

"Why do people say this stuff to me?? It's like they're trying to upset me," I raged in my diary. It's true that awkwardness around illness, especially mental illness, means people make the clumsiest of comments. But in truth, there was nothing anyone could say to me that wouldn't hurt me. If they told me to eat, I hated them. If they told me to do what I wanted, I felt in free fall. Anorexia Speak is not a very cheering language. For something more melodious, I recommend Italian instead.

Parents often ask me what they should say to their daughter. There is, sadly, no magic word a parent can say that will cure their child, and what seemed helpful yesterday might provoke screaming rage tomorrow (that's another thing about Anorexia Speak: it is a frustratingly mutable language). No one ever said a particular thing that helped me, but there were certain things that broke through the hard crust of the illness that encased my entire brain. Not the pleading, the reasoning, the anger or the crying, all of which bounced off my anorexia shield. Instead, it was comments about what my life would be like if I wasn't otherwise engaged with starving myself. Obviously, I hated those comments at the time and hated the people who made them. But I did hear them. So I hated it when my nurses Marie and Jocelyn asked me about what I was studying for GCSE or when my mother told me what my school friends were up to or when I'd hear about which school trip my sister was going on, because there was no way to translate those stories into Anorexia Speak, and so they were a reminder that I was stranded in no-man's-land. I twitched such comments away, but they still sank in and burned.

Parents need to learn Anorexia Speak not just to talk to their daughter but to understand her. During that first admission in Hospital One, the person I spoke to most viciously was the one I relied on the most, i.e., my mother. I felt safe to show her how miserable and angry I was because I knew she would never abandon me. So I blamed her for putting me in hospital, blamed her for making me get fat, blamed her for making me the way I was, blamed her for everything. I never got angry with Dr. R., and people around me back then assumed that this was because—unlike my parents—he knew how to "handle" me, but the opposite was true; I never trusted him enough to be honest with him. That is how it is when you're the parent of an anorexic (and of a teenager, full stop): the worse you're spoken to, the more you're trusted.

This doesn't mean that parents should passively tolerate their daughter's venomous tirades. But knowing that these Anorexia Speak rages, despite how they sound, are very much not an expression of hate can hopefully make hearing them easier to bear. My poor mother didn't know back then that my rage with her wasn't rage but love and fear. She didn't understand, and how could she? Neither did I, which is another problem with Anorexia Speak: the practitioners themselves don't fully comprehend it. But things were about to get a lot tougher for both of us, forcing us to become bilingual.

Chapter 9

The Real World

January–February 1993

"Where is she? I can fix her," a relative said to my father, standing on our doorstep. Not minded to wait for an answer, she pushed past him, walked into our home and marched upstairs toward my bedroom. Of course, I was in my bedroom. That was where I had spent almost all my time since leaving hospital. I'd been an inpatient for only ten weeks, but it felt more as though I'd been away for ten years, and tumbling back out into what everyone kept referring to as "the Real World" was as jarring as being yanked from a dream state to waking life. The streets all felt so wide and windy, the skies so dark after I'd become accustomed to the permanent lights in the hospital. So much noise, so much space, so many people asking me if I was so happy to be "back in the Real World." Instead of answering, I hid in my room, safe, enclosed, alone. Until one day I was invaded.

She was from the generation above me, and I'd met her a few times before. But even if she'd been my closest friend, I'd have been horrified at this sudden intrusion. I didn't even let my sister come in.

"Your parents can't understand you—only I can, because I've been like you," she said in a rush and sat down on my bed next to me. I jumped up and ran over to the far corner of my room.

"I can help you. You need to trust me and confide in me. Maybe you should come and stay with me? We can eat in our way together, I won't push you, because I totally understand," she continued, stepping toward me as I moved away from her, pressing my body against the wall as if to pass through it.

"Let's go for a walk—we can't talk with your parents around. Then you can tell me everything," she said, making a grab for my hand. But I snatched it away.

"I'm sorry, I can't, please, just leave," I said in a hurried whisper, cringing away from her.

She looked at me in shock, then in disgust, and then left the room, slamming my door behind her.

Mental instability can be merely an exaggeration of reality, and my complicated relative wasn't saying anything worse than what other people said to me in the Real World. They wanted to help, then were exasperated that I couldn't be helped, and then they were annoyed with me for making them feel like they should help more. One neighbor brought around chocolates "to give you a kick start." On my first day back at school, one of my classmates said she'd cried when she heard I was in hospital—not because she was sad for me but because she was jealous that I was successful at being anorexic when she had been trying so hard. Everyone wants to feel special. Some people told me that I looked great and shouldn't put on any more weight, when I still needed to gain another stone to reach my target weight. Others said I still looked too thin and it felt like their hungry gazes were feasting on my body. Some stared at me while I ate, as if I were a captive in a zoo, and said it looked like I was all better now. Everyone seemed to think this was just a physical problem and as long as I gained weight I'd be fine—so why wasn't I trying to gain as quickly as possible? Here, have some Maltesers, have some cheese, have anything. What's the problem? I was as unprotected as a freshly peeled orange, and every comment pierced me.

But there were things I wanted people to ask me, and they never did. Such as what were the nurses like in hospital (scary sometimes but also kind) and did I make any friends there (yes) and what were the weekends like (long and quiet and empty). They never asked anything like that. Maybe they saw it as an embarrassment—a psychiatric hospital? Gross! Either way, it was as though hospital was a blank space to them, a void I'd disappeared into, defined only by not being the Real World. They didn't understand that for me it had been extremely real and very safe. It had been home. And I missed it.

People talk about the viruses that people pick up during their stays in hospital. I picked up a superbug in there: Anorexia Turbocharged. Whereas before, my approach had been clumsily instinctive and blindly ignorant, I had emerged from hospital knowing exactly what I was doing and determined to keep on doing it. Being in hospital had saved my life, but it had also given me a defined identity—I was an anorexic!—and I understood now what that identity meant. This was in 1992, so I didn't, thank God, have online pro-ana (anorexia) groups to join or anorexic influencers to follow on Instagram, confirming my identity as part of a club. But the exercising returned, worse than before, and I was more obsessive about calories than ever. I developed a nervous tic—which still occasionally recurs in moments of stress, thirty years on—where I would circle my upper arm with my thumb and forefinger and see how far they could slide up before breaking apart. I'd do the same on my calves and then again on my thighs, making a circle with my two thumbs and forefingers. Seeing my wasted bicep easily slip through my fingers provided me with momentary relief, a form of self-soothing, although it had the opposite effect on my mother. I also knew how to cheat Dr. R.'s scales when I went in for my weekly weigh-in, slipping paperweights into my underwear and gulping down a gallon of water beforehand, my bladder desperately straining throughout the rest of our appointment (now I was grateful that he allotted only thirty minutes maximum to his patients). The hospital's dietician told me that I had to eat a certain number of calories for each of my meals and snacks, and I used that as an excuse to buy only microwave meals, which had the exact calorie information on the back. While my parents and sister ate my mother's macaroni and cheese, which I used to love, I insisted on microwaving a box of tasteless low-fat curry I bought from the supermarket and then ate it in the guest room next to the kitchen, because I didn't want anyone to see me eating (or leaving most of it on my plate). This, I assured my parents, was what was needed for my "recovery." While in hospital I'd also learned how to make myself vomit, and it wasn't my favorite thing or even a regular thing, but it was nice to know that I had it in my back pocket for emergencies.

Many patients relapse after leaving hospital and end up requiring multiple admissions. Four or five stays is average among the former patients I know. I needed nine, and in total I was in hospital for more than two and a half years over three years, with brief stays at home in between. Addicts know how hard it is to maintain recovery after leaving rehab, but anorexics don't need to just maintain—they almost always have to gain weight on their own. Addiction generally offers up good analogies when trying to explain anorexia, but the only analogy I can think of here is, imagine if a heroin addict didn't just have to eschew drugs when he left hospital, he had to put the needle in his arm every day and then pull it out before pushing the plunger. That is what it's like for an anorexic to put on weight out of hospital, having to do the absolute impossible thing day after day.

Anorexics have to continue their weight gain at home because hospitals just don't have the capacity to let patients stay for the amount of time it would take to get them to their target weight. Like many patients, I was released at the weight where I was deemed to be out of danger. It was also the weight where the hormones in the body kick back into action.

"It is very difficult for sufferers in adolescence to get above forty-one kilograms [ninety pounds], because at that weight your hormones start being released and all the feelings come rushing back, and they want to push them down. So forty kilograms [eighty-eight pounds] becomes the glass threshold that you can't get through," says Professor Lacey. "When people lose weight, the normal control mechanisms in their body become deranged," says Dr. Penny Neild, colead of the Adult Eating Disorders Program for London. "They lose their periods quite early on, then the blood pressure starts to not be regulated so well, the heart isn't being regulated, and the sex hormones are suppressed. As you start replenishing, the hormones kick back into action, and because anorexia tends to start [in adolescence] when so many other things are changing, and already people are in a big flux about how they feel about life and themselves anyway, when all that suddenly comes back, it can be very, very difficult."

The anorexia was clamped onto my brain more tightly than ever. The longer a person is ill, the more entrenched the illness becomes, and although hospitalization can be essential to save their life, it generally just attends to the physical problem while the mental one grows deeper roots. It's like repainting your house without dealing with the structural rot. I was so far down the rabbit hole that I now marveled at people I saw eating on the street, in restaurants, at school. Weren't they ashamed of their greed? How could they let other people see them do that? How could they show the world that they were arrogant enough to believe they were worth feeding and taking up space? It was genuinely inexplicable to me. I worked as a volunteer in the nursery of our synagogue on weekends, looking after the two- and three-year-olds while their older siblings and parents were at Hebrew school and temple. I'd always loved little children and loved especially the funny ways in which they saw the world. But now all I could see was how free they were of the thoughts that plagued me. They had no self-consciousness about their tummies, no hesitation about eating snacks or—the shame!—asking for more. "They don't even know what a calorie is," I wrote in my diary, when I'd barely known it myself a year and a half earlier. I couldn't understand how everyone else thought so differently from me. It was as though I'd woken up among some alien species—or, worse, I'd become the alien. This, I suppose, is what it feels like to be mad.

I became possessed by fear that anyone near me might be eating less or exercising more, and I constantly modulated my behavior accordingly: if I saw someone jogging on the street, I would start jogging, too, and it didn't matter if I was in my school uniform or walking with my parents. It pained me enormously to think that, somewhere in the world, someone was *always* exercising more than me, and if I allowed myself to think about this too much, I felt a deep ache in my brain and would gnaw on my fist to stifle my scream of frustration. Why couldn't I ever win? I urged food on people ceaselessly—

Have a cookie! Fancy a bagel?—partly for the vicarious thrill of watching them eat, mainly to ensure absolutely that I was eating less than they were. I'd always been competitive at school, wanting to do better than my classmates, and now that drive was channeled in a new direction. The leg jiggling reached new proportions, the exercising was out of control. My parents didn't have a scale, so I went to our local Boots pharmacy, which had a digital scale and, for a pound, would tell you your weight and if you were overweight. In one week, I lost five pounds, which briefly scared me but then thrilled me. (I was, the scale assured me, not overweight.) Finally, I'd found something I was the best at. I reread Maureen Dunbar's book about her daughter Catherine, and I felt no fear, only envy that she had been allowed to starve herself until her organs had failed. I imagined how people would talk about me if I starved myself to death: okay, they'd be a bit sad, but surely they'd also feel some awe, like how people spoke about explorers who died on a mission or astronauts who perished in space. Wasn't I doing what everyone wanted to do but was too weak to manage? I asked my sister if she was ever envious of me when I was at my thinnest, and she looked at me as if I'd finally lost my mind, but I smiled and knew she was lying: Who wouldn't want to look like me at my worst? I thought. Dr. R. told me that at the very least, I needed to maintain my weight and stop losing. I thought but didn't say, "But if I'm not losing weight, then everyone will know I must be eating, and that would be unbearable." I was supposed to keep a food diary and show it to him at our weekly appointments, but how was I supposed to do that when I couldn't even say the words "I ate"?

I'd missed the first term of my first year of GCSEs, but my school let me return in January. My books in my locker were just as I'd left them five months before, preserved like artifacts in Pompeii. Was I expected just to carry on as normal? My best friend, Esther, and I thought we could begin where we'd left off, but how could there not be a gulf? A therapist later told me that addiction is the opposite of connection, because the addict is too engrossed in his or her need for alcohol or drugs to form real relationships. Anorexia is an addiction to not eating and there was no room in my brain for anything else. Esther would be talking to me about what had happened the previous night on *Home and Away*, and I'd be mentally calculating how many extra jumping jacks I needed to do to work off that orange I'd treated myself to at lunchtime. A sparkling conversationalist I was not. Before, Esther and I used to spend all day every day sitting next to each other and then talking to each other on the phone for hours every night, but now I couldn't think of a single thing to talk to her about, and the only reason I watched *Home and Away*—or any TV at all these days—was in the hope of seeing someone eat on screen. I'd been away for three months, for reasons that were incomprehensible to her, so who could blame her if she felt betrayed? I'd broken the two most important best-friend promises: that I'd never change and that I'd always be there for her. Whereas once she'd gripped my hand, she now held me at arm's length, and I was grateful for that. I never held anyone's hand now. Who knew if they'd just been eating and the calories that might get on my hand?

I lost a lot by being anorexic: my hair, for one, which has never grown back properly, which a certain type of person on the internet still delights in pointing out to me; my teenage years, which were given to me as they are given to us all, but I burned them on a pyre. I did not know then that time is a gift that cannot be given again. But my biggest regret is the loss of Esther. We had been the tightest of best friends, and I loved her as I'd never loved a friend before. But I was asking too much of her, because I had changed so much and she was only a child herself.

When Dr. R. didn't let me go on the class skiing trip because I'd lost more weight, my father took Esther and me to Euro Disney for the weekend. We shared a hotel bedroom and laughed together as we hadn't in a year. But on the last night, I saw her noticing me drop pieces of my supper under the table, and something between us died.

Six weeks later, my weight had dropped back to almost what it had been when I'd been admitted the first time, and in February 1993 Dr. R. said I'd have to come back into Hospital One. This time I would stay for five months. I finally accepted the inevitable and dropped out of my school, and I said good-bye to Esther again, and that was the last time I would see or speak to her for many years. Unlike me, Esther was ready to grow up, and part of growing up is learning to put away your childish things, so I went off to be locked away, like a toy that has been outgrown. And the next day, as far as the Real World was concerned, I disappeared.

Chapter 10

Fritha's Story

I met a lot of girls during my various hospital admissions, and I remember the faces of many, the names of some. But Fritha Goodey stayed spotlit in my mind brighter than the rest, with her low, gravelly voice, her long, thick blond hair. I met her during my second admission to Hospital One, in the spring of 1993. She was, like most of the girls there, several years older than me, and I described her in my diary as "the most beautiful girl I've ever seen in real life." She also had the most beautiful name—who could resist someone called Fritha Goodey?—and it suited her, her ethereal elegance matching her breathy name, chosen by her parents in honor of the girl in Paul Gallico's elegiac *The Snow Goose*. She was tall, taller than the rest of us, and she had bright glittering eyes but a frequently distracted air; while the rest of us shrank ourselves to fit into the shrunken world, embracing our own institutionalization, she was often looking out the window, seeking elsewhere. She knew she did not belong in hospital with us.

There were more girls on the ward than there had been during my first admission and inevitably there were cliques. But everyone wanted to be friends with Fritha, even though she never seemed to notice. I went into the TV lounge one day and a bunch of the girls were in there, one group planning to go sit outside, the other wanting to watch a movie in the lounge. Both groups were asking Fritha to join them, but she didn't even hear them. Instead, as usual, she was lost in her own thoughts, completely uninterested in petty ward politics. To me, who was so desperate for anyone to ask them to join them anywhere, this struck me as deeply aspirational. Fritha was not playing it cool, she was—as she often was—in her own world, a world I desperately wanted to join her in, because I adored her. She was gentle, she was kind and she was beautiful. To me, she was perfect.

We didn't stay in touch—I was too shy—but over the past decade I've occasionally corresponded with her parents, Glenn and Sally, and one hot spring day I went to the family house in Southwest London to talk to them. As I arrived, they were packing up the home they'd lived in for several decades because they were moving closer to Fritha's older sister, Tabitha, to help her with their grandchildren. I mentioned that I was also about to move and told them my new neighborhood. "Oh, Fritha and I used to go there on our daily walks!" said Sally with a smile. Surrounded by photos of Tabitha and Fritha, I didn't need to prompt them for their stories about Fritha, because they were right on the surface for both of them.

"We lived down in Teddington when Fritha was born. She did horse riding, played the piano, did drama, dancing. Just a very full, happy childhood," said Glenn with an audible "So why?" beneath his words.

"There were things that made me think a little about autism, though. There was a floral wallpaper in her bedroom, and as a very tiny girl, she would point at it and scream, so she had to move bedrooms. One of our grandchildren has autism, and it's been interesting to watch them grow up. Fritha was very different from her older sister, much pricklier as a child," said Sally.

"But she was very popular, she had no trouble making friends and always wanted to give money to homeless people—I don't know where she got her generosity from!" added Glenn.

"She was kind even when she was ill, always kind. And she was academically good, a bit perfectionist but nothing over the top. That came later," said Sally.

As she grew up, Fritha's early prickliness changed into a strong sense of what was right and wrong, good and bad. When a bus driver once started to drive off while someone was still boarding, causing them to nearly fall over, Fritha went right up and told the driver off. "Once we were in Starbucks on Marylebone High Street," said Sally, "and a tramp came in asking for money, and everyone ignored him, except for Fritha. She said, 'Here's some money for a sandwich,' and he took it and didn't buy a sandwich, he left the shop. So I said, 'See! There you are, that's how it is.' Five minutes later he comes back in with a sandwich from Pret and says to Fritha, 'These are better.'" Sally and Glenn laughed fondly at the well-worn anecdote.

Before he retired, Glenn had worked as a high-ranking editor on national newspapers while Sally stayed home to raise the girls. "Fritha and I were very close, but she was much closer to Sally for obvious reasons. I used to leave the house at six a.m. and come home at eight p.m. most days, so Sally bore the responsibility," he said.

"We were very close, yes," agreed Sally. "She came to anorexia late, so we didn't have that so much in her teenage years—it didn't start until she was eighteen. But she was never a manipulative or awkward teenager. Everything seemed absolutely fine. Until the skin thing started."

When Fritha was a teenager, she'd developed some spots. This had made her so miserable that her mother had taken her to a specialist, who'd prescribed isotretinoin, which has been described as "an acne wonder ingredient." It has also been linked to increased risk of suicide, and many parents have blamed the drug for their teenage children killing themselves.[1]

"That was the beginning of the slow decline," said Sally. "I don't know if she began to lose weight because of that and she liked it or if it was all just anxiety on stalks. I remember she then went on vacation with a boyfriend, and she was taken ill with a kidney infection. I went to pick her up, and even in a week she was much thinner. Then we went through a series of doctors, thinking maybe it was the kidney infection, maybe ME [myalgic encephalomyelitis], but Fritha said nothing. It was a slow buildup. She had never said she felt suicidal or done any self-harm, but then she attempted suicide, and that's why she was in Hospital One."

When we were in hospital together in 1993, I knew Fritha wanted to be an actress and that she'd had a place at the London Academy of Music and Dramatic Art (LAMDA) but had had to defer it when she went into hospital. I hadn't given this too much thought when I met her, maybe because wanting to be an actress is such a classic pipe dream that so many girls talk about but rarely follow through on—the adult version of wanting to be a princess. But Fritha really did do it. After she left Hospital One—her only hospital admission—she worked briefly at Gap but struggled "to keep her head above water," as her mother put it. "Dr. R. told her to stop working, and he told all of us, the parents, that we should consider no lives for ourselves but looking after our daughter," said Sally. Fritha longed to go to LAMDA, and her mother came up with the idea of moving from the family home in Teddington to one closer to the drama school, making Fritha's commute easier. "We can change houses, but it won't change what's in my head," Fritha said. But she agreed, and they moved to the house where two decades later I would meet with her parents.

"That was 1994, and she had a tremendous time at LAMDA, made wonderful friends who are still in touch. It had been her goal in life to get there, and she passed after three years and started to make her way through the world of show business," said Glenn.

Fritha was cast in films such as *About a Boy* and Stephen Poliakoff's *The Lost Prince*, TV shows including *Sherlock* and *Randall and Hopkirk (Deceased)*. But it was really onstage where she got most of her work, joining Max Stafford-Clark's prestigious Out of Joint touring company. Glenn showed me a photo of Fritha in one of the plays. In it, Fritha is looking just as I always remembered her, and that's partly because she was as thin onstage as she had been when she was in hospital with me.

"They had to change her costume so that she had long sleeves, because her arms became so skinny," said Sally. "Tours were hard. There was always this buildup: how would she organize her food, what shops were there, which shops had the ready-made meals with the right number of calories. . . . So that was added pressure. Also, she didn't want other people to know that her life revolved around food, so she wouldn't go into digs with the other actors but had to stay somewhere else. It was all a source of anxiety."

Fritha had the looks, talent and drive to be an actor, but there are surely few worse professions for someone with anorexia, especially someone like Fritha. Constantly offering yourself up for judgment, being told that it's just professional when it all feels intensely personal, always being looked at.

"One thing that I think triggered something was she had a very brief part in the film *Alfie* with Jude Law, in which she played a nurse. Then it got cut. It sowed the seeds of doubt in her again. She started saying 'I'm not good enough, I'm not good enough . . .'" said Sally. Anorexia is generally born out of low self-esteem ("I need to be thin to be worth something, I don't deserve to eat"), and it then exacerbates it, locking the sufferer in her internal echo chamber of self-loathing and self-recrimination.

In 2004, Fritha was cast opposite David Suchet in a revival of Terence Rattigan's *Man and Boy*, directed by Maria Aitken.

"Everyone in the play told her how good she was, the director gave her a lovely letter, David Suchet sent her a note saying how glad he was that she was in it. But she kept saying 'I don't think I'm good enough, they don't like me,'" said Sally.

"Nothing would have reassured her," said Glenn.

Her agent phoned, and Fritha was certain that he was calling to let her know that she'd been fired from the play. He wasn't; he was telling her that the BBC had commissioned a second series of a radio drama she'd done the year before. Not even that could silence the spiral of self-doubt. She met up with her parents in Starbucks on the King's Road. She told them again that she wasn't good enough to do the play. Her mother said she didn't have to do it, but Fritha was adamant that she did. "It's my life!" she insisted. Glenn and Sally switched tack "to our usual cheerleading," telling her that she'd be great, she needn't doubt herself, she was wonderful.

"And I cuddled her and said, 'Give me a ring later,' and she didn't," Sally said. "It was so quick—she just slipped through my fingers. Suddenly in the blink of an eye, she was gone."

One September day, Fritha spent the day in rehearsals, and David Suchet later told Glenn and Sally that she had been "full of beans." She left at about 5 p.m. "Then she drove home, presumably knowing what she was going to do, the knife . . ." Sally said. Her father found her. In her suicide note, she had written, "I hope you will get over the shame." "Why would you think we would be ashamed?" Sally asked me, as if I were Fritha.

"She developed it at eighteen, and she died at thirty-two," murmured Glenn to himself.

Dr. R. contacted Glenn and Sally after Fritha's death, and he said it was the anorexia that had killed her, that she was so entrapped in it that her life was guided by it and she couldn't see her way out. But how can anyone untangle the anorexia from the anxiety, which had squeezed all the joy out of life for Fritha? The two were entirely enmeshed, exacerbating each other, draining all pleasure out of life for her. "Almost half of all individuals suffering with anorexia nervosa are also diagnosed with disorders of anxiety and/or depression. Regardless of age, one in five anorexia-related deaths is a result of suicide," says Dr. Penny Neild. "I think she was just so worn out by the constant anxiety," said Sally. "She never said anything about feeling suicidal, although she told her sister the day before she died, 'I feel like I did just before I went into Hospital One.' And then she was gone."

Maybe Fritha knew what she was going to do as she drove home from rehearsal, as her mother said. Maybe it was a split-second decision, caused by an overwhelming wave of desperation, "true madness, when you slip into something else," as Dr. R. later put it to Sally. It didn't matter; she was gone, when everyone had desperately wanted her to stay.

After she died, the *Guardian* wrote that Fritha's "was a successful career just waiting to burst into the big time; one special role would have done it."[2] "She had had problems over the years, but she was given so much support by her family and everyone hoped she had got through them. It's terrible," a friend told the *Evening Standard*.[3] Di Trevis wrote in the *Independent*, "Wider fame had yet to come; but it indubitably would have. Wherever she went, casting directors, producers and fellow actors murmured the same thing: 'A star in the making.'"[4] Of course, posthumous praise can be cheap. But seventeen years after she died, I still encounter actors who remember her. When I saw her obituary in the paper that I happened to be reading at work, I gasped out loud and burst into tears. Fritha is the starkest proof that anorexia really does pick off the best ones.

A few weeks after my meeting with Glenn and Sally, I sent them a note, asking how the house move had gone. "We have got rid of many things which have been collected over a lifetime and that has been hard," Sally wrote. "My biggest worry is that somehow I have left Fritha behind."

Never.

Chapter 11

No-Man's-Land

March–November 1993

When I left Hospital One in June after my second admission, everyone agreed I was in pretty good shape. Good enough, even, to be allowed to go to the United States and attend camp for a month by myself. I had decided to start a new school in the autumn, because I didn't want to return to my old school as I'd be in the year behind all my friends, and I liked the look of the crammer my mother had found, which was walking distance from our house. The plan was, I'd do my GCSEs in one year at the crammer, catch up with my friends, and then return to my old school for sixth form. Boom! Everything would return to normal, and we could treat this like the silly, reversible blip that it was, a crack in the wall we then painted over. This is what Dr. R. and my parents truly believed, and I was swept up in their optimism. I imagined myself at the camp and the new school, so popular and cool and happy. It wasn't until I arrived at the camp and went to the dining hall on my first night for supper that I remembered an awkward truth: I was still me.

Never is optimism more sweetly naïve than in the early days of anorexia. My father had to fly out and pick me up from camp early when my weight plummeted in two weeks, and I was checked back into Hospital One for the third time for a month's stay. Dr. R. said I should give up any idea of returning to education and focus instead on my recovery, but something in me knew that this was where my respect for the fancy diplomas on his wall ended. "If I quit school, what would I have in my life??" I wrote in my diary. A tiny flicker of self-preservation had flared up inside me, an insistence that I would have a future. Then it faded and I forgot about it for a long time.

My parents agreed with me about staying in school, and they decided to find me a new doctor. My father had never liked Dr. R. because he was arrogant and always late for appointments, and my mother had noticed that he played us girls off against each other in hospital, losing interest in those who recovered whereas those who stayed sick he blessed with the sunshine of his attention. And so we parted ways. But I stayed in touch with some of the girls who remained his patients, some of whom did adhere to his belief that staying in school was incompatible with recovery. Maybe that approach does work for some. But of the girls I know who left before taking their A levels or even their GCSEs, they either never recovered or believe it set them back years. What is there to recover for when the only thing in your life is illness and hospital? How can you rejoin the outside world when you've cut off all connections to your contemporaries and your future?

I never said goodbye to Dr. R., that man who had controlled my life for a whole year. But I did see him one more time. Almost twenty years later, I was at work, reading the newspapers one morning, and suddenly there he was: a giant photo of him next to a story saying that he'd been struck off by the General Medical Council because of his "blurred and secretive relationship" with an anorexic patient. A part of me wanted to pass out; another part thought, "But you always knew it was like this." The patient had gifted him large amounts of money, and he, in return, had prescribed her sedatives and sent her notes signed with love. The GMC criticized him for his behavior and also for his failure to keep "adequate records" about his patient, and that's when I knew the story was true, because he never kept records about any of us. For years, I cringed when I thought of the secret things I'd shared with him, back in the early days when I still hoped he might get me better. Finally, I realized that there was no need to feel shame because he'd never listened to anything I said anyway. I'd simply been screaming into the wind.

Dr. R. was not the only man I encountered in eating disorders health care who enjoyed blurred and secretive relationships with anorexics. There was the male nurse who took to phoning some of us on his days off and encouraged us to sit on his lap. When the other staff found out, they pressed us for details of his "inappropriate behavior," but we were all so desperate for validation that we weren't the best judges. It wasn't inappropriate; it meant we were special! He was quickly dispatched by the doctors, and some of the girls cried.

Over the years, I've heard from other former patients about a male doctor who ascertained whether girls were putting on weight by getting them to sit on his lap; a male nurse who insisted on conducting "pelvic exams" to check if a girl's period was about to return; another male nurse who made the patients strip down entirely every morning for the weigh-in; a male nurse who would leave notes for the girls on their beds.

Clearly, the vast, vast majority of men who work in eating disorders are not predators. But if you are the kind of man who feeds off the neediness and worshipful adoration of vulnerable women, then I can see that it could be a very tempting area in which to work. I never saw Dr. R. again, but I wondered occasionally how he ever explained his actions to himself. Did he think he had been a good doctor? A good man? I thought that he'd been a terrible doctor and my time with him had made me immeasurably worse—not because he had done anything but because he had done nothing. He had wasted my time in those crucial early days, and every minute wasted with an anorexic is another step deeper into the dark tunnel. I used to take some pride in the fact that I could always see through him. Of course he hadn't affected me—that silly, vain man? No way! But ever since I left him, I have always insisted on having female doctors. I guess he did affect me, after all.

With no doctor looking after me, I went careening off the cliff. If no one was weighing me every week, why would I eat at all? So I didn't. I loved my new school, a little crammer attended by kids who needed to retake exams or had been thrown out of their former school, where I could do my GCSEs in one year and therefore make up for the year I'd been in Hospital One. It should have been perfect for me, with its tiny classes and eccentric, passionate teachers who gave each student immense pastoral care, but it wasn't enough. Nothing was.

Every morning I ate my reassuringly pleasure-free breakfast of mini shredded wheat with one part skimmed milk to three parts water. Then, safely away from the anxious looks of my mother, I skipped lunch at school. I spent my lunch break standing outside the window of the bakery across the road from the school, staring at the buns and cakes. Please sir, I want some more, oh not really, yes really, not really, yes, no, no no. Anorexics say they don't want to eat, they're not hungry, eating makes them sick, and this is a complete lie. Of course we're obsessed with food—we're starving to death.

We long to eat, but we're terrified of how much we'll hate ourselves afterward. And so we starve, food dangled in front of our faces, our hands self-manacled behind our backs. I thought that when I stared at the buns in the bakery or spent all weekend cutting out recipes from magazines, I was proving how strong I was: Look, I can think about food all day and still not eat! But really, it was all part of the masochism that underpins so much of anorexia. As I gazed at the jam doughnuts through the window, a part of me got off on what I was doing to myself. I reveled in the exquisite pain.

There was a lot of schoolwork, because I was doing two school years in one. On this particular day I really felt the exhaustion, but I still had to do my exercises when I got home. (I had managed to do some in the toilets at school, but only sit-ups because I'd quickly discovered that people look at you funny when you come out of the cubicle after you've been doing jumping jacks.) Plus all my schoolwork, of course. It was a life as joyless as watery shredded wheat. In the few minutes of the day when I wasn't grinding through school and my thoughts weren't chaotically scattered, I fantasized about starving myself to death. I wasn't interested in suicide, which was the easy way out, but starvation fascinated me. At least then, I thought, I'd have achieved something. I'd mean something.

Before I was ill, I'd always had close friendships. I loved to feel like I belonged to a group or in a duo. How would I know that I existed if others didn't? Esther was the closest friend I'd ever had, as she was the first one I was old enough to really talk to, and the relief in that was immense. She was my bridge from being the little girl who told her mother everything to becoming a teenager who had her own world with her own friends.

The anorexia took all that away. I became secretive and

solitary. I avoided making friends at my new school, not just because I had no idea what to say to them but because I didn't want them to know me. I was terrified that someone might ask me to join them for lunch or hang out after school, and then I'd have to think of some excuse not to. I didn't want to seem rude, and so I tried to be invisible.

In late October 1993 I collapsed on the street. It was a dark autumn afternoon, although it always seemed dark to me then, the air heavy, and the wind blew through my bones. I was so cold then, all the time, shivering with blue hands and purple lips. Whenever I was inside, I would hurry to the nearest radiator and stand against it, so desperate for warmth I didn't notice when it scalded my skin. It's a cliché to say the cold was in my bones, but that is how it felt, as though I were freezing from the inside out, and I've never been able to lose that feeling entirely. As a child I loved the fresh air and snow. But now I dread the end of summer, and I always keep an electric heater next to my desk, just in case that cold comes back. Some people who suffer terrible deprivations become compulsive eaters when they get access to food again, or frantic hoarders. I am a heat hoarder.

On this afternoon, I was trudging down Cromwell Road in London toward my home. As I turned the corner to walk up toward Kensington High Street, I felt my chest go tight. Then my vision went. My lungs felt full of fire and my head was ringing, and suddenly I was on the pavement. At first I was worried I was having another seizure, but it felt more like a heart attack. Just as I was thinking, "Wait—no," the air rushed back.

"Here you go," a man said, grabbing my elbow from behind and pulling me up. "You had a bit of a tumble. Looks like you need a hot meal!"

I yanked my arm away from him—don't touch me!—and hurried away, embarrassed. After that, I had those semifaints fairly regularly, once every other week or so. I didn't tell anyone and certainly not my parents. This was when my GP, Dr. Kaye, told my mother to prepare herself for the very real possibility that I might die.

"Those were low days. I was very concerned about your electrolytes and your heart. And the sight of your poor scalp where you lost your hair. . . . All that suffering, all that exercise, not knowing why you were doing it—this disease really is a possession," Dr. Kaye later said to me.

I was having regular bone scans because I had such bad osteoporosis due to malnutrition, slowing my growth. Every scan showed that it was getting worse. Dr. Kaye would lecture me about this, but it made no difference. "It's not like I'm going to go home and eat a block of cheese, is it?" I wrote in my diary, my heart beating a little faster as I wrote the illicit word "cheese." But my bones were the least of my problems.

"When you lose weight, you lose fat first. But once there's no more fat to lose, you lose muscle, and not just the muscles in your limbs but the muscle that makes your heart pump and your lungs breathe. In addition to this, people become depleted of vitamins and minerals, which are important in maintaining the body's overall function in providing energy and stability to major organs, such as the brain, heart, lungs, kidneys and liver, and keeping the blood pressure at the right level. As the process of starvation continues and the body's energy and nutrient reserves are used up, the immune system starts to fail and it is much more difficult to overcome other illnesses such as infection. There is also an increasing risk of developing a fatally low blood sugar or a life-threatening heart rhythm disturbance," says Dr. Penny Neild. Abusing laxatives and purging put an extra strain on the heart, because they cause levels of potassium to drop, and potassium is a heart stabilizer, and to lose that when you're at a low weight with weak cardiac muscles is very dangerous. I didn't have that problem, but I was obsessively exercising.

According to Dr. Neild, "If you exercise when you have very weak cardiac muscles, it will put you at more risk of having a cardiac event and it may drop your blood sugar, which can cause death."

Dr. Kaye—who was now my only doctor—pulled me out of my new school and checked me in to Hospital Two, a private general hospital, where my blood pressure and heart could be constantly monitored.

The night before I went in, I asked my sister to photograph me in my knickers, because I knew this was the thinnest I'd ever been, and I wanted to preserve it forever. I also wanted close-ups, so alongside my schoolbooks and some changes of knickers, I packed a disposable camera in my suitcase and I spent my first night in hospital photographing every part of my body, as lovingly as a suitor: the sharp joints, the sighing hollows, the screamingly tight tendons. I knew how thin I was—not as a whole, but in sections—and I loved it.

Only the most acute anorexics are checked into a general hospital ward, yet general hospitals are profoundly unprepared to deal with anorexia. "In hospitals, patients generally want to get better. So it's very confusing for the staff to deal with patients who seem to be obstructing their recovery," says Dr. Neild. "Nurses don't want to be yelling at patients to eat, but then the patients don't eat, and they are put at further physical risk. Nurses end up being a mix of being strict and then not, and that's probably the worst of both worlds for the patients."

It is. At Hospital One, I'd loved Marie and Jocelyn because

they were firm but not cruel, kind but not pushovers, and they were always, always consistent. They took the responsibility for eating from me, because there was no negotiating with them, let alone any cheating. When one of them was supervising my meal, I knew what the deal was: I had to eat everything, and that was that. They talked to me like an individual as opposed to just another anorexic, but they also gave no concessions to my anorexia. That is what I needed in a nurse when I was anorexic. That was very much not what I was going to get in a general hospital. I would be watched to make sure I didn't die, but that was pretty much it.

Dr. Kaye had arranged for one nurse to oversee me. He told her I needed constant supervision, even in the bathroom, and that I was to eat everything of the meal plan that he had devised. But she didn't understand. How could she? Even those with specialist training had proven unable to handle me. I was off in my own land now, living according to an inexplicable system that set the rules, the voice in my head louder than ever. No one, let alone a poor nurse used to patients grateful for her administrations, could reach me.

The first morning, she brought me some toast with pats of butter on the side.

"I'll eat one piece of toast, no butter," I said, testing the water.

"Now, come on, you know what the doctor said," she said with a "let's not be silly" look, but I sensed a chink in her armor.

"I know, but just eating anything for breakfast is a big deal for me," I said.

She sealed her lips and gave a sympathetic nod. "Of course. Just eat what you can, dear," she said, patting my arm.

Eat what I can! There was no worse phrase. "But I can't eat

anything!" I silently screamed. My plan had worked too well, and now I needed to gauge the precise amount that would keep Dr. Kaye off my back but not bury my beloved ligaments beneath thick, rubbery layers of fat. I settled on two bites of dry toast and then gave her back the plate.

She made a tutting noise, but no complaint. "Tomorrow we'll try a little more, okay?" she said, and off she went, and I was left writhing in mental agony, wondering why I had eaten two bites when I probably could have gotten away with one.

She must have reported how breakfast had gone to Dr. Kaye, who in turn must have told her his thoughts on the matter, because when she came back two hours later with my morning snack of a high-calorie shake, she attempted a stricter pose.

"Now, you're to drink every drop of this, okay? No silliness," she said.

But the jig was already up. I'd seen her true self, and it was one I could manipulate. I didn't finish a single meal in that hospital and, as I flat out refused to be supervised in the bathroom and the nurse didn't have the wherewithal to fight me, I easily kept up my exercise routine, doing jumping jacks and sit-ups every time I went to the loo, which was now about thirty times a day. I told her it was because my body wasn't used to eating and that's why I spent so long on the toilet— a blatant lie I'd never have been able to get away with on a specialist ward. I should have been delighted, but instead I felt constantly anxious: at home I could do what I wanted, in Hospital One I'd had to do what they said. Here it was an unhappy mix of the two, and I felt constantly guilty that I was eating things that maybe I could have left on the plate, and the nurse felt frustrated that I wasn't eating enough. It was like being back home with my mother, but without the love.

I spent two weeks in that hospital, and I'm pretty sure that it was even less fun for the nurse than it was for me. When Dr. Kaye told me I was allowed to leave Hospital Two, I assumed I was going home, but he was checking me out only because he'd found a new eating disorders specialist for me, Professor Treasure, and she checked me into her eating disorders ward in an NHS hospital in London. Too tired to put up a fight, I agreed. And that was when I learned how dark life could be.

Chapter 12

Bedlam

December 1993–January 1994

Whereas Hospital One was in the pretty green spaces of Southwest London, and Hospital Two was in a quiet patch of West London, Hospital Three squatted on a chaotic street in one of the unlovelier parts of Southeast London. Just getting into the building was stressful, involving dashing across several lanes of traffic, and there was no respite from the pandemonium inside, only the swapping of bus screeches and car horns for shouting patients and visibly stressed staff. It was early December, so there were some halfhearted Christmas decorations strung up around the lobby, making as much holiday cheer as they could on an NHS budget. It was like someone asking weakly "Are we having fun yet?" at a wake.

My mother was with me, and we were led upstairs to the eating disorders unit. A nurse named Emma checked me in, and she explained that I'd be in "the dorm" with the other girls, which is also where I'd eat my meals. As at Hospital One, I'd be weighed every morning at seven, and on bed rest and half portions initially. This is still standard for all eating disorders wards, and it's to try to help the patient acclimatize emotionally not just to the food but also physically. A severely anorexic person needs nutrition, but it needs to be given slowly and with blood tests and careful monitoring of their vital signs, to make sure their body is coping with it.

Because Emma was kind, she said that even though I was vegetarian, she would write in my notes that I wouldn't have to eat egg dishes but could have alternatives. This was a huge relief and a big change from Hospital One, where the omelettes and quiches had made me retch and gag, and being forced to eat them in Hospital One had led to a lifelong not just loathing of eggs but a phobia of them. Being allowed to exclude something I genuinely disliked, a dislike that was not rooted in the anorexia but just a true personal dislike, would eventually help me learn how to enjoy food again. Emma told me I should say goodbye to my mother now. My mother was tearful, but I felt like an old practiced hand at this hospital shtick now—yeah, I got this, babe—so I hugged her good-bye without fear. Then I picked up my suitcase and followed Emma through a pair of double doors into the dorm. Toto, we're not in private health care anymore.

The dorm was a long, rectangular room into which they'd managed to cram in about twelve beds for patients. Each one had a curtain around it, but you were allowed to draw it only when you were getting changed, to prevent any surreptitious exercising, cutting or vomiting. Those few minutes of getting dressed and undressed were the only privacy any of us had. In the middle of the room was a long table, where we ate our three meals and three snacks a day, and there was a small kitchenette in the corner, where the nurses would plate up our food, which came up on a rattling trolley from the hospital kitchen. The toilet and shower were just outside the dorm, and most of us were chaperoned for that. The idea was that we would only eat and sleep in the dorm and spend the rest of the time in the TV lounge with the other general patients and on occasional trips outside the hospital, such as to the shops. This plan underestimated the patients.

In Hospital One, Selena, Alison, Kelly and I had thought of ourselves as a little team, but in Hospital Three it was every girl for herself, with everyone wanting to be the thinnest and the craziest. It was survival of the weakest. On that first afternoon in hospital, Emma told me to sit down at the table to eat my snack with the other girls, which I did. But by the time I'd finished my half portion of cookies, the others had barely started. They ground their cookies into crumbs and were either eating the crumbs individually, speck by speck, or chucking them onto the floor or chewing them up, then spitting them into tissues up their sleeves. Everyone seemed to be in competition as to who could eat the slowest, so that eating three cookies and drinking a mug of milk ended up taking two hours. I was bewildered. There had been nothing like this in Hospital One, where all of us had eaten our meals normally and never taken longer than thirty minutes. But in Hospital Three, meals took three hours, snacks two, each one bleeding into the next. Some days, we went from our beds to the table and stayed there all day until bedtime. The main instigators were three patients named Caroline, Tara and Nora, but soon everyone followed their lead and hid food: up their sleeves, in their pockets, under the table, kicking it under someone else's chair so they'd then get the blame. Butter was smeared under the table, mayonnaise flicked onto walls, biscuits and bread crumbled onto the floor. This was the room we slept in. It was disgusting and absolute pandemonium, and none of the nurses could control it, certainly not the gentle ones like Emma, but not the other kind, either.

A nurse whom I'll call Tessa worked most days, or at least it seemed so to us patients. She was probably only in her late twenties, and she was big—not fat but tall and solid—and she always wore biker boots, which she'd stomp around in, as if permanently furious, which she was. She never spoke, only bellowed, and she liked to slam her palms down on the table, making us all jump. If someone wouldn't eat, she would wrap one muscular arm around their upper half so they couldn't move their arms and then push the food in. It was genuinely torture. Tessa once threatened to do it to me when I had a seizure during lunch, insistent that I was merely faking to get out of eating. Fortunately, another nurse—not Emma but Gladys, another gentle one—realized what was happening and intervened to stop her from choking me with food. She would spend hours shouting in your face at the table, and then later, when she walked toward you in the TV room, she wouldn't glance at you but instead would stomp right past you. The other nurses—Emma, Gladys, Claire, Ann-Marie, Julie, Cherril and my favorite, Nicola—weren't just nurses but quasitherapists, and they would talk to us individually on our beds every week, holding us when we cried, listening to us as we talked about our lives. Tessa never did any of that, and the only time she ever said any of our names was to shout at us. She had no interest in us personally. To her, we were not people; we were reprobates to control.

We were badly behaved—of course we were, we were anorexic. Badly behaved, frustrating, determined to resist any efforts to help us get better. So when Tessa would force-feed us or scream at us, making us all cry and cower, I thought, "Well, we deserve it." What else can anyone do with us? I also thought this when I was small and adults would get cross with me and other children: we're annoying, adults know better. Now that I'm an adult and really know better, I feel about Tessa the same way I feel about parents who hit their children:

Why did you take on this job if you hate it so much? Tessa was such a throwback and a cliché it was hard to believe she was real at times—Nurse Ratched crossed with Miss Trunchbull. But she was, and those of us who knew her still talk about her to one another, in fear and in loathing. When we were in hospital, we all knew Tessa's work schedule, and even though there was no sense of solidarity among us, the nights before her shifts would start, we would feel the collective dread. The other nurses knew we feared her, and many of them had seen why for themselves. But with the patients behaving so badly, I suspect there was a general feeling of desperation: maybe, I imagine the thinking went, we need someone around to scare the girls, because nothing else seems to work.

This was not how the ward was meant to be. By having us eat and sleep all together—as opposed to on our own, as I had at Hospital One—the doctors and nurses believed it would foster an atmosphere of mutual support and that those early on in their treatment would be inspired and encouraged by those further along. And with previous groups of patients, it had worked like that. But this system didn't account for rogue patients and nurses who didn't see recovery as the end goal. Rather, what Caroline, Nora, Tara and Tessa all wanted, in their own ways, was control, and they got it. They controlled the ward.

The other patients in the dorm were easy to control because they were so vulnerable, even more damaged than the ones I'd met in Hospital One, having been anorexic for longer and, in many cases, coming from terrible situations. One girl, Joanne, had grown up in foster care and hospital was the only home she'd ever known, and so she kept starving herself to come back. Philippa was in her fifties; others were in their early thirties. The girls in Hospital One had certainly been unhappy, but in Hospital Three they were more broken, and the proof of that is that so many of them were bullies. You have to be incredibly broken to be an adult bully. Caroline, Tara and Nora were the worst offenders and also the most badly behaved at the table. Tara was twenty-seven but so thin and wasted that she looked about eighty-seven, and she reveled in her skinniness, always wearing leggings to show off her legs while the rest of us wore oversize sweatpants and long skirts. She refused to talk about her life, instead always changing the subject to weight. She loved to know how much other people weighed, and she regularly sneaked peeks at the weight charts in the nurses' office, gloating over who weighed more than her. Nora was twenty-six, and a few years later, when the Spice Girls became big, I thought for a brief moment that she was in the group, because she looked so much like Posh Spice. It was easy for me to imagine what she had been like at school, because that's exactly how she was in the dorm: the mean girl who reveled in her cool status and made sure others felt excluded. Do you know what makes you cool on an eating disorders ward? I'll let you in on that secret: it's if you've been fed intravenously. It doesn't matter if you've had seventeen admissions and you're riddled with osteoporosis. If you haven't had the tube, then you're just a day-tripper, and Nora made sure I knew it. For years I regretted resisting the tube in Hospital One. The one time in my life I'd had a chance to be cool, and I'd botched it. Typical me.

It was unnerving. I didn't know adults could behave like children. Before she was ill, Nora had suffered terrible personal losses, which were discussed only in whispers among us, and I tried to remember that. But it was hard when she made comments about how much I seemed to be enjoying my food or how much "better" I was looking and how she envied how good I looked with some weight on my face, knowing that every word was a knife in my brain. Who knows better how to bully an anorexic than another anorexic?

Caroline was the oldest of the trio and a devout Christian, and the only anorexic I ever met in hospital who was married. Despite her Christian values, no one lied more than her. She took hiding food to a kind of art form, slipping whole slices of pie up her sleeves so quickly that if she ever recovered she should have become a magician. But her preferred technique was to flick her food toward other people's plates and then watch as the nurses made them eat it, smiling to herself like a cat. Afterward, she would go to her bed and pray, maybe asking God for forgiveness or maybe just making sure He saw how she continued to resist temptation. Poor Caroline: she was born just a few centuries too late to get the holy veneration she craved. Caroline was the third evangelical Christian I met in hospital, yet I never met any observant Jews, Muslims, Hindus or believers of any other religion.

People say anorexia changes you, and parents especially say that about their anorexic daughters, and they're right, it does: good little girls become liars, cheats and terrors. Once people pleasers, they now cause enormous pain to those around them, and they refuse to stop doing so. They are willful and stubborn where once they were amenable and pliant. Tara, Nora and Caroline's bullying behavior was not part of their anorexia. It was probably, like the anorexia, a reflection of their unhappiness, but it was also partly who they were as people—traumatized, self-loathing people. I didn't understand that then, and so I only felt hatred toward them. It is only now, as I write about them, older now than they were then, that I feel what I always should have felt toward them: sadness.

Fewer than half of anorexics make a full recovery, and the number drops for those who have been hospitalized, and it drops yet further for adult anorexics. "By the time people are adults, the percentage of those who fully shake off the anorexia is very small. This is why I never say that recovery is the only end point of anorexia. It can also be about helping people who develop severe and enduring anorexia to improve their quality of life and reduce anxiety, and one way to do this is to take the pressure off full recovery," says Professor Lacey.

Up to a third of anorexics will remain chronically ill for the rest of their lives, and many of the patients I met in Hospital Three would do so; some of them knew it then, and their desperation was terrible. At times, it came out in terrible ways. "Why do the others affect me so much???" I wrote in my diary after I'd been there for a week. The answer was, I didn't have a strong enough sense of self to resist being influenced or bullied by them. Within days, I, too, was taking two hours to eat two biscuits and dissecting my meals as if they were scientific samples to be examined. I would slosh my soup all over my bowl and spread my food all around my plate, to leave behind as many dregs as possible. I pressed the grease out of my chips, squeezed the butter out of my toast, smeared the ice cream around the bowl, ensuring I could derive no pleasure from eating, only disgust. Unlike Hospital One, Hospital Three did not feel safe but rather was a constant test. All solid food had to be cut or torn into tiny, bite-size shreds before being consumed, like I was a baby at risk of choking. It took me decades to be able to bite directly into something—such as a banana or bread roll—even though I'd been perfectly able to do that in Hospital One. But when I did it once at Hospital Three, Nora told me that it looked like I was really enjoying my food, and so I didn't do it again until I was thirty, thirteen years after I'd left hospital—and when I finally did do it again, it felt forbidden.

Not all the patients were like Nora, Tara and Caroline. Nikki Hughes was checked in on the same day as me and she was also anorexic, although she didn't look especially ill to me. But she had diabetes, and her inability to maintain her blood sugar was making her a serious health risk to herself. Nikki alone resisted the temptation to eat like the other patients, instead maintaining her perfect manners (no squeezing of toast for her), finishing her meal in twenty minutes and then waiting for the rest of us to catch up, lecturing us about how stupidly we were behaving. "Lunch was samosas and I was able to smear some grease off of them until Nikki shouted patronisingly at me from across the table," I grumbled to my diary on December 15, 1993. She kept trying to make me be a better person than I was, and I resented her for it. "As long as I eat the fucking food, what does it matter to her?" I wrote furiously. But Nikki never got off my case, because she saw us as sisters, due to our simultaneous admission, and that felt like a curse, but really it was a blessing.

Nikki was twenty, and she came from Shropshire. She was small, only five feet, and she told me that she'd started to lose weight when she was fifteen because her best friend had told her she was fat. But Nikki was always so cheerful, so mouthy, and she had so much more to her than her illness. She was a talented artist, and she was funny, joking about "m' polys," by which she meant her polycystic ovaries. So it was hard for me to believe that she was *that* tormented by her anorexia. I was young and naïve, and I bought the lie peddled by the others that unhappiness must be expressed outwardly, visibly and performatively. She was only five years older than me, but she was twenty-five years more mature than all of us. Of course, Nikki was sometimes sad—mainly about her mother, who had died when she was young—and she worried about falling behind in her art career. But she never cried about food, so I assumed she was completely fine. I, on the other hand, longed to sink into the quicksand of craziness that the other patients dwelt in, fastening an easy identity out of illness and finding cheap validation in proving that I was more ill than anyone else in the dorm. Nikki refused to let me: her mere existence was a constant reminder that there was more to this world than the nuttiness within the four walls of the dorm and that most people did not behave as we did. "Why are you *doing* that?" she would scold me when she caught me trying to throw food under my chair. She was infuriating, but I was lucky she was there. She gave me much more than I ever gave her.

Only three years later, I was looking through a newspaper and there was a photo of Nikki. "Doctors Lose Anorexic Who Saved Others but Could Not Save Herself" read the headline, and my chest suddenly felt like an empty cave, because my heart didn't just stop—it seemed to shrivel up and disappear entirely. "Nikki Hughes knew what was good for others, but could not follow the advice herself, even when her life was on the line. She died in hospital with doctors and her family powerless to help," said the article. Because Nikki hadn't been sectioned under the Mental Health Act and she was an adult, the doctors weren't allowed to feed her without her consent, as they'd have been accused of assault. And so she died at the age of only twenty-three. She never got to be a graphic designer, as she'd wanted. I couldn't believe it, and for years, I couldn't talk about it. But when I let myself think about it, the question that terrified me was, had I made her worse? I certainly hadn't helped her get better. It is pure narcissism to think I played some definitive role in Nikki's life and death, but it is certainly possible that all of us in Hospital Three had entrenched her in her illness. That's the risk of coming into hospital: you pick up bad habits and validate your own. We all experienced that, especially at Hospital Three, which treated the worst of the worst, so we all learned the worst tricks, the worst thinking patterns, the worst ways to kill ourselves. But how could I have misunderstood Nikki so badly? All that time we were in hospital together, I thought of her almost like a nurse, but of course, she had always been a patient. All the care she gave me was care that she wanted for herself.

Nikki's death sparked a change in the law. In 2011 the Mental Health Act Commission issued new guidance for doctors about force-feeding anorexics, and it said that while a patient's consent should always be sought, some patients "may not be able to make an informed choice as their capacity to consent may be compromised by fears of obesity or denial of the consequences of their actions. The courts have ruled that feeding a patient by artificial means to treat the physical complications of anorexia nervosa can reasonably be regarded as medical treatment for a mental disorder."[1] The legal commission, it was reported, "took the decision to issue the briefing note after the case of Nikki Hughes, who died in January 1996." It's impossible to say how many lives have been saved because of Nikki, but "a lot" would be a safe bet.

My other friend in Hospital Three was Geraldine, whom I called Ger, and she was very much not like Nikki but also not like the others. She was two years older than me, and now she probably would have been diagnosed with autistic traits, because she refused to make eye contact with anyone, spoke only in a whisper and walked very slowly with her eyes always to the ground and her long hair in front of her face. All of those habits are long gone now that she's recovered, proving Gerome Breen's thesis that symptoms of starvation can sometimes look like symptoms of autism. But back then she was a mysterious mouse. I think what drew me to her was also what drew me to Nikki: she wasn't sucked into the cliquey dramas of the other patients. She ate very slowly, but she didn't care what the others thought of her. She was her own little island, and because I was so susceptible to peer pressure, I was fascinated by those who weren't. I have no idea why she decided I was someone she could confide in, but she became a real friend.

About a month after I was admitted, the consultant decided to move the eating disorders ward from Hospital Three to another hospital—partly, I assume, to remedy how badly things were going in the dorm, which had become completely unsustainable. One day we all nervously left the dorm and, closely chaperoned by the nurses, walked through the hospital lobby. Visitors and other patients stared at us as we went by. Anorexia is one of the few mental illnesses with an external and highly visible manifestation, and I could see them all thinking as we walked past, "Oh, look, it's the anorexics," as though we were a parade or a line of animals.

We climbed into a van and were all shipped out to Hospital Four, a psychiatric hospital made infamous by its frequent appearances in nineteenth-century horror stories. Despite its ominous reputation, Hospital Four was lovely, much lovelier than Hospital Three. Instead of being in the noise and grime of Southeast London, we were now in the quiet suburbs, with more space inside and out. We even had our own private courtyard, where we could sit on the grass in the sun. The gentle nurses Emma, Gladys and Nicola came with us, to my relief, but so did Tessa. Still, at least we now had a separate dining room, so we no longer ate where we slept.

Another new development in Hospital Four was that Professor Treasure—who oversaw all my treatment, from the food to the medicine to the therapy—assigned me a therapist, J.F. I've always fared better with therapists who are female, Jewish or American, in that order of importance, because it feels as though they have some understanding of my life, or maybe it just gives me the illusion that I understand them. Dr. R. was none of those things, and we never understood each other. J.F. was all three, and I'd never felt more understood by anyone in my life. Unlike every other therapist I'd ever seen, I couldn't fob her off by agreeing with everything she said or manipulate her into feeling sorry for me. She was the first one whom I knew for certain was much smarter than me, and that was annoying at first but, as with the nurses taking the responsibility from me about eating, J.F. put a stop to my exhausting people-pleasing pretenses, because she saw right through my game. She was in her early thirties and tall, and she always wore jackets and miniskirts. She was divorced and about to be married for the second time, which fascinated me because it seemed so racy. As well as being American, Jewish and female, J.F. had suffered from an eating disorder as a teenager. This in no way guaranteed that she would be a good eating disorders therapist. In fact, in my experience, it made her more likely to be a bad one. The therapist in Hospital One had been bulimic, and it had been obvious to me even then that working with people with eating disorders was her way of staying in the shrunken world after recovery and, maybe more important, staying close to Dr. R., who had been her doctor before he then hired her to be a therapist on his ward. But J.F. was different, and instead of viewing my illness through the prism of her own, she used her experience to better understand mine. She knew how the black snake in my mind worked and could always tell when I was lying or hoping to get away with something, but she never made assumptions. J.F. was the first person I told about the things that had happened to me at school, such as being caught in the toilet stall, and it was J.F. who told me I had done nothing shameful, which was the narrative I'd told myself for so long it had never occurred to me that maybe I'd written the wrong story. It had taken a long time to find the right therapist, and finding J.F. felt like finally finding true love after years of bad dates. I saw her twice a week for the next four years of my life.

Most patients, such as Nikki, had their own bedrooms in Hospital Four, which was another huge change—except those who were deemed to be a risk to themselves or their recovery, and that was me, Ger and another girl, a very sweet nineteen-year-old named Allie, who was, like me, a compulsive exerciser. The three of us shared a small dorm with twenty-four-hour supervision by a junior nurse (i.e., not Tessa). For the first time since I'd developed anorexia, I finally let go of my exercise schedule: no more endless sit-ups after every meal, no more thousands of jumping jacks a day. It was terrifying, sitting inert through those hours in which I'd once exercised, but it was also—I had to admit it to myself—something of a relief. The joy of lying on my bed and reading after a meal instead of frantically searching around for somewhere to do my leg lifts, crunches and jumps! Most amazingly to me, my body didn't change into a marshmallow overnight. In fact, I didn't actually look that different at all. I felt released. Released from myself, which was all I'd ever wanted. Being in the dorm, sharing a room with Ger, away from the others, all responsibility for exercising taken from me by the supervising nurse, seeing J.F. twice a week, I felt calmer than I had in years. I found peace in Bedlam.

Chapter 13

Geraldine's Story

Ger was very much the closest friend I made while I was in hospital, but after I went to university I stopped writing to her. J.F. told me I had to cut myself off from the girls I'd met in hospital so I could move forward with my life, and she was right. I needed to stop looking back over my shoulder. But I always missed Ger, and I was so pleased when I found her on social media while writing this book. I recognized her at once: in photos, she looked exactly the same with the same long hair, but—most shockingly to me—she was able to look straight at the camera. She'd never been able to look anyone in the eye when I'd known her, not even me, and we'd slept in beds next to one another for almost a year.

We exchanged messages and I asked if she would tell me her story for this book, and she agreed. Because we were in lockdown and Ger lives in Ireland, we could talk only on the phone, and over the course of several months and many long conversations, we caught up on each other's lives.

In all the time we spent together in hospital, we'd never spoken of our lives before, because we had been so locked in to the present moment, day by day, meal by meal. So I asked her what she had been like before I knew her.

"When I was in primary school, I was really loud and

vibrant, actually. And I had a great relationship with my parents—I was their only child—but there were some things I didn't talk about with them that I know now I should have done. Because there was nothing in particular that set me off, but looking back I can see there were lots of little things," she said.

Ger's mother visited her every day when we were in hospital, and the two of them were so close. Her father also came regularly, but he was much older and frail with what I later realized was Parkinson's. He had been married before, Ger said, but his first wife had died, and so she had a much older half brother and half sister. I said I couldn't remember any siblings ever visiting her, but maybe I'd forgotten them? She hesitated a little before answering "No, my half sister moved to Canada when she was seventeen, so I don't really know her. But I was very close to my half brother, and he would come around every other week or so. But when I was seven, he left his wife and he and my dad had a falling-out about it, and all of a sudden he stopped coming around. But I didn't know about all that, so I thought it was because he didn't want to see me, and that's what I thought for a long time."

Both of Ger's parents were Irish, but they lived in Middlesex then. When Ger made the shift to secondary school, she was bullied by some of the girls in her class. "Then when I was twelve, I looked older, like about fifteen, and I got involved with the bus driver who took me to school. I didn't know quite what was happening, but I knew I couldn't share it with anyone. Then he got married and it felt like such rejection, but I couldn't tell anyone," she said.

The anorexia kicked in when Ger was fourteen, and it took hold of her completely.

"I remember thinking that eating an apple a day was all I

needed, but I also remember before school leaving a bowl in the sink with bits of Weetabix in it so my mom would think I'd had breakfast, so on some level I knew what I was doing was wrong. But I didn't really know what I was doing until my parents took me to a consultant and he admitted me straight-away, and that was that."

I asked her something that I'd always been too shy to ask when we were in hospital: Did she think her father's illness had played a part in her anorexia?

"I think so. He became less approachable, and I think it was a bit of the two of us not knowing what to do. I know it tore him apart seeing me the way I was, and I was upset seeing the way he was going. But my mom was really my safety net. Even when I was sick, I could always talk to her."

In hospital, I'd envied the consistency of Ger's relation-ship with her mother. Whereas I had alternately pulled mine toward me and then pushed her away, wanting to tell her everything and also tell her nothing, Ger had always been close with her mother, the two of them talking to each other on her bed for hours at a time.

But even with her mom, Ger talked the way she talked with everyone: in a whisper, with her eyes always down. Speaking with her on the phone is the first time I've ever heard her voice properly. Can she remember what compelled her to whisper when she was ill?

"I think the trauma of being in hospital made me shut down completely, to be honest. I couldn't bear to look at myself, so I didn't want anyone else to look at me, and it was like, if I didn't look at someone, they couldn't see me: make yourself small, put your hair in front of your face. I wasn't like that before, but after I was hospitalized, I couldn't bear to look anyone in the eye, and it's still not something I'm good at. I have to make a conscious effort, but I find it easier to look at something else instead of at someone. My mom understands that, so I can do it with her," she said.

Anorexia cuts you off from the world. You become solitary, obsessive, unable to engage with others, and you live according to rules only you fully understand. Sometimes, with some people with anorexia, these feelings are not just experienced internally but expressed externally, too, such as through an inability to make eye contact or a reluctance to speak. These are also sometimes symptoms of autism, and when we were in hospital together, I know some people wondered if Ger was autistic, which she isn't. But it is unsurprising that the symptoms of one disorder can overlap with symptoms of the other.

I have never doubted that being hospitalized saved my life. Despite the bad habits learned and rogue patients, nurses and doctors, I know I would not have recovered without it. But Ger was more ambivalent. "I know hospitals keep you alive, but you're not the same after you've been in, because it changes your view of what's going on and what you're in the middle of. You pick up that competitive element from the other patients. I still have to make sure my food touches every bit of my plate and bowl, like we did in Hospitals Three and Four, and for years I couldn't eat meat and potatoes in the same bite—I would eat my way around the plate, like I learned in hospital. So I wonder if I'd have struggled so much if I hadn't been plunged into that atmosphere. And one thing I can never forget is when Tessa force-fed me at the table. It's the nearest thing I've experienced to being raped. I can still remember the smell of the banana Fortisip [a high-calorie shake], her holding me down, pinching my nose so my mouth had to open. Sometimes it felt like they enjoyed it. How you're treated in hospital really matters, because it affects how you see your-

171

self," she said. Ger had far worse experiences with nurses than I did. Before Tessa, and before I knew her, she had been in a hospital then known as the Peter Dally Clinic and had been looked after by a nurse named David Britten.

"He would worm his way into being your best friend, and he'd sit on your bed with his hand on your leg. Once, when he knew I was annoyed with him, he slipped a note under my door with a diagram showing the route to his office. Nothing happened between us, but it did with other patients," she said.

An investigation later found that Britten was a "manipulative predator who represents a clear danger to women," grooming the most vulnerable. He was sexually involved with many patients and in some cases impregnated them. He was sacked in 2002 and is thought to be living in France.[1]

I left Hospital Four before Ger and stopped communicating with her about six months later, so I hadn't known what had happened to her. She told me that she'd lost weight again and had been going to be sectioned in the Peter Dally Clinic again. By this point, Ger had gone through seven hospital admissions and her parents agreed with her, this system was not working.

"I'd always wanted to live in Ireland because it's where my extended family all live, and I said to my parents that if we went there, I would really, really try to get better. They thought, Well, why not? So we upped sticks and left, the day before I was going to be sectioned, and that's where I've lived ever since."

It would have been a tidy ending if Ger had recovered completely as soon as they arrived in Ireland. Too tidy for anorexia. After the move, she had two more admissions—once into a general hospital and once into a psychiatric facility that didn't have an eating disorders ward. When she left hospital for the last time, she was twenty-four and had been in and out of hospitals for a decade. She had no academic qualifications.

"At first, I was treading water for five or six years, with my weight being monitored, and I stayed steady for my mom and dad. But the more you go on, the more you realize it doesn't have to be like this, just getting through the days. I love being here in Ireland, because I have my family up the road and that means a lot, having support," she said.

When she was twenty-seven, she went back to school and did a degree course in clinical physiology. This took longer than expected, because Ger now suffered badly from fibromyalgia, as well as osteoporosis, which she'd developed during the anorexia. Even worse, her mom fell seriously ill. "But I got there in the end, and now I'm a clinical physiologist," she said.

I asked Ger if she felt the same as me, that we were lucky to get ill and treated when we were young, so it didn't dominate our adult lives.

"I don't know. It's hard if you get ill young, because when you get better, you don't have the background of growing up to go back to. Suddenly I was straight into my late twenties and hadn't had teenage experiences, like heartbreak. So I felt completely smacked in the face when that then happened to me, because I had no idea of how to cope with that. I still have a thing about rejection—that's massive for me," she said.

We talked more about our lives, and she gasped when I told her I have three children, because she still remembered me as the childlike adolescent I was. I asked about her parents. Her father had died several years before, but her mom was still very much around and still Ger's best friend.

"I live with her, and I worry about what will happen when something happens to her. I can't say with any confidence that the anorexia wouldn't come back and bite me on the bum.

Obviously, I'd try for it not to happen, but it leaves a residue. I know I have my three meals a day, and when I'm with my mom, I'm in that cycle. But on my own, I don't know what would happen," she says.

I told her how impressed I was with her for being so accomplished when she had gone through so much, and she instinctively laughed self-deprecatingly, embarrassed.

"I'm very regretful of all the years I wasted, but I am proud that I came out the other side. That stuff we went through, it wasn't the end of the story, and I was able to make something of my life. On the whole, yeah, I think I'm proud of myself. We got through it, didn't we?"

Chapter 14

Sickly Girl

January–March 1994

It was only when Allie painted the front lounge that I realized how long I'd been in Hospital Four. We'd transferred over from Hospital Three just after the new year, and our new ward was all white: white walls, long white corridors, everything as blandly anonymous as a travelers' motel, except with added panic buttons and the automatic locks on the doors, in case any of us tried to run away.

Allie, who shared the dorm with Ger and me, was a talented artist, and the doctors gave her permission to paint murals on the walls of our lounge. It was a big room, about fifteen feet by twelve feet with high ceilings. Allie went to work, sketching out sad-eyed pre-Raphaelite-style women in pencil on the walls before painting them in. One day, while sitting in the common room after lunch, I vaguely wondered how long we'd been in Hospital Four. I rarely wrote down precise dates in my diary, only days of the week, because our menus rotated on a weekly basis and all that interested me was what I was going to eat that day. Maybe two weeks? Then I noticed that Allie had painted almost the entire room, floor to ceiling. It was beautiful—glorious, really—and a little bit terrifying. How long *had* I been there? Three months was the answer. Just as when I was between hospital stays and I'd lose too much in a week, I initially felt scared, but then I felt pleased. Look at me, here in my sanatorium, sleeping through life! I was definitely a sickly girl now.

I'd always been fascinated by sickly characters in books, who spend most of the story wasting away from an unspecified illness, pale, interesting and beloved. Illness not so much as metaphor, but as evidence of a better self. Beth in *Little Women* is the classic example, but also Ruby dying of consumption in *Anne of Green Gables*, Mary's blindness in the *Little House on the Prairie* series, wheelchair-bound Colin in *The Secret Garden*, Tiny Tim in *A Christmas Carol*, and most of all, saintly Cousin Helen in *What Katy Did*, whose illness makes her "as interesting and unreal as anybody in the Fairy Tales: Cinderella or Blue-Beard, or dear Red-Riding Hood herself. . . . Cousin Helen was very, very good," the author Susan Coolidge writes. From these books, I learned that sick children were the best children, either because only good children became sick or because sickness made them good, it wasn't entirely clear, but it also didn't matter as the end result was the same. Even Ruby—whom Anne had previously derided as a fool—made "the handsomest corpse." The sickly children had irrefutable proof that they were good and everyone loved them. They were faced with no awkward social situations, no ego-crushing math tests at school, no gropes from boys—all they had to do was lie in bed and let the world pass by. One of my favorite novels in the past few years was Ottessa Moshfegh's *My Year of Rest and Relaxation*, in which the narrator attempts to regain control over her life by sleeping for a year. Moshfegh's book was a big best seller, suggesting I am not the only person still drawn to such a fantasy.

Time drifted in hospital. Every day was exactly the same:

weigh-in at seven, breakfast at eight, morning snack at ten, lunch at twelve, afternoon snack at three, supper at six, evening snack at ten. It was up to us to find our own entertainment in between the meals. If we had been well behaved, a nurse might take us on a walk, although I never really liked the walks, preferring to stay within the hospital's warm and safe walls, but if others were walking I had to go, too (I couldn't possibly burn fewer calories than everyone else). Mostly we just sat in the common room beneath Allie's murals, watched TV, read out-of-date magazines, wrote letters home, wrote in our diaries about what we had just eaten, and smoked. Nothing was asked of us, other than that we eat and that we choose between butter and peanut butter on our toast in the mornings (we all—without ever conferring or even thinking about it—chose peanut butter: fewer calories). I don't remember any sunny days; it was always gray outside, and our lives passed in a fog. We never watched the news—only soap operas and movies—keeping the Real World at bay. I refused to read any books about teenage girls because I had no wish to think about what I was missing. Instead, I read only Stephen King books for the entire time I was in hospital. They were scary, but not as scary as the Real World or reminders of it. To this day, what I lack in experience of life as a functioning teenager, I make up for in encyclopedic knowledge of Stephen King.

There had been a time when I didn't read horror. The year before I became ill, I read *Jane Eyre*, in which Charlotte Brontë set up the defining dichotomy of female illness in literature. On the one hand, there's Jane's schoolfriend Helen Burns, who—like Cousin Helen in *What Katy Did*—is a paragon of stoic, ladylike suffering: "By dying young, I shall escape great sufferings," she reassures Jane. And on the other, there is Bertha Rochester, that inconvenient bundle of womanly need

177

in the attic. These are the two ways of being not just ill but a woman, according to Jane: selfless, quiet, dependent but without desire or demands, versus a needy, impassioned lunatic. It isn't hard to glean which option is advocated by the book.

Anorexia combines both options: you are frail, and you are furious. You are striving for invisibility, and you are the focus of your family's anguished attention. It's physical (blameless, romantic) and mental (destructive, repulsive). You try to be Helen Burns, but you become Bertha Rochester. This is really the point of the disorder. Much has been written about anorexia being a desire for control, but it is also an expression of anger by a girl who has been taught—by books, by teachers, by parents— *society* that good girls don't get angry. There were lots of angry women around in the '90s—Alanis Morissette, Courtney Love, Kathleen Hanna—but they were largely laughed at by the public and media, proving the point, and anyway, good girls didn't want to be like them. The good girl wants to be good. So she turns her anger in on herself until she can take no more and it comes roaring out of her in a rage, like a dragon's fire breath. Not eating has the double effect of punishing herself and punishing those around her, thereby accomplishing two things at once. There are a lot of double effects of anorexia: for example, when I was ill, I saw not eating as proof of strength, which was just one reason why I didn't want to get better. It wasn't until many years later that I realized it was a weakness, because it came from a desire to hide from myself and the world.

I was confused by my burgeoning adolescent anger, but I was also angry that I felt so confused. I genuinely couldn't figure out how to grow up but still be me. I didn't want to take my top off and kiss boys at summer camp. But I also didn't want to be one of the weird kids who played on their computer alone in the dark all day, left behind while my friends all sped ahead of me. What do you do when you just want to fit in but aren't sure what you're trying to fit into? I told so many stories in my head about the kind of girl I wanted to be and the kind of girl I didn't, and I just couldn't find a narrative that worked. So I went with the narrative that allowed me to opt out without articulating my true feelings. Years later, as a grown-up, I still feel that temptation. As an adult, when I knew I had to break up with a boyfriend but didn't want to hurt his feelings, I thought, "Maybe I could just not eat for a bit and surely he'd get the message?" Being the sickly girl is—for those of a certain mindset, the kind that is terrified of articulating their desires—a tempting exit strategy.

Every time I went into hospital, after I got past the initial panic and fear at being made to eat, my anger would slip into the shadows, and that was because I had removed myself from the Real World, and it was the Real World that made me so confused, frustrated and angry. I hated the expectations I had of myself out there, and I hated how ashamed of myself I felt when I failed to live up to them. Instead, I lived a life that was like being permanently doped up with novocaine. Nothing was real in hospital, so nothing mattered. There wasn't anywhere else that I would have particularly preferred to be, so I dumbly floated along, those endless days and quick-fire months, focusing intensely on the tiny things in the short term (What were today's meals? Was my portion bigger than everyone else's?) and didn't think about the big stuff (What was I doing with my life?). It turned out those books from my childhood had been right, sort of: you do become a good girl when you're ill and in bed, because nothing is expected of you, so there's nothing to be angry about. And I probably would have continued to sleepwalk that way for the rest of my life had I not inadvertently shaken myself awake.

Chapter 15

A Gasp of Air

March–December 1994

It was breakfast time, so we were all in the dining room, but no one was eating. Caroline was hysterical, screaming, kicking, punching—the nurses, the table, herself—because there was more butter on her toast than on anyone else's. Scenes at the table were hardly uncommon, but Caroline was kicking the table so much it had become impossible for the rest of us to eat, so we all put down our cutlery and watched. It was August 1994, and this was my third admission to Hospital Four. Caroline was back in, too, as was—more happily—Ger, and we were in the dorm together again. Sticking with the same hospital for eating disorders treatment is a little like staying loyal to the same hotel for your summer vacations: you tend to see the same recurring faces.

Yet the ward felt very different this time compared to my first admission. Nora and Tara weren't there, and without their influence, cheating at the dining table was now seen by the new intake of patients as a shameful lack of solidarity, a breaking of the honor code. Caroline, who had been readmitted only the week before, was utterly flummoxed by this generational change, which is what had led to her meltdown that morning: she'd been called out—by another patient—for trying to smear her butter on the underside of the table, and now all she could do was scream.

"It's not fair, Emma! It's too much!" she sobbed as Emma the nurse tried to get her to take a bite.

I happened to be opposite Caroline, something I always tried to avoid so I wouldn't have to watch her shenanigans. But on that morning, I watched. It had been her thirty-second birthday the day before, and a thought appeared in my head—as unexpected and unbidden as the panic two and a half years earlier after I'd been told I looked "normal" in PE. The thought was this: "I will not be having temper tantrums over toast when I'm thirty-two years old. This will not be my life." It felt, just for a moment, like popping up for air after being suspended in dark water for so long. And then I slipped back beneath, like a submarine moving silently at night. But I'd had a glimpse, and something started to shift.

My first admission to Hospital Four had lasted four months, but when I left in March 1994, my therapist, J.F., yanked me back there after a week, because I refused to eat at home and was now getting up in the middle of the night to exercise, as well as doing it all day. I stayed for a further month and left in mid-April. I managed to do some of my GCSEs in June and then went back again to Hospital Four at the end of that month. It had become obvious months earlier that I wouldn't be able to do all of my GCSEs on the yearlong course as originally planned, because I was in hospital for almost the whole academic year. The crammer where I was still enrolled suggested that I do just half of them in June and then take the rest in November on a three-month course starting in September. Then I'd finally start my A levels in

January 1995, only one term behind my year group. That, anyway, was the plan.

The day before Caroline had her meltdown at the dining table, I got the results of the clutch of GCSEs I'd taken in June. There was a phone box on the ward, just by the smoking room, which probably dates this story even more than the phone box. After breakfast, I put money into the phone and called up my school to get my results. I'd felt detached about my exams until that point, being far more concerned with more practical issues, such as whether at lunch for pudding I'd get a corner piece of the apple pie (Extra pastry! Nightmare!), rather than the theoretical vagaries of Biology GCSE. Now that I was calling my school to get my grades, my competitive spirit bloomed, but suddenly, for the first time in years, it was not about eating the least. For a moment, I stopped thinking about the apple pie.

When I walked back into our dorm, Ger could tell from my face that I was pleased with my results, and even though she never normally allowed anyone to touch her, she hugged me. So did the nurses. Caroline felt the need to tell me that she didn't know how I sat still for two hours at a time to take each of the exams. "I'd have felt so fat," she said. But I didn't care. I didn't understand it at the time, but a window had opened and a voice whispered on the wind, "This present moment is not all there is for you. A different future is still waiting for you, if you want it."

Life, unfortunately, is not like an '80s movie, in which a character has an epiphany, a triumphal rock track plays on the soundtrack and everyone smiles at one another: roll end credits. If my teenage years were a movie, they were more like an extremely depressing and directionless European art house film that goes on for ten hours with no logical character motivation. So I did not get better after getting my GCSE results. In fact, after being discharged in September, instead of grabbing my future, I shoved it away by refusing to eat. I went back to Hospital Four only a month later and stayed until Christmas, thereby kiboshing the plan that I would start my A levels in January 1995. But I was lucky: unlike Dr. R., J.F. was adamant that I continue with my studies, and so she and my crammer let me do the accelerated three-month GCSE course from hospital, with teachers sending me my lessons and my mother shuttling my homework and coursework between hospital and school. As I said, I was very, very lucky.

A new voice inside me quietly liked that I was the only patient on the ward who was doing her schoolwork, that I was the only one of my age group who hadn't dropped out of school. Counterbalancing this was the anorexic part, which resented the implication that the doctors had hopes for my recovery, when surely I'd already proved to them that no one had ever been more ill than me. (I win! The trophy of death is mine!) I'd always wanted to feel special, and once I'd gotten that from the anorexia, but there's nothing special about being anorexic when you're on an anorexia ward. Maybe there were other ways to be special. I ostentatiously carried my textbooks around, flaunting them needlessly, as how I used to do my Hebrew school homework while at my English school or exaggerate my English or American accent when in the other country. I want to be different, was the message, and it was the first time I'd wanted to convey it in hospital, whereas previously all I'd wanted was to fit in and prove my anorexia credentials. Doing my math homework in the common room was the healthiest gesture I ever made in hospital and certainly the only positive experience I have ever had with trigonometry.

183

My teachers had hoped I'd be well enough to come into school to take my last remaining GCSE exams in November. I wasn't, so they somehow got special dispensation from the exam boards for me to take my exams on the ward, supervised by a teacher, while the nurses tried to keep everyone quiet in the corridor outside. I was delighted by this setup because every time I sat an exam paper, I missed a snack. It wasn't until years later that I realized there were other benefits to taking my GCSEs besides skipping some cookies.

Something was shifting in me, but it was not in a straight trajectory toward recovery. I had now spent more than two years in hospital, and I was—I knew it, even though I couldn't bear to say it—fully institutionalized. We all were. People become institutionalized for two reasons: they have been in the institution for too long, or they prefer it to the outside world. With us, it was both. Ever since my very first admission to Hospital One, I'd dread the day I would be discharged. When asked why I was crying, I'd say I was scared about how I'd cope outside. But the truth is, I hated leaving hospital, because that was the only place where I didn't hate myself for eating and not exercising, because it wasn't my fault there. Back home, everything was my responsibility—the eating, the exercising, the living. Who needed it? The nights before I was readmitted, I would tearfully stroke my soon-to-disappear hip bones and think, my heart beating fast, about the foods I would soon be made to eat: plum crumble, buttered toast, cheese and crackers. My eyes would widen in the dark with eroticized horror—but only on my own at night, because no one must ever know that a part of me loved being in hospital. I couldn't even admit this to the other patients—in fact, especially not to them—even though we all felt the same. But to admit that would be to admit that we liked food, and that was the one thing we could never, ever say. "You really make yourself at home here, don't you?" Caroline said to me when she saw my bed in the dorm of Hospital Four, which I'd decorated with photos of my dog and the school friends I no longer saw. And she was right, I did, but I knew what she was really saying: that I clearly liked being in hospital because I was greedy. I was too flooded with shame to make the obvious retort that she obviously liked being in hospital, too, given that she had been in more times than me. A part of me wondered if I'd end up like Lesley from Hospital One, who lived in hospital forever. Another part of me thought, in those moments at home when I had to decide what to eat and whether to exercise more, that wouldn't be so bad.

The illness had had its teeth in me for too long, and I was on the verge of becoming chronic. Caroline had been anorexic for sixteen years. Others had been ill for more than twenty. There were two male patients on the ward, Gordon and Simon, who were in their thirties but looked like they were in their sixties, both quiet and gentle, and they had been ill for a decade and a half. There was never any oddness about their being there, or none that I noticed anyway. We'd all been ill for so long that we'd rendered ourselves sexless, in both senses of the word: not interested in sex and without biological sex. It wasn't that we were female and Gordon and Simon were male, we were all anorexics, and that was our only identity. During my first admission to Hospital One, I'd taken it for granted that *of course* I'd get better and be back at school in time for A levels, but that was a long time ago now. Ever since I'd arrived at Hospital Four, I'd thought of this as my life now, obsessing over the weekly menus, seeing my parents only during visiting hours. But then there were my exams and then that morning in the dining room with Caroline fighting about the toast, and it was like I'd been in free fall and someone had suddenly caught me in a net. Before, Hospital Four had normalized chronic anorexia for me; now it acted more like a warning: "Look at these thirty-, forty- and fiftysomethings whom you live alongside in here," the hospital whispered to me. "Look at them crying over mashed potatoes, hiding bags of vomit under their beds, sneaking in jumping jacks in the shower. Look at them, because unless you finally do something, this will be you." The part of my brain that controlled self-preservation had long ago gone dark, but suddenly it started to glow, an old machine cranked back into life. I'd been right at a crossroads, and I could have gone in one direction, but something kicked inside of me, and I went in another.

Initially, this made my life much more difficult. Before, I could slouch through the days half conscious, letting time pass like gently falling snow. Was it April or September? 1993 or 1995? It didn't matter, because I was where I was supposed to be, in hospital, being anorexic. Awareness that maybe this wasn't the end of my story made me itchy and anxious. Hospital Four now felt like an incarceration that was sucking the years of my life away. But I was stuck: I didn't want this life forever, but that meant I would have to eat. Once, the idea of feeding myself had been unimaginably worse than the prospect of hospital. Now the two were equal, which meant I had no good options. For the first and only time during my illness, I slipped into a depression. Previously, I'd only ever felt wild and anxious, but now I felt despair, knowing what I wanted but not how to get it. J.F. promised me that as long as I kept thinking about the kind of future I actually wanted, there would come a point when the eating wouldn't seem so bad, but I wasn't sure. I couldn't imagine myself without the anorexia, all that comforting furtiveness and secrecy that kept

186

me separate from others. It was who I was, surely. But realizing that I didn't want to be having tantrums over toast in my thirties, that I liked keeping up with my schoolwork, slowly made me think that there might be a little more to me, maybe.

The cliché of recovery is that the patient has to hit "rock bottom" before it begins. People often talked to me about "rock bottom" during my illness, and I liked it because it felt like they were giving me permission to make myself as ill as possible. I can't *possibly* get better until my kidneys have started to fail! I would use this as an excuse between hospital admissions to lose weight again: You see, doctors, I will always feel frustrated that I didn't get to *x* weight before quitting the anorexia for good, so let me just have this last blowout, watch my liver start to pack in, and then I'll spring up like a bungee jumper flying upward into the sky after the plummet. But it never, ever worked like that for me. Recovery happened only when I was well enough to get glimpses of what it would mean, and you can't get those when your organs are failing.

"No one knows who will recover and who won't, and no one knows which treatment will help someone to recover. I'm often embarrassed to read my initial assessment letters, thinking this person would get better, then they become very ill, or the other way around," says Professor Lacey. "Sometimes the oddest approach works, such as yoga. More usually, those who recover will say something like 'I was speaking to a nurse on a Friday, and she was telling me what she was going to do that weekend and I suddenly thought, I want a part of that life.' And that might seem strange, that a little comment could make such a difference instead of all the expensive treatment that patient has had. But the expensive treatment wasn't wasted, it gave the patient the posture to change rather than making the actual change itself." Sarah McGovern, the eating disorders ward manager, says that "the saddest part of the job" is seeing the patients going into and out of hospital: "You discharge them, and then later you hear about them being referred to another hospital. That's the hardest thing about working in eating disorders: the low rate of recovery. Sometimes it takes a couple of admissions before something clicks for them."

What that click is and why only some patients hear it are just two of the many things doctors still don't know about anorexia. Just as no one really knows why some people develop anorexia and many don't, no one knows why some patients recover and some don't. There are factors that can contribute to the onset and the cure, but there are no universal truths. "The longer you're ill, the more resistant to treatment you'll be and the harder it will be to recover. But there is always hope. Early intervention helps a lot, as does having a supportive family, but the problem is when families get fragmented by this illness, which can easily happen. But often patients who are anorexic are very bright and have talents, and that can carry them through," says Professor Janet Treasure. Although the problem there is, Dr. Kaye says, when those patients use that intelligence "to attack themselves." "Patients with anorexia are normally highly articulate and highly intelligent, and they then use those qualities against themselves by defending the anorexic behavior," he says.

"A lot of people think patients grow out of anorexia, but not everybody does," says Dr. Agnes Ayton at the Royal College of Psychiatrists. "The general rule is that one-third of patients with anorexia recover, one-third may survive but struggle with difficulties, and one-third live with chronic anorexia. The chronicity of anorexia is partially related to the maintenance of malnutrition. It's like if you have type 1 diabetes: you need to get your blood sugars to a normal range, or otherwise you will suffer chronic long-standing consequences in your body and brain."

Sometimes patients find a reason to eat that is stronger than their anorexia, such as wanting to get their degree. Sometimes they simply become fed up with the limitations the anorexia puts on their lives, although "starved up" is perhaps the more accurate term there. They hear about what is going on in the Real World, and it sounds a lot better than the world they're in. It's like having physiotherapy after a serious break or sprain: moving the limb is painful, and you'd rather just rest it, but then you'd never recover. You have to exercise it to get it back to normal. With anorexia, many patients would prefer to hide inertly from life, their connection to normality decaying every day. By talking about the outside world, the people around them are strengthening that connection, doing physiotherapy on a mind that has been broken by anorexia.

But there is no way of knowing who will recover, when or why, and this is a very hard truth for patients and their families to hear. Having a glimpse of the future helped me then, but it hadn't before. In Hospital One, an art therapist told me to picture my life as an adult, and I imagined myself as a mother in a beautiful house, but the real excitement of this fantasy for me was the prospect of feeding my children and watching them eat. Watching other people eat was my favorite hobby then, and unlike my sister, my children couldn't complain, I thought, if I stared at them while they ate grilled cheese sandwiches. I imagined greeting them at the door when they came home from school with chocolate milkshakes, cheese on toast, cookies so freshly baked the chocolate chips melted as they bit into them. The anorexia was still fixed so tightly around my brain that it strangled every thought I had. It even strangled my dreams: for years, I had a recurring nightmare that I'd eaten a whole cake without realizing it. It came so regularly I would awake with a jolt just as I started to look down at the empty, crumb-scattered plate. The feeling of pure relief when I realized it had just been a dream was almost orgasmic. After I took my exams, other images of the future started to come into focus for me (university! friends!), but if I'd taken them a year earlier, maybe I wouldn't have been ready and the stress would have sent me spiraling deeper into the illness. There is no universal cure. There isn't really a cure at all; there are only luck and circumstances.

And even those are no guarantees. After I left Hospital Four for the fourth time, I lost weight again. When I went below a certain threshold, J.F. said that she was not going to send me back to hospital, because I was too comfortable there. I'd never told her how much I liked being in hospital—it was my most shameful secret—but she knew me well enough to guess. Instead, she said, if I lost two more pounds, she would tell my parents that they would have to pay for a nurse to live in our house and to supervise my meals. This was a big gamble on her part. After all, maybe I'd see this as the best of both worlds, in that I'd be at home with my mother but I wouldn't have to take responsibility for the food. Maybe I'd live like that forever, a kind of Boo Radley figure in the neighborhood, accompanied on my daily walks by a nurse, while my sister went to university and got on with her life and I stayed at home obsessing over whether Heinz baked beans had more calories than Sainsbury's own brand, fighting with a nurse about whether cleaning the plate meant licking up all the toast crumbs. I might have loved such a prospect. But I didn't—I hated it. It was one thing to opt out of life, hide away in hospital and live in your own little institutionalized world; it was quite another to live among the living when you are half dead. Even worse was the idea of my parents having to pay for a private nurse (thousands of pounds a year? millions?) who would live in our house and my parents then seeing me fight with her about portion sizes and corner pieces of pie. The horror was overwhelming, the prospect all too plausible, and this was the final push I needed. And so I did something I hadn't done in almost four years: I stopped losing weight at home. I ate just enough that year to stay exactly the same. Staying in the same place had never taken such effort, not even when I used to run for miles on the treadmill.

If I'd developed anorexia simply because I didn't want to grow up, living at home with a nurse would have been perfect. And that *was* partly why I developed it, but it was also because I wanted to grow up but didn't know how to do so, and that part had, over the past year, taken precedence. The idea of staying home forever was the opposite of what I wanted. I had, at some point, crossed over from being a scared little girl to a tremulous adolescent, and it was J.F. who'd helped me to do so, and if it hadn't been for her, I'd be dead or, more likely, still living a twilit half-life, hopping back and forth between my parents' home and hospital, uneducated, unhappy, unable to travel anywhere out of fear of unfamiliar foods and supermarkets, an empty, friendless, joyless life. I can picture that life so clearly it is like a shadow that follows me, something that is happening in a parallel universe. It still feels like a miracle to me that it is not happening in this one.

J.F. suggested that maybe I should go to boarding school instead of returning to the London crammer and living with my parents, as we'd planned. As soon as she said it, I knew she was right: to get better, I needed to be in a new environment, and what would feel safer than another institution? My doctors and parents were less convinced: leaving home is often when anorexia first takes hold or worsens. But J.F. and I were both so determined that this was right that they gave in. My crammer found a similar school for me that offered boarding in Cambridge, and as soon as I visited it and met the teachers, I knew this was the right decision. I signed up for the one-year A level course starting in the autumn of 1995. J.F. said I would be weighed by the school twice a week, and if I started to go down, I'd be brought home and my parents would hire a nurse. I agreed to the conditions but said there were three things I needed from the school: I didn't want them to let any of the students know that I'd been in hospital or why; I wanted to keep a minirefrigerator in my room, so I could take care of my own meals instead of eating with the other students; and I wanted to change my name while I was there. I accepted that I had to eat to go to school, but the idea of me, Hadley, eating felt like such a heartbreaking self-betrayal, I could eat only if I could pretend I was somebody else. J.F. and the school agreed and asked what I would like to be called. I chose the most anonymous, most un-Hadley name I could think of: I chose Clare. I knew that to find myself again, I would first have to lose myself entirely.

Chapter 16

Home and Boarding School

March–December 1995

My mother put a loaf of bread onto the counter. After taking out two slices for herself, she put it back into the fridge. She then got out a basket of cherry tomatoes for me, put them down in the same spot where the bread had been and asked if I wanted some hummus with my salad. No, I replied, I had to go out and get something first, and then I'd make my own lunch. I walked out of the room, my face immediately crumpling as soon as my back was turned, went up to my room and shrieked in rage into my pillow. How could she have put the tomatoes where the bread had been? Now I'd need to go out and buy new tomatoes and get rid of the contaminated ones without her noticing. How could she have done this to me?

It was March 1995, and I'd been home from hospital for two months, waiting for the clock to run down to September, when I would start school in Cambridge. I fantasized extensively about what my life would be like there: I'd have a boyfriend who would drive me around in a convertible, we'd meet my friends for dinners in cafés where he would feed me French fries and I would laugh and eat them with adorable abandon. My fantasies were heavily dependent on my suddenly not being anorexic and turning into a character from *Beverly Hills 90210*.

This dream was the carrot that persuaded me to eat just enough to keep my weight steady during my nine months at home. I was a tightrope walker, calibrating every single calorie to make sure I didn't tip too far one way or the other. (People told me it was fine if I put on weight as I was still too thin, but those people were clearly insane: Why on earth would I weigh even an ounce more than I absolutely had to?) It amazed me how everyone else was apparently able to maintain their weight naturally: Why weren't they all constantly gaining or losing weight? How did they know the right amount to eat?

"You eat until you're full," my mother said, as though that meant anything to me at all. In any case, I knew—and this was my new shameful secret—that I was never full. No matter what I ate, I was still hungry. I didn't understand then that this was because I was still about twenty pounds underweight and my body was constantly asking me to eat more. I just assumed I was unnaturally greedy and I'd developed anorexia because I needed to loop some reins around my outsize appetite. In my more panicky moments, I worried that eating all those big meals and snacks in hospital had permanently stretched out my stomach. My punishment for developing anorexia, I anxiously thought, was that I would forever after be cursed with excessive hunger.

So I ate. Just enough. It was a source of enormous humiliation to me that my no-longer-skeletal body told everyone that I ate food, my most private activity. How other people would feel if a red cross appeared on their forehead every time they masturbated to porn is how I felt about having a visibly healthy(ish) body. Oh, the pain of this public proof of appetite! This confirmation of weakness, of entitlement, of gluttony. It was mortifying. But I ate, so that in nine months' time I would transmogrify into Shannen Doherty and make out with Luke Perry, a prospect I increasingly saw as a promise. I blocked my ears to the screams of the serpent inside, who wailed in horror every time I put food in my mouth. But he soon found a new way to consume me.

Whereas once I had anguished over my stomach, my upper arms, my thighs, my butt and my legs, now it was my hands. What had they touched? Who had touched them? Because I was so precise in the amount I ate, I worried enormously about extra calories somehow sneaking in and tipping the balance. I imagined crumbs of other people's food somehow transferring to my hands, either from their touching me or my touching a place where food had been and my then accidentally consuming those crumbs. This quickly extended to other people touching any part of my body—someone brushing past me in the street, say, or giving me a friendly pat—or my food being anywhere other food had been. My brain wove frantic stories about how other people's calories might get inside me, having taken journeys more elaborate than that of Gulliver: some mayonnaise from a sandwich got on a stranger's hand, then he touched a pole on the bus, then I touched the pole, then I put my hand in my mouth. Once I saw this transference in action, when my sister was making some pasta and sauce from her thumb got on the fridge handle. As I watched my worst nightmare in action, I honestly thought I might faint.

I was socially distancing long before everyone else jumped on my bandwagon. I flinched when anyone got within three feet of me, because who knew where they had been and what they had been eating that day? I demanded my own shelf in the fridge. My parents' and sister's food was kept at a safe distance from mine and I had my own loaf of bread, so I would never eat anyone else's crumbs. I became more dexterous than Daniel Day-Lewis in *My Left Foot* at opening doors with my feet, and I turned off taps with my elbow because obviously I couldn't touch a tap after just washing my hands, as then I'd have to wash them all over again. It would have been a never-ending Escher drawing of washing and tap turning, washing and tap turning. I wore gloves, even in the summer, to keep the world at bay, although I then had the problem of figuring out how to take the gloves off at the end of the day when they had been *touching everything*. And I washed—oh boy, did I wash. Once I had exercised obsessively; now I applied that same obsessiveness to washing my hands. I washed them so much that the skin around my knuckles split and bled, just as I had broken the skin around my spine from too many sit-ups. I was always trying to shed my flesh. Instead, I just mortified it, like the saints. I had permanent rashes around my wrists because my cuffs were always wet from all the washing, and I wore only long sleeves because I couldn't bear for anyone to see the flesh of my arms. But I couldn't roll my sleeves up before washing my hands because that would mean I'd have to pull them down afterward, and then I'd have to wash my hands all over again. It looked nonsensical, but it was actually very carefully thought through—although the result of all this thinking was that I had bright pink rings scored into the skin encircling my wrists, like bracelets, which itched and burned constantly.

I feared anywhere and anything that other people had touched—who knew what had been on their filthy flip-perlike hands that day? Public transport became a huge source of anxiety (all of those people, all of those food wrappers), shoes a nightmare (who knew what they'd stepped into on the street?). So I washed and washed and washed, determined to be pure, free of any external contamination. With my stringy and patchy hair and now constantly bleeding hands, I took on a striking resemblance to Edward Scissorhands.

I knew I wasn't behaving in an entirely reasonable way—most people, I understood, did not have tubs of liquid hand soap (never a bar, not hygienic enough) in their bag when they left the house, so they could wash their hands in public toilets without having to touch the soap dispenser. (The only thing more contaminated than public soap dispensers were refrigerator handles. And restaurant tables. And taps.) Because this all seemed to me to be a fear of calories, I thought it was anorexia. I didn't understand that the unhappiness and anxiety that lay under the anorexia was now leaking out of me through obsessive-compulsive disorder.

Anorexia often mutates into something else as the patient recovers. Bulimia is common, as is binge eating, as the anorexic rebels against themselves by going from eating nothing to eating everything and thereby attaining new levels of self-loathing. Alcoholism is a common comorbidity with eating disorders, although the rates are higher among bulimics (45 percent) than anorexics (10 percent).[1] OCD is perhaps anorexia's most natural—purest, even—bedmate, because it strips the latter down to its essence. It shows that the illness is not really to do with food but is about anxiety and unhappiness. Sometimes the former comes first, sometimes it's the latter, but each leads to the other. The mind coins tricks to distract from those feelings, only for those tricks to become a new source of anxiety. With anorexia, that trick is starvation; with OCD, it's the compulsions. My still anorexia-riddled mind took the classic OCD obsession with germs and transferred it into an obsession with calories.

My fixation on these extra, floating, unseen calories and my compulsion to protect myself from them were so paralyzing that I—inevitably—became agoraphobic. The small joys I had started to rediscover, such as going to the cinema on my own or walking in the park while listening to my Walkman, were locked away behind a steel door by my killjoy mind, which whispered scenarios of how they might lead to the inhalation of invisible calories. (Cinemas were especially perilous—who knew what people had been eating in those seats? Or what the person behind me was eating?) The one outing I allowed myself was to the supermarket, because God forbid anyone else do my shopping and touch my food. I made that daily excursion count, though. The supermarket was at the end of the road, but each trip took about two hours, because doing the shopping was an obstacle course. I could buy only items that had touched no other food products, thereby reducing the risk of transferred calories, and also were unlikely to have been touched by other shoppers, so I would dig through to the back and the bottom of the shelves. I held my shopping basket close and tight, as if protecting my ready meals from muggers, ensuring it didn't touch anything else in the aisles. If someone put their items too close to mine at the checkout or just stood too close to me, I'd take everything off the conveyor belt, pretending I'd forgotten something, suppressing my fury, put everything back, and start the process all over again. It was like being on *The Crystal Maze* but a lot less fun.

Like anorexia, OCD can be hereditary—but unlike anorexia, no one in my family ever suffered from OCD, or at least not to the extent that I did. As with anorexia, it can be sparked by abnormal levels of serotonin in the brain, which can lead to greater anxiety and the ensuing obsessiveness that accompanies that. I was undoubtedly hugely anxious at this point in my life, not least about eating, and obsessing about magical flying calories was both an expression of that and an attempt at distraction from it. There was perhaps a bit of time filling going on here. I had eight months at home, with no school and no friends, as I'd long ago lost touch with people from my private school and I'd barely attended the London crammer. The only friends I had were the girls I'd met in hospital, and I wrote to them every day.

Eating disorders inpatients are mainly girls and young women in their teens and twenties, and they are hospitalized for months at a time, so it's inevitable that they become friends with one another in a way that, say, patients on an A & E ward don't. You don't have to squint very hard when you look at an eating disorders ward to see what could well be a boarding school, with all the cliques and tight friendships that come in such a setup, and these friendships can last well beyond hospitalization. I stayed in touch with several of the girls after I left hospital, because who could better understand what I was going through? But after I left for the last time and made up my mind I wanted to go to boarding school, they started to feel more like weights pulling me backward. "Got a letter from Rosie today. She said she feels guilty if she stays in bed after 6 a.m. Thanks a lot! Like I don't struggle, too!" I wrote in my diary.

"We always tell the patients, 'Don't become friends with people in hospital," because it can be really damaging," says Sarah McGovern. "But the younger ones all become friends on Facebook, Instagram and Snapchat, and then you have them posting images of themselves after hospital when they're losing weight, and the patients in hospital then feel fat. They often know when someone's coming back into hospital before we do. Staying in touch can be a form of support, because they understand one another, but it's so easy for the eating disorder to get its claws in again and make them competitive with one another. Sometimes we have to tell them to block certain people on social media."

J.F. told me I needed to break off contact with people from hospital, and I knew she was right, so then I no longer even had those relationships or the identity they conferred on me of being part of a group. But without any friendships at all, what else was I going to do with my time other than take pots of hummus on and off the shelf at my local Marks & Spencer and keep vigilant guard in the kitchen over who put what on which part of the counter?

By July, I was able to take enough of a breath to realize that OCD was simply not going to be sustainable at boarding school and certainly not if I was going to eat French fries with Luke Perry. And so, as with the anorexia, I didn't magically recover from it, but with enormous will, I pressed it down inside myself just enough so I could live a semblance of a life. As J.F. had promised, the moment had come when living a life was more important to me than purity and perfection. In practice, this meant people were still not allowed to be near or touch my food, but I no longer avoided public spaces, because even I could see that wouldn't really work in a boarding school. I balanced on the edge of anorexia, on the cliff face of OCD, and I stayed rigid with the effort of not falling into the abyss. It wasn't especially relaxing, but I was able to exist in the Real World, which was more than I'd managed for a long time.

When I finally went to boarding school, I didn't turn into Shannen Doherty and I didn't eat French fries. It turns out that even if you move home and change your name, you don't completely transmogrify. Just as I was anorexic in London, so I was anorexic in Cambridge. You're always still you. But

I was, to everyone's astonishment, including my own, a functioning anorexic, and I didn't lose a pound the whole time I was there.

Crammer boarding schools tend to attract two kinds of kids: those who need help retaking their exams and those who just need help. I lived in a house of about twenty other teenagers, all of whom were taking their A levels in a year, and both types of crammer kids were firmly represented. In the first term, one boy stabbed another in the TV room, and another boy was then thrown out for stalking the girl whose room was next to mine. If I hadn't spent the past three years in and out of psychiatric institutions, this would have felt a little overwhelming; instead, I felt right at home.

It takes a certain kind of teacher to want to teach kids who are all, in various ways, fuckups. There was little prestige or glory to be gained from working at this crammer. The teachers were there for the challenge, and we the students were happy to give it to them. They knew that I'd spent the past few years on psychiatric wards, but next to kids who had been expelled from their former school or were flat-out violent, they didn't see me as an especially interesting case, which was just what I wanted. I no longer wanted to be special; now I wanted to blend in, and that was partly so people wouldn't watch me and comment on how rigid my eating patterns were. But it was also because I—at last—wanted to get on with my life. To move forward. To no longer be a child or defined by the past. I was determined to maintain the pretense that I was totally normal. No longer did I fear that word. Now I aspired to it. The school was happy to collaborate with me on that, as long as I maintained my weight. One of the many reasons I didn't stay in touch with any of the friends and teachers from my original private school was that I feared their treating me like the freak they remembered me as being and I still feared myself to be.

Before the anorexia, I had always been a good student but never a great one. I'd wanted to be, desperately, but I had gone to high-pressured, extremely academic private schools, and I could have studied until my eyes fell out, but I would never have been the best in the class, because there were always girls there who were more disciplined, more driven and just smarter than me. Things were different at my boarding crammer. The ethos was to do your best, not the best, and without that thumb on my neck I was able to breathe. The other students weren't the hothouse girls I'd always gone to school with, and they had other life goals than being top of their class. I didn't, because that's how I'd been trained since the age of five, and so I was quickly seen as the school swot, and I gratefully seized on this as my identity. Skinniness no longer felt like the only thing I had to offer—suddenly, unexpectedly, I was the academic one. But it wasn't just the school that was different. I was undoubtedly a different person from the one I'd been last time I'd been in a school. For a start, I now had all this anorexic/OCD energy churning inside of me that needed to go somewhere, given I couldn't release it anymore by starving myself or washing my hands fifty times a day. I wasn't eating in a way anyone would describe as normal—the same things at the same time, in my room, on my own, every single day, keeping my food in the little fridge I hid under my desk—but I was eating, so I couldn't distract myself from my anxiety with starvation. Instead, I channeled it into studying. I never went out, partly because—well, obviously no, due to anorexic/OCD mentalness (Someone might touch my food! I might touch theirs!). Also, what on earth would I talk about with other kids? "What have you been up to lately?" . . .

"Cool. Me? Well, I've been locked in psychiatric institutions for the past three years." "Fancy seeing a movie sometime?" "Oh, I can't, because I still have a phobia of cinemas. Bye!" It was only when I was alone at my desk studying that I felt safe and in control, which meant it was the only place I felt calm. Studying became my new starving. I spent my evenings memorizing *Hamlet* quotes and French verbs instead of sitting with my housemates, who were snogging, smoking and watching TV (which may have been for the best, given the stabbing and stalking). I was no longer a raging skeleton, but I was the madwoman in the attic, rarely seen and never heard. Incredibly, my housemates didn't seem too weirded out by me, or at least they never said so to me. They were only ever kind and accepting. This was another benefit to going to a crammer instead of the type of school I'd gone to before: here, outcasts and neurotics were the norm. I don't blame my old schools for what happened to me. Plenty of girls go to private schools and don't develop anorexia, and some find reassurance in school rules and feel in free fall at more lax institutions. But I will say this: there's a lot to be said for schools for weirdos.

When I received an offer from a university, the obsessiveness spiraled to new proportions. Whereas with losing weight or handwashing, there was never any defined goal—which was part of the problem, because it meant I didn't know when to stop—now I had something specific to aim for: I had to get the grades. There was a fixed point, a finishing line, and I focused so hard on it that the anorexia and OCD became backing music as opposed to the deafening soundtrack. They were still very much part of my life, but not my only life. My eating was fanatically controlled, but I was eating, my hands were clean but not bleeding, and I studied, and that was how I spent my final year at school. If that sounds a bit joyless for an eighteen-year-old, well, compared to the past three arid years, it was pure hedonism. I was living a real life, one with an actual future laid out in front of me that I was reaching out with both hands to grab. It was exciting. True, I was spending sixteen hours a day learning French vocabulary and the dates of Renaissance paintings, but only six months earlier I could never have imagined such freedom.

Chapter 17

University

December 1995–June 1999

Almost all the universities I'd applied to had turned me down flat, which wasn't a massive surprise. "Wait, what's the problem here?" I wanted to ask them. "Is it that I've spent three years on a psychiatric ward? That I'm extremely likely to relapse again? That I'm currently at a school for juvenile delinquents? Come on, Bristol and Durham, give me a clue!" I did, however, get asked by Oxford to come up for an interview, which was a shock but later turned out to make a lot of sense.

Oxford's fondness for overconfident and bluffing boys has become very well established, thanks to the prominence of well-known graduates such as former prime ministers David Cameron and Boris Johnson. But it also—at least when I was there—had a penchant for good girls, the kind who could be relied on to read the whole of the set reading list and also several texts beyond it. I didn't meet any other girls who had been hospitalized for anorexia during my time there, but I met many other good girls who were very similar to me, pulling their hair in front of their faces, pulling their jumper sleeves over their knuckles. The university libraries were filled with them, all anxiously reading every book they could find related to their course. Oxford liked these girls, because they

205

were pliable and hardworking, but it rewarded the overconfident bluffing boys with firsts and university awards. That was Oxford University in the late twentieth century, or my experience of it, anyway. This may or may not explain a lot about modern British politics.

In order to be offered a place, I first had to be interviewed, and this caused me enormous anxiety beforehand. Most teenagers are nervous when they are summoned for an interview by a university, but probably not for the same reasons as me. "How will I cope with the food?? Maybe I'll ask Mom to come with me and for us to stay in a hotel. At least then I won't have to share a room with another candidate, and I can control the food," I wrote in my diary. After several nervous calls to the college, in which I was assured I would get my own room in the halls, I arrived with a suitcase packed with crackers, apples and tinned chickpeas, which is what I ate for three days, spooning the chickpeas cold out of the tin. No way was I using the college's shared kitchen. Who knew what other foods had been in there?

This anxiety about having to share a room overshadowed not just the interview but my entire university application process and as a result dictated my future. I applied only to universities which promised every student their own room. My room was where I ate, so obviously another person couldn't be in it. They might try to use my precious little fridge! They would see me eat!

"I really regret applying to Oxford instead of Cambridge. At least in Cambridge I know where Marks & Spencer and Sainsbury's are," I wrote after the interview. I chose my Oxford college with similarly sound reasoning: in the brochure, it said that many of the students prepare their own food, so I thought my absence from the school dining hall wouldn't seem so remarkable. It wasn't until I arrived that I realized no one at university gave a damn where I ate.

Despite spending an incredible amount of mental energy worrying about shared rooms, I did manage to get into the university, and so off my little fridge and I went to Oxford. While other first years spent the first week getting to know one another and locating the college bar, I headed out to locate the Marks & Spencer and Sainsbury's. They were both reassuringly easy to find.

I was still clearly unwell at university. As at boarding school, I spent most of my time huddled next to the radiator in my room, and I counted every single calorie that went into my mouth. And yet despite that I managed to have a pretty good time. Not the fun that people tend to associate with student life, no. But I made some friends, ones who were kind enough to pretend not to notice the little fridge in my room the (very) few times I let them in. I was still a people pleaser and good at guessing what people wanted from me, so I could do a decent imitation of a bubbly eighteen-year-old girl. But I was also still very much an introverted anorexic and so afterward would run gratefully back to my room, soothing myself by being on my own, writing in my diary and eating bags of raw vegetables. The snap of a raw broccoli stalk between my teeth and the bitter taste that followed reassured the still present anorexic part that I was still me, furtive and self-denying and weird. I worried that everyone could tell what was wrong with me, and a few people could: girls, invariably, and usually privately educated, so they'd encountered it before. But the majority and especially the boys were oblivious, and they were shocked when, years later, I told them about my past. I don't know if eighteen is early or late to learn this lesson, but that is when I learned that it was absurd to worry about what people were thinking of me, because they were too busy worrying about what other people thought of them.

It would have been easy—so easy!—to lose weight then, because no one was watching me at all. J.F. was on maternity leave, and after the first term I was no longer obliged to get weighed at the local GP's surgery twice a week. But I didn't. I didn't put any weight on, nor did I lose any, because I rigidly ate the same things every day—if they didn't make me fat yesterday, they won't make me fat today—gripping onto the life that I had so nearly lost. I no longer thought all the time about what I would be doing at that moment if I were in hospital, no longer checked my diary to see if they were on Week One menus or Week Three ones. I had found a way to maintain strict control but also to go forward. Instead of obsessing about exercise and losing weight, I obsessed about my studies, and Oxford welcomed my obsessiveness.

To casual observers, I looked fine. Thin with permanently dry lips, lots of bald spots and an absolute refusal to eat in public, but fine. But some things weren't quite right.

The awkward rock face of puberty that I had, so far, successfully deferred scaling still loomed ahead of me. If anorexia is in part a means of avoiding female adolescence, and it certainly was for me, then being anorexic traps you in the liminal state where you have not gone through the hormonal and physical changes but are stuck in perpetual anxiety about them. It's like having a fear of flying and living forever in an airport, watching everyone else board the planes while you pace nervously around the duty free.

Doctors have since told me that I was lucky to develop anorexia so young, because it meant my bones had time to rebuild and recover from the osteoporosis that set in during my years of starvation, and that is true. My hair has never regrown properly, and doctors tell me that this is because although I wasn't severely anorexic for long, I was severe enough that some things were permanently affected, and I should be grateful it was just my hair and not my bones. I try to remember this when I delete another photo on my phone because you can see my bald spots too clearly. It is also true that I was extremely lucky to stay in my academic school year, thanks to my crammers. But while my outward body was in the right year, my internal one was very much not. I hadn't gone through any of the social or hormonal developmental stages of my peers but instead had placed myself on ice when I was just fourteen. I had disappeared just as boys were starting to be interested in me, and that is not a coincidence, but it also meant that I arrived at university without ever having held hands with a boy or experienced an unrequited crush or a boy liking me whom I didn't like back. I had no idea how to handle any of these things. Anorexia freezes time, and that may have been the sufferer's intention from the start, but difficulties emerge when the ice thaws.

In recent years, there has been much written about delayed puberty because of the increased interest in puberty blockers for gender dysphoric children. Puberty blockers have been widely touted as a consequence-free option for anxious young people who wish to delay puberty to decide whether their physical body matches their internal gender identity. They are seen as the perfect way of stopping time before a young person goes through the bodily changes that then make changing sex more complicated. On the website of the NHS's Gender Identity Development Service (GIDS), blockers are described as "a physically reversible intervention: if the young person stops taking the blocker their body will continue to develop as it was previously. However, we don't know the full psychological effects of the blocker or whether it alters the course of brain development."[1]

In fact, researchers have found that blockers can have serious long-term physical effects on adolescents, such as reduction in bone density,[2] and can possibly affect the young person's sexual function.[3] But GIDS was right to say that the psychological effects of delayed adolescence are unknown.

"Whilst the impact of delayed puberty is an active research field, it's remarkable how little is written on the psychological side of delayed puberty," says Dr. Sallie Baxendale, professor of clinical neurology at University College London. "The way the brain develops, there are windows of opportunity in which the brain is primed to develop specific functions at certain chronological ages. Different areas of the brain get ready to respond to different features in the environment, at specific ages. So in adolescence, for example, the window of opportunity is all about making social connections and working out where you fit in social groupings and how to talk to people outside of your family. That's why we get crushes in adolescence; these incredibly intense connections are the result of the brain testing things out. If you don't go through this in adolescence, either because there's no one to connect with or hormonally it's being suppressed or in the case of anorexia there's not enough energy for your body to move to that state, things get confused. Even if you go through puberty later, you've lost that key window, so you'll always be playing catch-up to some extent. So you might be feeling not as socially adept as other people; perhaps you're more prone to making poor choices or failing to pick up on red flags in relationships because you haven't been through adolescence, when you do make poor choices and you then learn from them. If you go through puberty in your midtwenties and you start having relationships, it can be difficult because hormonally you're in your teenage years, but a teenage relationship is very different from one in your twenties. You're coming at it from a delayed stance."

This tallies so much with my own experience that I nearly cry when Dr. Baxendale tells me this. I'd never before heard my inner mood music articulated. Ever since I left hospital and until I had my children in my late thirties, I felt about a decade behind my peers. "I just feel on the fringes of everything, not part of real life, and it is totally my fault, but I don't know what to do about it," I wrote in my diary. "I've never been drunk, never kissed a boy, never been to a club or festival, never done anything spontaneously. I can blame the anorexia but as I'm almost 20 for god's sake, I think I should take some responsibility." Outwardly, I was at university, but inwardly I felt fourteen. I was still terrified of boys, but I also became painfully aware that I was, in my second year, a nineteen-year-old virgin. So I determinedly slept with the first person who offered, and because I hadn't started my periods yet, I thought I couldn't get pregnant, so I said nothing when, the next morning, I found that the boy had stuffed the condom I had given him under my mattress, still in its wrapper. It wasn't until twenty-five years later that I learned an actual crime had been committed against me. The local GP at university told me that, despite not having periods, I could still get pregnant from unprotected sex, and so she fitted me with a coil to prevent any possible conception, and I cried the entire time. I couldn't even get this right, I thought to myself. After that, I slept with any boy whom I thought was pretty, whether he was kind to me or not. This was never about pleasure, and it resulted in predictably miserable experiences. But because I was emotionally fourteen, it didn't occur to me not to sleep with those boys again. Instead, I kept pursuing them, because I had adolescent crushes on them. I don't blame any of those boys, even the condom-averse one, because they were young, too. Many late teens and twentysomethings are childlike, but I felt as though I were in one of those body-switch movies they were so fond of making in the 1980s and I was a child who had somehow been dropped into an adult's body, because that's what I was. Sometimes when I was in my college room on my own on a dark Saturday night, I would look around and think, "Where's my babysitter?"

Then there was the added embarrassment of still not actually having gone through puberty. Once, when I was out walking with a friend and she said she needed to go to Boots to buy some tampons, I sympathized. "I'm always running out, too, it's a nightmare!" I declared, just that little bit too loudly. I was Steve Carell's character in *The 40-Year-Old Virgin*, comparing women's breasts to bags of sand in an attempt to sound like a womanizer. Once I'd been horrified at the idea of being normal; now I was terrified of revealing how abnormal I was. That I was still sexually a child at university compounded my self-image that I was weird, not like other people, not normal.

"Going through puberty very early—such as at eight or nine—is associated with later depression. Going through it much later brings its own complications. It is so much easier to go through it at the same time as your peers," says Dr. Baxendale. I ask Dr. Baxendale if my experience of delayed puberty due to anorexia is analogous to that of kids who go on puberty blockers.

"No, because with anorexia everything has been suppressed. This is the body's naturally evolved response to an environmental situation. The reason women don't get their periods below a certain weight is to stop them from conceiving during a time of famine; that's a naturally evolved response. But puberty blockers are not natural, and they suppress the natural production of hormones. Without this, the brain development gets out of sync. People think medicine can stop time, but it can't," she says.

One winter morning in my second year at university, I woke up in what felt like a pool of wet syrup. I looked down and saw that my sheets were full of blood. Too embarrassed to ask for help and too shocked to think clearly, I got up, stuffed the sheets and my pajamas into a plastic bag in my room, washed myself off, got dressed and walked to a laundromat a mile away, so no one from college would spot me. While my sheets were in the machine, I went to a chemist and, just about suppressing shocked giggles at the absurdity of what I was doing, I bought a box of tampons. I was nineteen years old, and I had just gotten my first period.

"Maybe it happened because I had a gin and tonic in the college bar last night?" I wrote in my diary, thinking that the rare allowance of extra calories (sugar! alcohol!) had finally unblocked my puberty. More likely I was confusing the cause and effect: the happiness I was feeling at university is what led to me having a drink in the bar and also, probably, my hormones kicking in. The more the light got in, the less dark and dusty I was inside. It was a bit unnerving to see this unarguable biological proof that I wasn't dangerously underweight anymore or at least not so much that I could console myself in difficult moments that I couldn't be as obese as I felt, given that I still didn't have my period. But this was outweighed by my desire to stay at university and be a typical girl—a normal one, even. So when I got my period, I was Pinocchio, turning from wood to flesh.

213

Chapter 18

Fashion

A few years later, I was at a fashion show in Milan. Models marched past me, each with legs so spindly they looked—as one fashion writer wrote admiringly—like baby fawns learning how to walk. Their elbows bulged out of their arms, just as their knees did from their legs; you could see their hip bones through their clothes. They didn't look unhealthy the way the anorexics I knew did, with crepelike skin and sunken eyes and thinned-out hair. But they were extremely thin, and if they'd been in hospital, I'd have guessed they'd been in for about two months and were still on one high-calorie shake a day. But they weren't, they were working, and they were paid to look this way. I'd been working as a fashion journalist for long enough now to barely notice the models' bodies, and, to be honest, they'd never really interested me anyway, any more than drunk people outside a pub bother reformed alcoholics. When you've been a professional, you tend not to care about the dabblers. But suddenly, one model walking past set off an internal alarm. My ano-dar.

Since leaving hospital, I occasionally—maybe once or twice a year—spotted a severely ill anorexic out in the wild. Sometimes I saw them on the street or wandering dead-eyed through health food shops or frantically stretching their tense

214

and exhausted bodies in yoga centers (one day, someone will write a PhD thesis about the heavy overlap on the Venn diagram mapping out anorexics and yoga fans). They were always bundled up in winter clothes, whatever the season, and their drawn and sunken faces looked as if they'd seen at least eighty summers, but they were probably all in their late twenties. As soon as they appeared, they were all I could see, as if they were spotlit. But they seemed to be invisible to everyone else, because no one but me did a double take on seeing them. No one gasped, "Dear God, why is that woman not in hospital?" Instead, their eyes skated right past them. They were like half-dead wraiths moving among the living unseen, visible only to those who themselves had once dwelt in the underworld. Even when I pointed them out to friends, they only vaguely seemed to take them in: "Oh yeah, I guess she is pretty thin" or "Isn't she just an old lady?" Almost everyone notices thin or even slim women, and often they crane their necks around, looking at them longingly. But anorexics are high-pitched notes out of the public's hearing range, and only the specially attuned can detect them.

So despite all the popular theories about the connection between fashion and eating disorders, this was the first time in my half-dozen years of going to fashion shows that I'd seen an acutely ill anorexic on the runway. It was also the first time that others around me noticed, too.

"Wow, look at Olga. She's tipped over into anorexia," said the fashion editor next to me, in the sympathetic-but-irritated tone of a barman faced with a client who can't hold his drink.

"Oh yes, what a shame," said the editor on my other side, carefully writing down her thoughts about what Olga was wearing.

In so many ways, I was a classic anorexic—well, I always

was a rule follower. But in one respect, I went against the grain: once I started to recover from anorexia, and after I finished university, I went to work in fashion. It was a reversal of the more commonly assumed trajectory, which is that proximity to fashion will give you an eating disorder. Instead, I took my newly hardened hide and entered the mouth of the dragon.

When I'm asked why I started my career as a fashion journalist, I give the glib answer that it was because I was offered a job. But going into fashion had absolutely been a conscious decision on my part, and I remember making it, one morning, shortly before I graduated, when I was sitting at my mother's kitchen table and reading a fashion story in the *Guardian*. "Being a fashion journalist would be fun," I said to my mother. "Mmm, okay, sweetie," she replied cautiously. I was still thin enough to make my parents fearful of saying anything to me that might be construed as unsupportive.

Anyway, I was right: being a fashion journalist was fun. In some ways, it was like being in hospital, in that I was surrounded by women and everyone was obsessed with one thing to the point of monomania, although whereas in hospital it had been food, now it was fashion. Once when a group of us flew to Paris for fashion week, a colleague asked me why there were so many signs in the airport for the Japanese label Comme des Garçons, not for a moment thinking that the "CdG" acronym probably referred to, in this setting, Charles de Gaulle, the name of the airport. It reminded me of the time an inpatient and I were allowed out to a café and she asked why they put the calories next to each item on the menu. I reassured her that they were just the prices. When your head is full of hammers, the world is a giant nail.

But it was undoubtedly bizarre to be recovering from anorexia while working in fashion, like a diabetic in a sweet factory. Your colleagues might be lovely and the work a laugh, but you can't deny you're swimming in sugar. Of course, I knew what people outside the industry thought about fashion and anorexia, and I could see why. I didn't talk about my medical history with my colleagues, but I knew that my still residual thinness gave me extra credibility with some of them and compensated for my obvious lack of fashion knowledge. PRs sent me clothes in sample sizes—i.e., the same size as the models wore—and fashion bloggers photographed me going to the shows. It wasn't my still patchy hair that attracted their interest.

I've met a lot of people who've recovered from anorexia who work in restaurants and catering, some who work as personal trainers, and a lot who work in adolescent mental health, all taking aspects of their history and putting it to use. But I have yet to meet another former anorexic who went into fashion, and at times I wondered if I was a poacher turned gamekeeper.

I started working in June 2000. By this point, the media was extremely excited about what they saw as the direct connection between the fashion industry and eating disorders. Fashion editors were hauled in to give peevish interviews on Radio 4 about it, conducted by ill-informed presenters who seemed to think all that was needed to cure anorexia was for Kate Moss to eat some chips. No one ever came out of those encounters well, and nothing ever changed, other than anorexia becoming a mainstream conversation, whereas when I had been in hospital it had still felt vaguely on the fringes. It's the one time in my life I was ahead of a trend.

It was strange to hear and read theories about an illness I suffered from and its connection to an industry I worked in, invariably put forward by people with experience of neither.

For a while, I spent an inordinate amount of time writing articles for my newspaper insisting that no, fashion doesn't cause anorexia, any more than beer ads cause alcoholism, and could people please stop belittling a serious mental illness in this stupid, sensationalist way? I wasn't, I don't think, quite as dismissive as those fashion editors when they spotted an anorexic on the runway, annoyed that one of their own had let the side down. They were trying to defend fashion, and I was . . . well, defending anorexia is not the right way to put it, but I was trying to explain that anorexia is not about wanting to look like a model. But the fashion industry does have a connection to eating disorders, it's just not the simple shallow causation that people often assume.

So much of anorexia stems from the environment, and that means the culture we live in. Fashion is a part of the culture and a distillation of it, and its boss-eyed obsession with skinniness reflects how deeply the association between female self-denial and perfect femininity is entrenched in our culture. This doesn't cause anorexia, but it gives it a softly fertile ground in which to breed. The trend for ultraskinny models has invariably coincided with social movements in which women have ostensibly been granted more freedom, such as the birth of the flappers in the postwar 1920s, the rise of Twiggy in the sexual revolution of the '60s, and the emergence of Kate Moss in the postfeminism era of the '90s. It's a classic give/take tactic, a brilliant ploy to make sure women know they're never entirely free of the shackles: "Yes, ladies, you can run free now! But you should hobble yourselves first by trying to look like this." That backlash doesn't only come from fashion—it comes from a wider mood, a societal shift, and fashion catches it, exaggerates it and perpetuates it. Self-starvation is an act of self-hobbling, and anorexia begins during adolescence, just as the child is about to experience the liberation of the teenage years and adulthood. It can feel so much easier to hide in hunger than to experience all that unimaginable freedom.

Models today are skinnier than those in the 1940s, but the supermodels of the '80s were bigger—or at least curvier and more athletic—than the waifs of the '60s. Ideas about female thinness change over the decades, but it never stops being idealized by society and promoted by fashion. Designers don't use thin models to hurt women's feelings—they use them because they sell clothes. We say it's because the clothes look better on them, but that's just because we think they do: in a different culture, one that fetishized female fatness, we would think clothes look better stretched out and squeezed around overweight models. If women didn't want to look like the skinny models, if they were inherently repulsed by them, designers wouldn't employ them. That designers use thin models as emblems of aspiration makes them look more aspirational to women's eyes, but women's desire to be thin—to look self-denying—had to exist in the first place. Every designer on the planet could use overweight models in their ads, and that wouldn't change the fascination with thinness (although it would probably dull some of the edges). This is clearly bad for women and girls and terrible for the models who work in the industry and must balance on that knife edge of looking almost anorexic in order to work. But anyone who thinks that only fashion magazines idealize skinniness has clearly never read a children's book. Good children (Matilda, Anne Shirley, Harry Potter) are thin; bad ones are plump or outright fat (the Wormwoods, Josie Pye, the Dursleys). It's universal shorthand, and children learn it quickly (especially if they read Roald Dahl, the Anna Wintour of children's literature when it comes to fatphobia). Everyone, I understood from the earliest possible age, wants to be thin. The movies I watched as a kid, even the cartoons, reinforced that message. Ariel in *The Little Mermaid*, Belle in *Beauty and the Beast*, Jasmine in *Aladdin*—all of them have emphatically concave tummies, while, say, Ursula the Sea Witch is laughable in her fatness, monstrous when she morphs from the (thin) princess and back into her original form, waddling around in front of a plainly revolted Prince Eric. When an actress dares not to be skinny, she has to make herself an object of mockery in order to work, from Roseanne Barr to Melissa McCarthy. When I was about nine, I had a sleepover, and one of the games my friend and I played after dark was lifting our nightgowns and showing each other our bodies. My friend was already an accomplished ballet dancer and more elegant and graceful than me, it seemed to me. When I lifted up my nightgown, I made sure to suck in my tummy. It was all I had to even up the balance.

The badness of fatness is not the only message about bodies that children learn: skinny women are generally witches and evil hags in children's books and movies. Unlike in fashion magazines, in children's books there is such a thing as too thin. Yet the message ultimately is the same: body size is a language, it communicates who you are. This is especially true with female characters, who tend, still, to get less to do in children's books than male ones do. The prince can fight dragons and conquer lands; the princess waits in the tower and tries to be neither too fat nor too thin. As girls grow up, graduating from *Matilda* to *Anne of Green Gables* to *Pride and Prejudice*, many will learn that their body is the loudest thing about them. It's what people pay attention to more than anything they say, any achievement they attain. The much-vaunted "return to curviness" that the media trumpets occasionally, as heralded by Sophie Dahl/Gisele Bündchen/Kim Kardashian (delete according to your generation) is no better than the focus on skinny women, as represented by Kate Moss/Jodie Kidd/Kaia Gerber. The body might be different, but the message is identical: all you are is your body, and your body had better be someone else's idea of perfect. From this perspective, an anorexic can be seen as both the victim of this message and also its defier: she is taking her body and making it nobody's idea of perfect.

Before I became ill, I had no interest in models. I still don't. They were never the point for me. The first time I looked at a fashion magazine was during my second admission to hospital, when a well-meaning aunt sent me one to read during the long days locked up inside. It was *Harper's Bazaar*, and inside it had a feature about the "future supermodels," who were all teenagers deemed by the magazine to have the right look. My fellow patients and I were especially interested in that feature, because the models were roughly the same ages as us, and it gave us details about their lives ("a keen horse rider," "teased at school for having skinny legs"). I was looking at it one day with Nicola, a nineteen-year-old inpatient who was being treated for bulimia, and I pointed to one of the models, who was wearing a crop top.

"Her tummy sticks out," I marveled.

"Yeah, but you just know that's pure muscle," Nicola replied. That's when I understood the difference between bulimics and anorexics: bulimics think a toned stomach looks good; anorexics want a stomach so shrunken and sunken it becomes a sagging hammock strung between the hip bones. It's an entirely different mentality. "Bulimia is conflated with anorexia, but bulimics often say they just want to lose a few kilos, so it's an extension of fairly common emotions among women. Anorexia is different," says Professor Lacey. Anorexics don't want to look like the models in magazines; they want to look ill.

The celebrity world is just as obsessed with female skinniness as the fashion business is. Fasts, juice diets, a preference for food that is not actually food (chia seeds, bee pollen, activated charcoal): these are common features in a celebrity's "What I eat" Q & A. In one interview, Victoria Beckham claimed that her favorite meals were "whole grain toast with salt or steamed vegetables with balsamic vinegar."[1] No one ever admits that they have to eat a certain amount in order to maintain their weight, otherwise they'd eventually be hospitalized. Or maybe some people don't. Once, for work, I spent some time with a famously thin celebrity, and every day her diet was as follows: pineapple for breakfast, edamame for lunch, whitefish for supper, supplemented throughout the day with champagne and lots of Marlboro Lights. I ate the same as her while I was with her, because I knew that by my doing so she'd feel that we were similarly inclined and therefore feel comfortable with me. There's always a risk, of course, that eating like this will suck me back into the anorexia. But because I was doing it deliberately to mirror someone who—to be blunt—I had never aspired to resemble in any way, it felt more like a cunning trick than an unhappy tic. Watching someone unknowingly dabble in the shallows of anorexia when you've knowingly plumbed the depths made self-starvation and self-obsession look silly as opposed to strong, so there was never any temptation for me to fall back into it. I know others have a different reaction to permanently half-starved celebrities. But I'll let you in on a secret: by the end of three weeks with her, I'd lost almost a stone, but she never changed in size. So the only conclusion I could draw was that either she was bingeing every night and I didn't see it or she had the world's slowest metabolism. I find this a useful way to think whenever I read another interview with a celebrity talking about how they don't eat after 4 p.m.

The fashion world's obsession with skinniness was never an issue for me—until I left hospital the first time and was expected to gain weight at home. I absolutely didn't want to, and so I looked for encouragement and permission not to do so, and I found plenty. My parents and doctor had told me that my obsession with skinniness was deluded, but it seemed to me that they were the deluded ones. Every time I left my house, I saw models on advertising billboards who looked like my former fellow patients, celebrities giving interviews about their preholiday fasts, TV shows laughing at fat people. I felt like the paranoid in the horror movie who wakes up to realize her worst fears are in fact real.

It is a shame that the fashion industry has become so synonymous with conformity and an obsession with women who have the bodies of little boys, because that is the opposite of what it should be. Fashion should offer girls and women fun ways to express themselves, to experiment with different personae, to enjoy themselves, and to enjoy being a woman (no matter what *GQ* says, women's fashion will always be more fun than men's). One of the things I loved about fashion in my twenties was that it allowed me to escape myself, just as changing my name at boarding school allowed me to pretend I wasn't Hadley anymore. I could play at being English in Liberty prints, French in little black dresses. This was originally what made me want to work in fashion: it seemed like a place where I could wear costumes and be someone new. I was working at a national newspaper and going to glamorous fashion shows, but in my mind, I was still that terrified fourteen-year-old being checked into a psychiatric hospital. Putting on clothes that helped me be someone else was extremely beneficial.

I was able to mine the good from fashion and leave the bad because I'd already exhausted the latter. I'd fully explored the promise that thinness leads to happiness and seen what a mirage that was. I suspect there was a part of me that found fashion appealing because I knew that my still-thriving food neuroses would be easier to camouflage among fashion journalists than they would among, say, news reporters. But I was lucky that my closest colleagues were, in regard to food and body size, so unexpectedly normal—and my immediate boss, Jess Cartner-Morley, so exceptionally lovely—and so, by gentle example, they encouraged my recovery. Who knows how things would have turned out if I'd gone to work at the fashion magazine whose office I visited once, where all the journalists had cups of ice on their desks because the editor didn't allow anyone to eat while they were working and the bathrooms were out of service because the pipes were corroded by vomit. Fashion does not cause anorexia, but it definitely doesn't discourage it.

Discussions about social media and eating disorders today have taken on a similar hue as ones about the fashion industry back when I was ill. It is clearly undeniable that social media have an impact on the mental health of adolescents (and adults). Whether it causes eating disorders is a more complicated question. One young woman with anorexia whom I spoke to put it to me like this: "Instagram didn't make me anorexic, but it made it harder to stop being anorexic. People would like my photos and posts about being ill and would tell me how brave I was, and I had a little online community. Those things were hard to give up." If you're looking for an excuse to stay ill, social media, like fashion magazines before, will provide it—but that doesn't mean it makes you ill. The mediums change, but not the emotions, and anorexia is deeper and has a longer history than either *Vogue* or Instagram.

After almost a decade as a fashion journalist, I was no longer so strikingly thin, and the free clothes and fashion bloggers disappeared. Fortunately, I had grown sufficiently disenchanted with fashion not to care and sufficiently well enough to laugh at how unashamedly the fashion industry loves those who are able to balance on the brink of anorexia but scorns those who succumb to it. I was reminded of this later in life when I learned that the cool kids love girls who take cocaine but are repulsed by drug addicts. The fashion industry rolls its eyes at anorexia for many reasons, not least because it makes it look bad. But the real problem is that fashion pretends that extreme thinness is, if not exactly effortless, then at least natural and normal; anorexia makes it look extremely effortful indeed.

Anorexia and fashion have a glancing interest in each other and some overlapping origins. But fashion reflects the culture; anorexia is much more personal, its causes more complicated than Kate Moss or Snapchat. The temptation to look at those who represent our own personal physical perfection and think our lives would be glorious if we looked like them is hard to shake, whether they're in a magazine or on social media. That if we change our bodies, we change our selves. I don't feel that when I look at models. I do, however, feel it when I see an anorexic, and a voice from a dark and tender part inside myself says, "Lucky her, she is free to eat whatever she wants, and she'll still be perfect and free." But then the light comes in and I remember that the reverse is true: the more perfect I was, the less free I was to do anything. That's something no one tells you. I had to learn it for myself.

Chapter 19

Amanda's Story

Eating disorders aren't the only kind of mental illness prevalent in the fashion industry. Addiction is at least as much of a problem. I'd been thinking about the overlap between anorexia and addiction ever since I was in Hospital One, drinking my high-calorie shake in the TV room while an alcoholic went into withdrawal on the sofa next to me and Chris, the cocaine and heroin addict, cried about the mess he'd made of his life. I met Amanda at the end of my first admission to Hospital One, and she was in the room next door to mine. I didn't really get to know her, because she was still on bed rest by the time I left, but we never forgot each other, sending one another occasional little messages late at night on social media. It never occurred to me to wonder why she was awake so late, which is odd, because I certainly knew why I was. One night—not so late—I messaged her to ask if we could meet up, as I was writing a book partly about our time in hospital. She instantly agreed. One warm spring afternoon, we found each other in Waterloo Station in London and hugged each other like the old friends we always should have been. We found a café in the station and didn't stop talking for the next three hours as we caught up on the past thirty years.

Like Geraldine's and mine, Amanda's anorexia had set in when she was fourteen, but she hadn't been hospitalized until she was seventeen. "I was a slow burner, but once it took off, there was no going back for me. I remember the first time I left Hospital One and Dr. R. said to me, 'You'll be all right now,' and I thought, 'Ha-ha, I don't think so!'" In the end, Amanda was in Hospital One five times.

Despite some therapists' claims that anorexia can be predicted by birth order, Alison and Fritha both had an older sister, Geraldine was an only child with much older half siblings, I have a younger sister, and Amanda has a twin brother. So there is not much of a pattern there.

"My brother and I were really close. But when we were seven, my parents sent him to a different school from me, and that was really hard for me, because I felt like I must have done something wrong, and I went from being happy and confident to teachers asking me if something was wrong. I started being picked on at school and I felt so alone, and my parents just didn't pick up on it," she said.

She and her brother didn't go to school together again until sixth form, by which point they'd grown apart. It was a mixed-sex college, and Amanda dated a boy there. But when he ended the relationship, "it was like a switch went off in me," she said. "All those negative feelings I'd carried around completely overwhelmed me, all those negative thoughts I had about myself, all that low self-esteem."

Amanda had barely started her A levels when her weight began to drop. On the advice of Dr. R., her parents pulled her out of school.

"That was the worst thing that happened, because once I lost that, I had nothing. Then all my friends were going off to university and I had nothing, no structure, nothing," she said.

This was the period when I met her, when she was on her third or possibly fourth admission to Hospital One.

Desperate for a change, she eventually went to America to work as an au pair but discovered, as many of us learned before and after her, that getting away from home doesn't always mean getting away from yourself.

"I became really, really bulimic when I was there. Just so out of control, more out of it than with the anorexia. It was the first time I'd ever binged, and it was awful. I just couldn't stop and I hated myself," she said.

Still searching for a way to be happy, she went to Israel to work on a kibbutz. When she returned to the United Kingdom, she embarked on a serious relationship.

"But the truth is, I didn't know what a real relationship was; it was just somebody liking me, and things became very chaotic in my twenties. I smoked a lot of weed, did coke. I saw Dr. R., and he said, 'Are you taking drugs?' and I said yes, and he said, 'I don't blame you, really.' Not very helpful, was it? Then I found out I was pregnant," she said.

She had her son, Jake, but when he was two, she was readmitted to hospital for anorexia. When she was discharged, she made a serious suicide attempt and was in intensive care for several days.

"It was the anorexia that prompted the suicide attempt. I just thought there was no way out, and I had a two-year-old and I thought he'd be better off without me. It's those feelings of anxiety and you think, 'Just get me out of this.' But the suicide attempt turned things around for me—I suddenly had the fear. I was very lucky that Jake's father—who I was no longer with—didn't take him away from me, because he probably could have," she said.

Amanda told her life story fluently, like someone who

was accustomed to reciting it for therapists and health care workers, but also with the frantic speed of a woman who had been desperate to off-load it onto someone she trusted would understand and not judge her for it. I asked if she was able to talk with her family about what she'd been through.

"Not really. After I got out of hospital, Jake and I came back to Surrey to live with my parents, and I wasn't having any counseling, no one talked to me about my anorexia. I think my parents were scared, too, so I was really lonely."

As a kid, before the anorexia, Amanda had loved sports, especially tennis, and had been good enough to compete as a county player. Whereas I'd been a kid who hated exercise but took it up when I was anorexic as a form of self-punishment, Amanda had always exercised but stopped when she developed anorexia, because that was her form of masochism.

"This was the problem with the one-size-fits-all approach they had at Hospital One, treating us all the same. I get why they were stopping you from exercising, but it would have been healthy for me to be encouraged to get back into it, helping me to be the person I was," she said.

Instead, Amanda found her own way back to being the person she was. While living at home, she trained to be a tennis coach, which she found she loved, even more for the teaching than the tennis. This then led to her studying to become a primary school teacher, which is what she is now, working especially with vulnerable and neurodiverse children.

She met and married a man and had two more sons with him.

"My youngest son is autistic, and that changed everything, because he needs a lot of support," she said.

I told her about the theories suggesting that anorexia is a form of autism, and she nodded with enthusiasm.

"Yeah, I think about that a lot. I see so many similarities between anorexia and autism: the black-and-white vision, the lack of empathy, the social withdrawing. I know of at least three other mothers who had anorexia and now have autistic sons. There has to be something there, don't you think?"

There may be. A 2022 Swedish study found that children of mothers with eating disorders are "significantly associated with attention-deficit/hyperactivity disorder and autism-spectrum disorder," even in families with no history of ADD or autism.[1] The authors of the study reached no conclusion about this other than stressing the need of giving "support to women with eating disorders and their children."

Amanda isn't in treatment for anorexia anymore, but she's still, she says, "self-destructive": "I drink too much and self-sabotage, but I think that's improving. I don't drink all the time, but sometimes when I start, I can't stop, but then I can stop for weeks. If I'm drinking, it can be fine, but if something upsets me or I get thrown off course, then it's all night. I find it more shameful than the eating disorder, because I get completely out of it. That's much more of a problem than the eating now. I'm just glad I don't live in America, because if I had a gun I'd have killed myself years ago," she said.

I asked her if she thought much about Hospital One, as I do every day.

"Oh, God, yes. I remember it so clearly and also how I thought back then. Like, I used to say I don't see other people as fat, just me as fat, but that was absolute bullshit—I wanted to be thinner than everybody and I was just saying what they wanted to hear, as usual. And I still think about the target weight that Dr. R. set for me and I think how much heavier I am than that now, and I wonder if that's okay."

I told her I think about that, too, and that's why I refuse

to weigh myself and why I turn around when doctors weigh me so I don't see the number: because I'm so scared to see how much heavier I am than the target weight I was set when I was fourteen years old.

She nodded and reached across the table to take my hand: "There's always a bond between those of us who have been anorexic. I really think of us as survivors."

Chapter 20

Addiction

June 1999–June 2009

An underrated bonus of anorexia is the sense of achievement it gives you. Not just in losing weight, although there is that, of course. But also the little things, so small no one else would even see them, let alone experience any emotion about them, but for the anorexic they can provide the purest, most ecstatic high. Finding out your pot of diet yogurt is twenty calories less than you'd assumed; sneaking in extra jumping jacks without your parents catching you; your mother buying you a regular Coke in the cinema but you see—although she doesn't—that the man accidentally puts Diet Coke into your cup instead. So sure, it was nice to be back in the Real World, but what could ever give me such comparable blasts of serotonin?

Not food, that's for sure. Sex? Don't make me laugh. I was not the only twentysomething young woman who saw sex as a source of validation rather than pleasure, but I perhaps had a head start on most, as I'd never considered pleasure to be a priority. Spontaneity was impossible for me; my meals were monotonous, and friends were kept at arm's length so they wouldn't see or, worse, comment on my still extremely rigid eating patterns. All I had to focus on was getting through each day, meal by meal, hour by hour. And unlike in hospital, I did not find this comforting. I found it boring. I really didn't want to go back into the anorexia, but I needed something new to obsess over, to make me feel fantastic 10 percent of the time and terrible 90 percent of the time, just as the anorexia had, so that was a ratio that felt familiar to me. Something that would swap the incessant anxiety in my head for a different kind of self-loathing and misery. Enter stage left: drugs!

I didn't go from being a tightly wound anorexic who planned every minute of every day to becoming a chaotic hedonist overnight. For a start, there were serious efforts on my part to fill that self-destructive void with other things before drugs. Bad boyfriends worked for a while, as they hit that anorexic sweet spot of making me more miserable the closer I got to my goal. The more unavailable and unkind the boy, the more consumed I was with the belief that my happiness depended on him. By now I was working as a journalist and my newspaper's travel desk gave me the most incredible assignment of a week in a luxury spa in St. Lucia with one other person. My then boyfriend preferred to spend the week getting high with his friends, and so I took my best friend, Carol, whom I'd met at university. One evening, we sat on the hotel's private beach, sun setting in the distance, restaurant setting up for dinner, and I sobbed and sobbed, telling her I just couldn't see a way out from my own feelings for that ridiculous boy. It was my family vacation to the South of France all over again, a perfect trip poisoned by my own crazy brain.

Heroin addicts became a specialty of mine, yet I was not the least bit interested in heroin. In fact, I never knew the men were taking the drug until a few months into the relationship. At the time, I thought this was just one of those weird things, like meeting two people called Nicola in one day. I keep dating heroin addicts! What a co-inky-dink!

I dated heroin addicts because I was a functioning anorexic. By now I was living on my own—I'd tried having flatmates, but the combination of my terrible boyfriends and my neuroses about sharing a refrigerator with other people made me less than ideally suited to shared domesticity. So I rented a small flat from a friend and began my new wild and crazy life as a single twentysomething in London. I was still underweight and my periods were erratic at best, and although I insisted I ate normally, this was true only if having a mortal terror of carbohydrates is normal. My body was screaming for me to eat more, but how could I do this and yet not gain weight? I found the solution: binge on vegetables.

Every evening, I would come home from work, boil some water and steam vegetables: whole broccolis, entire cauliflowers, bags of carrots, Brussels sprouts, peppers, spinach, zucchini. I could easily get through all that in one sitting. I especially liked cauliflowers because I discovered if you steamed one for long enough, it almost tasted like a forbidden potato. Sometimes I couldn't be bothered to wait to steam and I'd binge on raw vegetables: green beans and carrots were my favorite for that, and I eventually added cherry tomatoes to the mix, even though they're technically a fruit. (How much sugar does your favorite fruit have? You might be surprised!) This was how I spent my time and my money (turns out vegetables aren't cheap). God knows what the supermarket—let alone my neighbors—thought. Eating bags of vegetables probably doesn't sound wildly exciting to most people, but the thrill of feeling full—stuffed!—more than made up for any blandness in taste. Then I'd lie nearly comatose from all the food, and I loved this part almost as much as I loved being full, because—for the first time in my life—my mind was quiet, all anxieties gone, because I was too full to think, just as I'd once been too starved to think. Once again, I'd been taken out of myself, which is what I always wanted, and my poor shrunken tummy strained to cope with this deluge of watery vegetables. Eventually, I would get up and look admiringly in the mirror at the profile of my belly, distended and tight, nine months pregnant with broccoli, and it was terrifying but also fun, because I knew it would soon be gone and I'd be back to my usual underweight self. That killjoy of a black snake whispered that the bingeing and bloating would stretch me out and I'd be left with all this loose skin (just the phrase chilled me). But even I couldn't really believe that cabbage would make me fat, and after five or so binges my skin appeared unchanged, so I stocked up on the green beans and carrots. Whenever I occasionally went out after work, I would sit in the pub, sipping at my vodka and soda, and think with furtive glee about all the cauliflower bingeing that awaited me at home.

You might think that heroin addicts don't have much to recommend them as romantic partners. Actually, they come with a lot of advantages. For a start, they don't notice if you slip off at the end of the night to go and binge on vegetables. Distractedness was something I very much looked for in a man, someone who wouldn't notice what I ate and what I didn't and that I clearly didn't enjoy sex at all. The other quality that made someone boyfriend material for me was if he needed to be repaired. I loved boys who were broken, because it meant all of the attention would be focused on him, and neither of us would think about me at all, and I could continue on my happy, vegetable-strewn, functioning anorexic path. Because they were often addicts, emotional connection was impossible with them, which was great, because it was impossible with

235

me, too. I desperately needed a new and fruitless obsession into which I could channel all my anxious energy, and what is more fruitless than dating an addict? On top of all that, they had a very low sex drive, asked nothing of me other than that I asked the same of them, and were almost as emotionally stunted as I was. Was it my fault that heroin addicts ticked all of my boxes so well?

After several years of this nonsense, I could no longer convince myself that I felt anything for these men other than a narcissistic belief that if I fixed them and got them clean, that would prove how special I was (better than heroin!). Something new was needed in my life, something a little less boring and a little more effective as a distraction from the constant self-doubt in my head. Maybe even something that would stop me bingeing on vegetables because, along with heroin addicts, the charms of Brussels sprouts were waning. So—with a certain amount of efficiency, if I do say so myself—I cut out the middleman, in the form of my addict boyfriends, and threw myself directly into a massive pile of drugs.

Not heroin, thank God (it turned out that even my self-destructive impulses had limits). But everything else was fair game, especially the stupidest and shallowest drug of all, cocaine. At first, in my midtwenties, drugs were terrific for me. They stopped the internal noise because—oh, blessed relief—they took me out of myself and gave me the confidence to do all the things I'd longed to do but was too insecure and neurotic to try sober: Stay out dancing all night! Have really intense conversations with friends and strangers! Have sex and not entirely hate it! Before, I had felt so helpless, like a collapsed marionette doll after the strings dropped, and drugs gave me an inner scaffolding. Cocaine turned out to be especially good at helping me do something that I especially didn't want to do but needed to, which was be honest with people about the past fifteen years of my life. I rarely talked about my years in psychiatric hospitals, not even with people I'd been at university with.

I'd always felt a little socially awkward, worrying excessively about what to say next in a conversation and certain that whatever I did say was boring and stupid. At school, I would look enviously at the kids I thought of as "the cool girls," by which I really meant the confident girls, because they seemed to talk with such ease to one another, even to boys. I overthought everything in my head before saying it, only to then come out with a nervy "So has anyone seen a good movie recently?" Somehow it always sounded better in my head. I spent so much energy trying to figure out what it was the other person wanted me to say that I often barely listened to them when they were talking. I didn't confide in friends. I didn't know how to do small talk. It seemed to me that surely my attempts at anything deeper would be even worse.

Anorexia had been one cure for my self-loathing awkwardness, because it made me curl up inside myself, like a caterpillar that had just been prodded. It didn't help me connect with people, but it stopped me from longing to and hating myself for failing at it.

Yet it proved not to be a long-term solution. Drugs provided me with an alternative approach because it turns out that what people say about cocaine is true: it makes you talk about yourself a lot. So now I was telling everyone about my past, and instead of looking at me like I was Hannibal Lecter, muzzled and strapped to the gurney, they reacted only with kindness and poured out more drugs. It was incredible. That double burden of shame about my illness and my inability to converse was gone. It also did not go unnoticed by me that drugs kill your appetite, but rather than triggering my anorexia again, it made me a tiny bit more relaxed about eating, because I knew I hadn't eaten anything when I'd been high. I even ate the occasional carbohydrate (forbidden potatoes!), and the really eye-opening revelation was that I didn't turn into Jabba the Hutt. In fact, my body didn't change that much at all. Wow, I thought, twirling around, surrounded by friends and good times, drugs are great! And then, by my late twenties, they became very much not great.

When an anorexic starts to recover, her eating may stabilize but not necessarily her emotions. The unhappiness and anger that drove her to starve may leak out in other symptoms, and often, by this point, the sufferer is no longer seeing her eating disorder doctor or therapist, meaning she is under little or no medical supervision. I occasionally tried to save myself, making appointments with whatever hypnotherapist or nutritionist or acupuncturist someone recommended to me, all of whom were an equal waste of money. I even tracked down J.F. to ask if she could see me again, but she gently explained that she treated only adolescents. I had yet to find a J.F. for adults, which is what I needed at this point. I strongly recommend to anyone who is recovering from an eating disorder to try to find a therapist once they stop seeing their eating disorder specialist. You might not be underweight anymore, but you still need help.

"We sometimes see misuse of alcohol and drugs, cutting, sexual disinhibition among people recovering from eating disorders. One behavior is dominant and then another recessive, so you go from food to alcohol, men to cutting," says Professor Lacey.

"There is a reasonably established rate of drug abuse among eating disorders, but more in binge-eating groups than purely

238

restrictive anorexia, which is what you had," says Dr. Gerome Breen. But drugs appealed to me because of my anorexia: they, unlike alcohol, were a calorie-free way to get out of my head. They helped me to break away from the still anxious little anorexic that I was and become a more fun-loving twenty-something like I wanted to be. "You'd been to university, you were meeting friends, you were realizing there was a world away from steamed vegetables. You also recognized that to have that world you needed to change, and the drugs gave you the posture to change," Professor Lacey says to me.

When I started taking drugs, it wasn't that I didn't believe they were addictive, it was that I thought I was too strong to be addicted. After all, I'd got myself out of anorexia. Who was stronger than me? No one. And it's true, I was strong. Strong enough to go for days on drugs, longer and harder than anyone else. But I wasn't strong enough to stop.

I don't want to exaggerate. I wasn't an Irvine Welsh character—did I mention that I wasn't doing heroin? Still, if "not doing heroin" is the best you can say, you've let the bar drop pretty low. I was out of control, but I managed to keep my life ticking along pretty well. As with the anorexia, the drugs destroyed my happiness but nothing else. I wasn't taking them all the time, but on nights when I did, I would do them all night and beyond. I realized I was addicted when I couldn't imagine having fun without drugs, but I also knew that they spoiled my fun, because every night out ended with my taking drugs on my own, unable to put them down and go to bed. I was back in the land of no fun, and the drugs had taken me there just as surely as I'd once thought they had rescued me from it.

The real problem, though, was the epileptic fits. I was still having seizures regularly, about twice a year, and I now had seizures whenever I got high, which meant every week. That does seem, in retrospect, like a pretty clear sign that I should probably have stopped taking drugs, but it was one I very much ignored. Every time it happened, it took me about two days to recover and I felt as though another chunk of my brain had died. People got used to my keeling over at parties and twitching on the floor. I always felt utterly mortified when I came around—oh, God, did I ruin the party atmosphere with my embarrassing seizure?—but not so much that it slowed me down. To spare myself this increasingly frequent social faux pas, I skipped the parties and took drugs on my own at home. Given that I'd originally started taking drugs to stop staying at home and go to parties and talk to people, this wasn't a decision anyone would call logical, but I was too high at this point to think logically.

The one downside to staying home to take drugs so no one would see me have a seizure was that no one was with me when I seizured and thus no one could check if I was choking or had hurt myself or was breathing. One morning, I woke up on the floor of my kitchen and realized that, at some point, I'd had a seizure and been passed out for several hours on the linoleum floor. I was supposed to be meeting my sister at the Natural History Museum, so I got up and went to the bathroom to make myself look as good as I could on three hours of sleep on the kitchen floor. But I dropped my toothbrush in the sink when I saw my reflection: I had an enormous black eye, a visible lump on my forehead and a split lip. I had smashed my head on my countertop when I had the seizure and then fallen directly on my face. I looked like a domestic abuse victim. But I refused to cancel my plans, because that would be an admission that something was wrong and something very bad had happened last night. So even though it was April and cloudy I pulled on a winter hat, put on my darkest sunglasses, grabbed some lip salve and went out to meet my sister. She sighed when she saw me. I was so contrite that I didn't do any drugs the following weekend. But I did the weekend after that and the one after that and the one after that. For more than a decade, I thought that maybe this was something I would never overcome. I'd finally found the thing that would crush me.

Chapter 21

Recovery

New York, 2009–2012

I'm probably the only person in history to move to Manhattan to get away from drugs, but I did, and it worked. Fourteen years earlier, I'd changed my name so I could eat when I went to boarding school, and now I'd changed my home to stop being a drug addict. And both times, my slightly extreme plans worked. I didn't have any dealers' numbers in New York, and I didn't really know anyone, either, given that I'd last lived there twenty years before, when I was eleven, so I wasn't going to parties. Instead, I stayed quietly in my little apartment, got on with doing my work, and got used to sleeping regular hours again. It was nice not to feel like complete garbage most of the time. And so, of course, that's when the anorexia came back.

My fantasy of recovery hadn't changed that much in the years since I'd dreamed of eating French fries with Luke Perry, except this time instead of a man that saved me, I dreamed that it would be a place. As I packed up my flat in London ahead of my move, I felt certain—positive!—that this would be the thing that would rescue me. I had images of myself eating brunch in downtown diners, not wired and hungover from the night before, not anxiously picking at my food to avoid all carbohydrates and fats (and sugars, and dairy, and

242

oils . . .). But eating happily, while yellow cabs whooshed past outside and New Yorkers shouted at one another. Hey, I'm *wawkin'* here, I'm *wawkin*! (Despite originally being a New Yorker, I harbored images of the city that were about as cli-chéd as scenes from *Crocodile Dundee*.) Of course, everything would be fine in New York, because everything was fine when I used to live there, I reasoned as I boarded the plane. Things had started to go wrong when we moved to London—it was all London's fault. Stupid London! I heart NYC, the city that never sleeps, the greatest city in the world and so on.

The flaw in this brilliant plan, which I didn't understand until too late, was that I wasn't trying to move back to New York, I was trying to move back to my childhood, and sadly, British Airways doesn't do flights to there. That's what the anorexia had been about all along, trying to stay a child, run-ning away from the terrifying complications of adolescence. It's a testament to how happy my childhood really was, but I needed to move on.

Still, if I couldn't go back to New York City 1989, New York City 2009 wasn't the worst alternative. As I said, I didn't take any drugs, I made some nice, nondruggy friends, got a dog, wrote features for the *Guardian* and had pretty much everything I'd ever wanted. But I just couldn't figure out how to live. How do people get through those awful hours of 2:00 p.m. to 4:00 p.m., when the afternoon feels so long and empty and repetitive? Or 10:47 a.m., when it feels like you've lived so much of the morning already but still have so much to get through? Or the evenings, when you just wish the hours would speed past so you could go to sleep already. The anxiety that you've left the stove or the tap or the gas on, the front door open, the windows unlocked, the dread that you've done or not done something that will cause irreparable damage? Or the shame, the constant sense of shame, that you're stupid, an embarrassment, that everyone finds you awful, and that even thinking this proves what an overly privileged, narcissistic fool you are who should just vanish? The inner noise, which I'd silenced before by first starvation, then drugs, came rushing back. So what choice did I have? Of course, I ran back to the anorexia.

Not drastically. In fact, I didn't even lose much weight. But I became more obsessive about food than I'd been in a long time, and the vegetable bingeing returned. I was in The Most Exciting City in the World, and all I was doing was buying vegetables over and over again. By making my day entirely about food, I didn't have to think about how uncomfortable I still was in myself. At one point, desperate, I went to a nutritionist, just wanting them—anyone!—to tell me what to eat so I could stop trying to figure it out for myself. It turns out—and I really should have thought of this before—that most people in Manhattan go to see nutritionists because they want to lose weight, so they're little more than one-to-one Weight Watchers services. I went to the nutritionist's office somewhere in Midtown, tearfully told her my story and explained my desperation to stop making life so miserable for myself. She nodded solemnly and asked me to step on the scale. I explained I'd turn my back, as I couldn't bear to know my weight. I got on.

"Well, you're xyz pounds, which is healthy, but you could lose some if you want. Shall we get you on the light reduction plan?" she said.

When I was back on the sidewalk outside, I laughed and cried so hard and simultaneously that a passerby asked if I was unwell.

My sister and I often quote movie lines to each other that

we loved as children, and one of our favorites is "The Schwartz is in you, Lone Starr. It's in you!" It's from Mel Brooks's bafflingly underappreciated 1987 *Star Wars* spoof *Spaceballs*, and it means that you don't need help from outsiders because you're strong enough on your own.

It was shortly after the nutritionist incident that I accepted that the Schwartz was in me. If I really wanted to stop making life so difficult for myself, I would have to stop trying to outsource my recovery, imagining that Luke Perry or boarding school or New York or a dodgy nutritionist was going to fix me. Only I could do it.

I'd known that all along—all anorexics do, I think. That's one of the reasons we become anorexic. We're so scared of the power we have, the choices we can make once we're no longer children, the responsibilities suddenly given to us. If we make just one mistake on this exam or at this party or ever, our entire lives will be ruined! So we shrink our worlds down so that we have no power, no choices, no freedom, and other people tell us what to do, so if things go wrong, it isn't our fault. It's also partly why getting better is so hard. We know that no one else is going to get us better. They can hook us up to feeding tubes and give us menu plans and weigh us and put us on bed rest and listen to us and analyze our drawings and tell us what our childhoods meant and what our parents did wrong and take away our education and put us on antidepressants and anti-anxiety meds and antipsychotics and take our blood and scan our bones and tell us it was always going to be like this, but it doesn't always have to be like this because there's hope, there's always hope. But we're the ones who, out here, back in the Real World, have to get up every morning and feed ourselves breakfast and then lunch and then dinner. And we have to go to the supermarket to buy our food and somehow pretend to be normal people when we do this, not people who don't want to eat anything and simultaneously people who want to eat everything. Anorexia is not about the food, it really isn't. But it becomes about the food, and the only way out of it is through the food: you have to eat in a healthy way every day, over and over and over and over, for the rest of your life, and eventually, one day, after a few months, or a few years, it won't feel like you're eating your own heart every time you do it. I know, because that's what I did, and that's what happened. The Schwartz was in me, and it got me almost to the end of recovery. And then, at the final yard, I got the push I needed over the finish line from an unexpected source.

Chapter 22

The Final Chapter

London, 2012–2022

After three years in New York, I moved back to London. I missed my friends and my family, almost all of whom were in London. I needed to go back, once again, to the Real World. And a few years after I moved back, my old fantasy of recovery came true, when I finally met a handsome prince. Two princes: I gave birth to twin boys.

I was in my midthirties and in a relationship with a man who was (a) nice to me and (b) not a heroin addict, so progress had clearly been made. He didn't change me, as I'd always dreamed. Instead, I wanted to change, and he was there at the right time, and so I changed while I was with him. After two years of dating we moved in together (more progress), and although he was definitely taken aback by my still somewhat eccentric eating habits, compared to how I'd been eating just a year before, I was pretty much a gourmand. Plus, I wasn't stinking out our flat by steaming kilos of vegetables every night, so, really, he should have just been grateful for that. The only way to stop being scared of eating something, I realized, was to eat it. Each time I took the first bite, it felt as though I were breaking a law, which I was, and I was always quietly but genuinely astonished that I didn't become instantly obese.

And because I didn't, that made it less scary to eat the next time. You don't just change overnight and find eating simple, as I'd always vaguely imagined: you have to get there yourself, by eating. So that's how I continued, timidly eating new things but always keeping a running tally in my head of what I'd eaten what day and how I could compensate for it tomorrow. Outwardly I was recovered; inwardly I wasn't quite. And then I got pregnant.

It probably helped that I was pregnant with two very big, very hungry babies who plowed past all my residual anorexic barriers with their insistent appetites that could not and would not be denied. A whole baguette as a midafternoon snack? A giant chocolate bar? A bag of sour lemon candy? I ate it all while pregnant, because the babies demanded them. Some women tip back into anorexia after the baby is born, and I can understand that: your body has obviously changed, and your life is terrifyingly out of control. But for me, it did the opposite. I had the boys at thirty-seven and then a daughter at forty-one, so I was a long way from the illness at its most heated, despite my best attempts to hobble myself with drugs. Because I am not Ozzy Osbourne, drug binges and parenthood were not a combination that was going to work for me. Neither was anorexia and parenthood, and it's hard to imagine how I would have maintained, say, my decades-long phobia of touching other people's food or other people touching me while raising toddler twins. I suppose I could have—avoiding their sticky hands reaching for mine, doing jumping jacks in the kitchen anytime I touched food I was preparing for them—but I didn't want to. I didn't want to. It was as simple as that. Once that would have felt like a weakness—a surrender, an excuse for greed. Now it just felt like a relief. To this day, whenever I bite into their pasta to see if it's ready or see some peanut butter one of them has gotten onto my hand, I recall, faintly, the anguish that would have once followed, the compensations I'd have had to make to calm myself down, the meals I'd have skipped. It's like recalling a long-ago, deeply misguided relationship, and all I feel is relief that I'm not there anymore, just as I'm relieved not to be washing my hands hundreds of times a day, or exercising all day, or feeling cold and thinking about food all the time, or throwing my life down the plug hole of hospital. And it's not just for my sake. I am all too aware of the family legacy my children live with in regard to eating disorders, and I know that the best way to break that chain is for me not to let shadows of the past into their home.

I resisted writing this chapter for a long time, because it seems such a silly, Hallmark movie end to this particular story. "Sick for decades, then having kids made her all better!!!" Children are not a cure for eating disorders, and mine didn't cure me. (If anything did cure me, I'd like the credit to go to *Spaceballs*, please.) It was time. I had outgrown that scratchy, self-made jumper of self-defeating self-destruction, and I no longer believed that holding on to splinters of anorexia made me special or that bingeing on drugs made me fun. I truly wanted out, but I needed something to yank me out of it other than the needs of my own body and life, because I had never cared about them. My children did the yanking. I at last found something I cared about enough.

When my boys were little, I often read to them *We're Going on a Bear Hunt* by Michael Rosen, about a family who face constant obstacles—long grass, a river—in the search for a bear. My children's favorite part, which we all sang together, was about the family conquering the obstacles: "Can't go over it / Can't go under it / Oh no! / Got to go through it!" I tried to get around recovery by swapping the anorexia for drugs, but it didn't work. It seemed to at first, but I was kidding myself. I had to go through it.

I assumed I'd never fully recover. I didn't actually believe it was possible. To experience no anxiety about food? Not google a restaurant's menu before agreeing to meet a friend there? Not check the calorie and carb count of everything before putting it into your shopping basket? Who even is that person? I used to say I wanted to eat "normally," but this proved to be an unstable foundation on which to build my future. "Normal," once again, as I should have learned back in that 1992 PE class, means different things to different people. Sure, I had a few female friends who could unthinkingly sit back on a sun lounger in a bikini, pop open a can of Pringles and contentedly eat until they'd had their fill. But they were far outnumbered by women who avoided carbs; women who avoided sugar; women who made just that little bit too much fuss when they ate something sweet ("Ooh, chocolate! Don't tell my personal trainer, ha-ha!"); women who "just aren't hungry in the mornings"; women who "get tired if they eat lunch"; women who "can't do wheat/dairy/gluten"; women who define themselves by being the opposite to wheat/dairy/gluten avoidants (Twitter bio: "Always eating cheese"); women who skirt the edges of anorexia but hold it together just enough to look fashionably thin as opposed to annoyingly ill; women who "never eat after 4 p.m."; women who eat food that is pretending to be another food (cauliflower rice, zucchini); women who go on "fasts"; women who go on "detoxes"; women who binge; women who starve; women—so many women—who think just that bit too much about food. Thinking too much about food is normal to too many women, because it's how so many of us learn to express our feelings and to judge ourselves.

I could have used that as an excuse to stay in my narrow

little underground bunker, shielded from the sun. Hey, if everyone else thinks like this, why should I change? Alternatively, I could have reacted violently against it and dedicated my life to preaching about how awful it is that we live in a diet culture in which you can't even open a newspaper these days without seeing an article encouraging readers to lose weight. But I didn't, because I didn't want my life to be defined by anorexia in any way, whether I was reacting to it or against it. Also, even I understood, on some level, that the ubiquitous encouragements to lose weight were never aimed at me and taking them personally was as absurd as being outraged that there were adverts for blond shampoo on TV when I'm a brunette. More people are overweight than underweight in Western society, so inevitably there are more ads on TV for Diet Coke than for high-calorie shakes. This can be difficult when trying to recover from anorexia, as it seems to confirm the anorexic idea that everybody wants to be thin. But at some point, I had to make the decision that I wasn't going to use the noise around me—around all of us—as an excuse to be unhappy. It wasn't always easy, and it still isn't. But it is a choice I and all women must make for ourselves.

Recovery doesn't mean eating "normally," whatever that even means now, when everyone knows someone who is into fasting or doing the 5:2 diet or juicing, and so on. It means not going to a farther away supermarket because its brand of yogurt has fewer calories. It means not being overwhelmed by panic when a friend invites me over for supper or when I'm about to go away on a work trip or on vacation. It means not dragging myself out of my hotel, jet-lagged and exhausted, to a vegan café seventeen miles away but instead just eating whatever is in the diner across the road. It means not being ashamed of appetite and also not being obsessed with it. It means food not defining how I feel about myself and also not defining myself through food. It means not constantly compensating for food I ate or will eat so that my brain feels like a giant calculator totting up my sins. It means being able to eat spontaneously as opposed to knowing what I'll eat that day from the moment I wake up. It means freedom.

There is still something in my brain that tries to stop me eating. Not to lose weight, but that internal voice from thirty years ago that tried to make food seem repulsive to me is still there. Mostly I tune it out. At other times, I work around it, eating something else before the voice can make the new thing seem nauseating, too. Because that voice isn't trying to make me thin, it's trying to stop me enjoying food—experiencing pleasure, in other words. It's a literal killjoy. I spent years killing my own joy, with starvation and then with drugs, and I just won't do it anymore. To quote that inexhaustible fount of life lessons *Lethal Weapon*, I'm too old for that shit.

In 2022, twenty-seven years after I was last there, I visited Hospital Four. I had resisted thinking about the place for years, but as soon as I was approaching the front gates, it all came back: the tearful but stony-faced drives with my parents in our family car so that I could be readmitted, the newsagent on the corner where I would go with the other girls when we had permission to buy newspapers and lottery tickets, the view from the dorm window on those endless afternoons. There were more buildings on the lot than when I had last been there, and it all looked much whizzier, with more gleaming medical facilities among the gloomy Victorian halls. But so much had stayed the same, including the location of the eating disorders ward. I walked down the path toward it, a path I had walked down so many times with nurses and other patients, and opened the door.

The public phone box where I'd gotten my GCSE results was now a store cupboard, and the smoking room where I'd hung out sometimes to look cool to the older girls was now a therapy room. The dorm that I'd shared with Ger and Allie was now a group therapy room. But really, it felt as though I had stepped back thirty years. The nurses' station was in the same place; lurking all around it were skeletal women wearing leggings or jogging trousers, all trying to find out who would be on duty tomorrow and who would be supervising lunch, just as I used to do. One of the women hugged her arms around her body and stared down at the floor, just as Ger used to do. Another paced back and forth, just as so many others I had once known did. Nothing had changed. The same illness, over and over.

Sarah McGovern, the ward manager, was in her office, which had been a bedroom when I'd been in. But the ward had cut bed numbers recently—not because fewer people needed admission; on the contrary, there were more patients on the waiting lists and in a worse physical state than ever. But because of Covid, they'd cut the numbers of beds to try to maintain some social distancing on the ward. McGovern had been working there for three years, and we talked about how things were when I had been in and she laughed and said she'd heard about my era, when the girls would take three hours over their meals. They'd learned from their mistakes back then, she said, and there are now strict time limits on the meals. She showed me around the ward so I could see what else they'd learned since my time there. We went to the dining room, which was still the same, except now there was a kitchen where the food could be prepared, as opposed to arriving lukewarm from the hospital kitchen. I looked at the list of what was on the menu today, and each of the girls was getting a different meal, such as cauliflower cheese or beans on toast, which they chose from a long list of options, including a vegan option. McGovern told me that the doctors felt that if they could teach the patients to eat meals that felt safe to them, they were more likely to continue eating on their own. She also told me that they were soon to move the eating disorders ward back into a very refurbished Hospital Three, because it had been decided that the patients need the nicer individual rooms they have there now, because being anorexic is not a crime and the patients shouldn't feel as though they are in jail. There, they would all have their own rooms with en suite bathrooms, to give them a sense of dignity. I remembered our dorm when we were in Hospital Three, that disgusting big room where we slept and ate, where Tessa screamed at us and pounded the table, and it was like looking back on a Victorian-era asylum.

We talked about other elements of anorexia beyond the not eating, such as exercising and purging, and she said that exercising was still the most common problem they saw, with girls secretly doing jumping jacks and pacing around rooms and jiggling their feet, just as I did. We also talked a little about the comorbidity between anorexia and autism spectrum disorder, and she said that sometimes the ASD symptoms abated as the girls put on weight and sometimes they didn't. There was no predicting it.

We walked down the corridors together, and I felt the ghosts of girls I'd once known shuffling alongside me, feeling so trapped and also so alone. I could see Nikki Hughes striding ahead of me, refusing to be performative in her sickness, and she walked quickly and with strong steps, and then she went through the door that had been her room and disappeared. I went into the lounge, where we used to sit after meals, and I looked out of the window toward the woods. I must have spent hours staring out of that window during my admissions, looking timidly out at the Real World, longing for it but also terrified of it, trapped inside, safe inside.

McGovern asked me what I used to think about when I was ill, and I told her how I couldn't bear the thought of someone eating less than me or doing more exercise than me. About the nights when I would anxiously add up everything I'd eaten that day and cry and cry. How it was the moments afterward I feared the most: the moment after eating, the moment after not exercising, the moment after seeing how much I weighed. How do people cope with such feelings? I couldn't. So I jiggled my foot or did jumping jacks so I wouldn't feel them anymore. McGovern nodded.

"It's so interesting to me seeing how the patients think so similarly. People think anorexia is just about social media or body image, but it's not. Ultimately, it's about the thought patterns," she said. In other words, it's about unhappiness and anxiety, and body image becomes the way it's expressed.

I didn't stay long—she was busy, lots of patients to look after and everything—and as I left, I realized it was the first time I'd walked out of that ward, in all my time of living there, on my own. Not with a nurse, not with my parents, just me. And then I got into the car and went home.

It is now three decades since my first hospital admission, so my experience—back in the dark analogue era—should have as much in common with that of young anorexics today as Ernest Shackleton has with Elon Musk. Certainly, there are some differences: I was obsessed with diet magazines and aerobics classes; they spend hours on Instagram and taking selfies. But when I talk to the women with anorexia, their emotions and thought processes rarely vary that much from what mine were, just as one person's bout of chicken pox will have much in common with someone else's. One told me that she had stopped eating because she was so embarrassed at being the first person in her class to need a bra and she thought she could diet away her breasts. Another described her father leaving the family for another woman, and she thought if she made herself ill he would come back. A third remembered how her mother only ever ate one meal a day and refused to change, even after her daughter was hospitalized.

One dark winter afternoon, I met up with Daisy, twenty-two, who had recently left hospital, and I asked her if she understood now why she had stopped eating. "I really don't blame my parents, but I do remember them sometimes saying things like 'I don't want you to grow up, I want you to hold my hand forever and just be my little girl.' I felt that. It was really hard to grow up. As a teenager, you need to have little outlets of anger and fights with your parents, that's a normal part of growing up. But I found it really hard to be angry, especially with my parents. I wanted to be their perfect, problem-free child. Then when I got sick, I got really, really angry with them, and it was almost like the anorexia was an excuse to be angry because in my head I could tell myself, 'That's not me, that's the illness.' I think I needed to find some way to be angry, and having an eating disorder presented itself as the optimal opportunity."

Anorexia takes different forms for different people, but the crux of the illness itself is unchanging, and no matter how life and technology and society changes around it, the thick black snake slithers on through, unaffected. More than a millennium after Wilgefortis, despite all our social and feminist advances, so many girls and women are still horrified by the prospect of womanhood and the feelings and expectations that come with it. And still they can express it only by punishing their bodies, an act that is either obtusely misunderstood or misguidedly validated, depending on the social mood of the time.

When a mother asks me for advice on what to do with her suddenly self-starving daughter, I always say the same thing: get professional help as soon as you can, and don't become her caregiver. Don't let your relationship with her revolve entirely around anorexia, and don't be the food police. All parents want to save their children, but in this case, you save her by handing her over to someone else so that you can still be her mother. It is not a failure. It just means she is sick, like so many other girls have been before her.

More generally, I've thought a lot over the decades about why so many girls still struggle with becoming women and why they still get such terrible messages about what girlhood and womanhood mean. We can't always change the world, and we can't shield girls from every potential influence. But we can equip them with tools to deal with the world as it is. I wish we were better at explaining to girls what growing up involves: not just bras and bleeding but all the things we say good little girls don't do. It means getting bigger, hungrier, smellier, sweatier, greasier, spottier, hornier, angrier, and everyone goes through it, even if they don't look like it, and it passes, and life gets better. I wish we would tell them that they don't need to be perfect, and that means sometimes they will let people down, even their parents, and that's okay, and they will experience rejection, loneliness, loss, disappointment, injustice, pain, and that, too, is normal, and it is not shameful. I wish we would tell them that, contrary to what they see in movies and on TV shows, boys are not all desperate for any girl, and they may well at some point be rejected by a boy, and sexual rejection is painful, but it does not mean anything is wrong with them. It just means boys are human, and so are they. Growing up means freedom, and this can feel very scary to many young people. Not every young person is desperate to go out late, have sex, smoke and drink. Some want to stay home and watch films with their parents, read books in bed and go to sleep by ten, and feeling as though you're behaving wrong can be as unsettling as feeling as though you look wrong. I wish we would tell them that everyone grows up at different rates and in different ways and there is never just one way of being, even though it often feels like it. I wish we would tell them that it is true, people do talk a lot about how girls look, and life is easy in some ways for the pretty and the slim, but it's very much not if that's all they think they have to offer, and anyone who says differently is selling something. I wish we would tell girls that their bodies are not an outward show of who they are. I wish we would tell them that it's not their job to be pleasing and pretty and the world will not end if they disappoint or anger someone (even their parents) and they don't have to make themselves ill to be forgiven or to be angry—in fact, it's better if they don't, because being ill is really tedious, for them and for those around them. I wish we would tell them that they don't have to make themselves small to speak up and also to be really careful which stories they choose to tell themselves about who they are, because it *is* a choice and they can be their own worst narrators. I wish we would tell them that they don't need to hide how strong they are, and because they are strong they are not the helpless victims of external influences: they are stronger than Instagram, stronger than fashion models, stronger than diet culture. I wish we would tell them that just because others—even maybe their parents—praise them for being good little girls, it doesn't mean they will be loved only if they are good and little. I wish we would tell them that they are not how others perceive them and certainly not how they think others perceive them. I wish we would tell them that no teenager knows who they are yet and it's normal to feel like nothing right now and one day that will change, but only if they are kind to themselves. I wish we would tell them that they don't have to lock themselves into a single identity, because no one is a single identity and everyone changes all the time. I wish we were better at telling girls that there are endless ways to be a girl, and I wish we were better at convincing them that there are endless ways to be a woman. And most of all, I wish we, the grown women, were better at believing all this ourselves and would stop self-deprecating, stop apologizing before we speak, stop expressing self-doubt through body anxieties, stop believing that male approval is the ultimate validation and stop being far more critical of women than we are of men. Because how else will the younger generations stop hating themselves if they're learning it from us? And I wish we would tell them that starving themselves to be perfect is as nonsensical as punching themselves in the face to turn orange. But we don't. Not enough. Not yet.

A few weeks after my visit to Hospital Four, my two-year-old daughter and I went to one of my favorite streets in London. We did a little book shopping, a little window shopping, I bought a pullover for her and some trousers for me, and even though it was before noon, I was hungry and so we went to a Greek restaurant. Lunch used to be my easiest meal to skip, and even in my twenties I would often just eat vegetables for it and then wonder why I was so completely exhausted by midafternoon. It is wonderful to no longer live in a permanent state of semistarvation, so that all you think about is food. There is so much more to life! The calorie counts were listed next to each dish on the Greek restaurant's menu, but I didn't look at them—blinkered my eyes to them, just as I had learned to blinker myself to so much in the world once I'd made the decision to recover—and ordered exactly what I wanted. Sometimes I still feel as though I'm playacting a fake life and my anorexic self is still my true kernel, because that was when I felt most myself, or maybe it was just when I thought about myself the most. I ordered a glass of wine with my lunch, which I never normally do, but I felt like it, and so I did. Noon now, the girls in hospital would be sitting down to their lunch and looking around to see who got the biggest and smallest portions, the corner and the middle pieces. I looked down at my plate, piled with beans and salad and pita bread, and at my daughter happily playing with a piece of halloumi. Sometimes I miss the simplicity of hospital, and I often think of the girls, especially those whom I spent months sleeping next to, only to learn later from newspapers that they had died. Why them? Why any of us? What did we do that was so bad? It still feels like an hourly miracle to be free of the cold and the hopelessness and the loneliness and the palpitations and the exhaustion and the exercising and the guilt. But even though I'm free of it, I will never forget it, and even though I'm recovered, the splitting never fully mended, so I'm always standing a little to the side of myself, looking at the life I have and thinking about the one I don't. I looked at my daughter, smearing hummus on her face. Thirty years it took me to get here from when I first became ill, exactly thirty years. I raised my glass, to the past, present and future, and I ate.

Acknowledgments

I have many people to thank, from then and now. Let's start back in, then.

Thank you, definitely, but more than that, a massive apology to my family for all I put them through and continue to do so now (yes, sorry for all the stuff you didn't know but then found out in this book). I'm so sorry for being the teenager from hell and I'm incredibly grateful that you never gave up on me, even when I came home one day with seven body piercings (at least I left that story out of the book). I wouldn't be here without you.

Thank you to my wonderful teachers, whose support and kindness made all the difference: Pamela Shadlock at Godolphin and Latymer, Alastair Boag and David Bainbridge at MPW, Charlie Ritchie, Ali Lake and Berenice Schreiner at CCSS.

Extremely overdue thanks to the extraordinary nurses who looked after me: Marie, Anita, Theresa, Jocelyn, Geraldine, Nicola, Emma, Anne-Marie, Clare, Julie, Cherril, Gladys. Honestly, I don't know how any of you do what you do, but I am incredibly grateful that you do.

To the doctors who saved my life: Dr. Georges Kaye, who was with me from the beginning and still is; J.F., who knows who she is; Professor Janet Treasure, my miracle worker.

To all the girls, women and men whom I met in hospital:

we were too ill then to understand how important we were to one another. I understand now. Thank you.

And now for the now.

When I finally decided to write this book, I knew that I didn't want this to be just my story. It's so many women's story, and the women I most wanted to include in this book were those who were in hospital with me. Thank you so much to Alison, Glenn and Sally Goodey, Geraldine and Amanda for trusting me to tell your stories. Spending time with you for this project is something that will stay in my heart forever. We're still there for one another, thirty years on.

To my mother, for being so generous with her insights, allowing me to write about some of the most personal experiences in our lives and being so supportive, as she always is.

To Professor Treasure, again. Thank you for everything.

Enormous thanks to all the doctors and experts who gave up their extremely valuable time to answer my endless questions: Dr. Georges Kaye, Professor Hubert Lacey, Dr. Agnes Ayton, Dr. Kate Tchanturia, Professor Gerome Breen, Dr. Dasha Nicholls, Dr. Penny Nelid, Stella O'Malley, Sarah McGovern, Professor Christopher Fairburn, Dr. Anna Hutchinson, Dr. Melissa Midgen, Anastassis Spilliadis, Dr. Sallie Baxendale and David Luck.

Thanks to the team of wonderful women around me: my agent, Georgia Garrett; my editors, Louise Haines (4th Estate, United Kingdom), Emily Graff and Mindy Marques (Simon & Schuster, United States). They were assisted by Honor Spreckley, Mia Colleran, Hana Park, Amber Burlinson and Martin Bryant. Thank you to all of you for saving me from excesses and tolerating my stubborn ways.

Thank you to all those who contributed so much to this book with their thoughtful suggestions, edits of early drafts and so many WhatsApped reassurances: Carol Miller, David Baddiel, Dolly Baddiel, Debbie Hayton, Janice Turner, Susanna Rustin, Jonny Freedland, Amelia Gentleman, Marina Hyde, Helen Lewis, Sarah Ditum, Catherine Bennett, John Harris, Sonia Sodha, Rachel Cooke, Isobel Montgomery, Rafael Behr, Trevor Phillips, Laura Craik, Adam Phillips.

And as ever, thank you to my partner, Andy, and our children, Felix, Max and Betty. You are the bright lights at the end of a very long tunnel.

Notes

INTRODUCTION

1. "Anorexia Nervosa," NHS, https://patient.info/mental-health/eating-disorders/anorexia-nervosa.
2. Hristina Petkova et al., "Incidence of Anorexia Nervosa in Young People in the UK and Ireland: A National Surveillance Study," *BMJ* 9, no. 10 (October 22, 2019): e027339.
3. Andrew Gregory, "NHS Unable to Treat Every Child with Eating Disorder as Cases Soar," *Guardian*, January 5, 2022.
4. Denis Campbell, "One in Five Young Women Have Self-Harmed, Study Reveals," *Guardian*, June 4, 2019.
5. Andrew Gregory, "Thousands of Girls as Young as 11 in England Hiding Signs of 'Deep Distress,'" *Guardian*, February 28, 2022.
6. Ibid.

CHAPTER 1: THE TRIGGER

1. Rudolph M. Bell, *Holy Anorexia* (Chicago: University of Chicago Press, 1985).
2. Joan Jacobs Brumberg, *Fasting Girls: The History of Anorexia Nervosa* (New York: Vintage, 2000).
3. Terry Atkinson, "TV Review: 'Karen Carpenter Story': Close to Her," *Los Angeles Times*, December 31, 1988.
4. Mat Whitehead, "Experts Warn Netflix's 'To the Bone' May Be Potentially Harmful for Audiences," *Huffington Post*, July 13, 2017.
5. Mevagh Sanson, Deryn Strange, and Maryanne Garry, "Trigger Warnings Are Trivially Helpful at Reducing Negative Affect, Intrusive Thoughts, and Avoidance," *Clinical Psychological Science* 7, no. 4 (March 2019): 778–93.

CHAPTER 3: CHILDHOOD

1. Rudolph M. Bell, *Holy Anorexia* (Chicago: University of Chicago Press, 1985).
2. Samuel Fenwick, *On Atrophy of the Stomach and on the Nervous Affections of the Digestive Organs* (London: J & A Churchill, 1880).
3. Hilde Bruch, *The Golden Cage: The Enigma of Anorexia Nervosa* (Cambridge, MA: Harvard University Press, 1978).
4. J. Hubert Lacey, "Anorexia Nervosa and a Bearded Female Saint," *British Medical Journal* 285, no. 6357 (December 18, 1982): 1816–17.
5. Maria Makino, Koji Tsuboi, and Lorraine Dennerstein, "Prevalence of Eating Disorders: A Comparison of Western and Non-Western Countries," *Medscape General Medicine* 6, no. 3 (September 2004): 49.
6. Zhen Hadassah Cheng et al., "Ethnic Differences in Eating Disorder Prevalence, Risk Factors, and Predictive Effects of Risk Factors Among Young Women," *Eating Behaviors* 32 (January 2019): 23–30.
7. Anne E. Becker et al., "Ethnicity and Differential Access to Care for Eating Disorder Symptoms," *International Journal of Eating Disorders* 33, no. 2 (March 2003): 205–12.
8. Margarita Sala et al., "Race, Ethnicity and Eating Disorder Recognition by Peers," *Eating Disorders* 21, no. 5 (2013): 423–36.
9. Pat Gibbons, "The Relationship Between Eating Disorders and Socioeconomic Status: It's Not What You Think," *Nutrition Noteworthy* 4, no. 1 (2001).
10. W. H. Kaye et al., "Altered Serotonin Activity in Anorexia Nervosa After Long-Term Weight Restoration. Does Elevated Cerebrospinal Fluid 5-Hydroxyindoleacetic Acid Level Correlate with Rigid and Obsessive Behavior?," *Archives of General Psychiatry* 48, no. 6 (June 1991): 556–62.
11. Ibid.
12. Walter H. Kaye, Julie L. Fudge, and Martin Paulus, "New Insights into Symptoms and Neurocircuit Function of Anorexia Nervosa," *Nature Reviews Neuroscience* 10, no. 8 (August 2009): 573–84.

13. P. Gorwood et al., "The 5-HT2A-1438G/A Polymorphism in Anorexia Nervosa: A Combined Analysis of 316 Trios from Six European Centers," *Molecular Psychiatry* 7, no. 1 (January 2002): 90–94.

14. Ursula F. Bailer et al., "Amphetamine Induced Dopamine Release Increases Anxiety in Individuals Recovered from Anorexia Nervosa," *International Journal of Eating Disorders* 45, no. 2 (March 2012): 263–71.

15. Dimitrios Kontis and Eirini Theochari, "Dopamine in Anorexia: A Systematic Review," *Behavioural Pharmacology* 23, nos. 5–6 (September 2012): 496–515.

16. Drew Westen and Jennifer Harnden-Fischer, "Personality Profiles in Eating Disorders," *American Journal of Psychiatry* 158, no. 4 (April 2001): 547–62.

17. Helen Bould et al., "The Influence of School on Whether Girls Develop Eating Disorders," *International Journal of Epidemiology* 45, no. 2 (April 2016): 480–88.

18. Anna M. Bardone-Cone et al., "The Inter-relationships Between Vegetarianism and Eating Disorders Among Females," *Journal of the Academy of Nutrition and Dietetics* 112, no. 8 (August 2012): 1247–52.

19. Azeen Ghorayshi, "Puberty Starts Earlier Than It Used To. No One Knows Why," *New York Times*, May 19, 2022.

CHAPTER 4: THE SPLITTING

1. Joan Jacobs Brumberg, *Fasting Girls: The History of Anorexia Nervosa* (New York: Vintage, 2000).

2. Youssef Kouidrat et al., "Eating Disorders in Schizophrenia: Implications for Research and Management," *Schizophrenia Research and Treatment*, November 18, 2014, 791573.

3. Johanna Keeler et al., "Hippocampal Volume, Function and Related Molecular Activity in Anorexia Nervosa: A Scoping Review," *Expert Review of Clinical Pharmacology* 13, no. 12 (December 2020): 1367–87.

CHAPTER 7: MOTHERS AND THE WOMAN PROBLEM

1. Hilde Bruch, *The Golden Cage: The Enigma of Anorexia Nervosa* (Cambridge, MA: Harvard University Press, 1978).

2. Anne Harrington, "The Fall of the Schizophrenogenic Mother," *Lancet* 379, no. 9823 (April 7, 2012): 1292–93.

3. Phillip Inman, "Three-quarters of Mothers Now in Work, Figures Reveal," *Guardian*, October 24, 2019.

4. Juliana Menasce Horowitz, "Despite Challenges at Home and Work, Most Working Moms and Dads Say Being Employed Is What's Best for Them," Pew Research Center, September 12, 2019.

5. George Guilder, "Women in the Work Force," *Atlantic*, September 1986.

6. J. Hubert Lacey, "Anorexia Nervosa and a Bearded Female Saint," *British Medical Journal* 285, no. 6357 (December 18, 1982): 1816–17.

7. Hilary Mantel, "Some Girls Want Out," *London Review of Books*, March 4, 2004.

8. Emma Hartley, "Why Do So Many Teenage Girls Want to Change Gender?," *Prospect*, April 2020.

9. "Gender Identity Development Service Referrals in 2019–20 Same as 2018–19," Gender Identify Development Service, https://tavistockandportman.nhs.uk/about-us/news/stories/gender-identity-development-service-referrals-2019-20-same-2018-19/.

10. Andrew Gregory, "Thousands of Girls as Young as 11 in England Hiding Signs of 'Deep Distress,'" *Guardian*, February 28, 2022.

11. See, e.g., Kathrin Nickel et al., "Systematic Review: Overlap Between Eating, Autism Spectrum, and Attention-Deficit/Hyperactivity Disorder," *Frontiers in Psychiatry* 10 (October 10, 2019): 708; and Varun Warrier et al., "Elevated Rates of Autism, Other Neurodevelopmental and Psychiatric Diagnoses, and Autistic Traits in Transgender and Gender-Diverse Individuals," *Nature Communications* 11, no. 1 (August 2020): 3959.

12. Vicky Holt, Elin Skagerberg, and Michael Dunsford, "Young People with Features of Gender Dysphoria: Demographics and Associated Difficulties," *Clinical Child Psychology and Psychiatry* 21, no. 1 (January 2016): 108–18.

13. Elizabeth W. Diemer et al., "Gender Identity, Sexual Orientation and Eating-Related Pathology in a National Sample of College Students," *Journal of Adolescent Health* 57, no. 2 (August 2015): 144–49.

14. Carly E. Guss et al., "Disordered Weight Management Behaviors, Nonprescription Steroid Use, and Weight Perception in Transgender Youth," *Journal of Adolescent Health* 60, no. 1 (January 2017): 17–22.

15. I contacted multiple UK organizations for LGBT people and trans youth, including Stonewall, Mermaids, the Mosaic Trust and the Tavistock and Portland Trust, to ask about overlaps between gender dysphoria and eating disorders, and whether a young person's gender dysphoria can ever be an expression of anxiety and unhappiness, as anorexia is. None would talk to me.

16. See, e.g., Bethany Alice Jones et al., "Body Dissatisfaction and Disordered Eating in Trans People: A Systematic Review of the Literature," *International Review of Psychiatry* 28, no. 1 (November 30, 2015): 81–94.

17. "Statement in Response to Coverage of DfE Guidance in the Mail on Sunday," Mermaids, https://mermaidsuk.org.uk/news/statement-in-response-to-mail-on-sunday-and-sunday-times-coverage-of-dfe-guidance/.

18. Ibid.

19. Elizabeth Sweet, "Toys Are More Divided by Gender Now than They Were 50 Years Ago," *Atlantic*, December 9, 2014.

20. Carol J. Auster and Claire S. Mansbach, "The Gender Marketing of Toys: An Analysis of Color and Type of Toy on the Disney Store Website," *Sex Roles* 67, nos. 7–8 (2012): 375–88.

21. Andrea Long Chu, *Females* (London: Verso, 2019).

22. "A lot of gay men are gay men as a consolation prize because they couldn't be a woman." Matt Cain, interview with Juno Dawson, by *Attitude*, Summer 2017.

23. Sam Ashworth-Hayes, "Detransitioners Should Sue the NHS," *Critic*, June 30, 2022.

24. Deborah Cohen and Hannah Barnes, "Gender Dysphoria in Children: Puberty Blockers Study Draws Further Criticism," *BMJ*, September 20, 2019.

25. "Treatment: Gender Dysphoria," NHS, https://www.nhs.uk/conditions/gender-dysphoria/treatment/.

26. Azeen Ghorayshi, "Doctors Debate Whether Trans Teens Need Therapy Before Hormones," *New York Times*, January 13, 2022.

27. *File on 4*, Radio 4, November 26, 2019.

28. A. Hutchinson and M. Midgen, "The 'Natal Female' Question," Woman's Place UK, February 17, 2020, https://womansplaceuk.org/2020/02/17/the-natal-female-question/.

CHAPTER 10: FRITHA'S STORY

1. Sarah Marsh, "Suicides Linked to Acne Drug Roaccutane as Regulator Reopens Inquiry," *Guardian*, December 27, 2019.

2. Michael Coveney, "Fritha Goodey," *Guardian*, September 10, 2004.

3. Luke Leitch and Justin Davenport, "Suicide Actress 'Terrified of Failure,'" *Evening Standard*, September 8, 2004.

4. Di Trevis, "Fritha Goodey," *Independent*, September 13, 2004.

CHAPTER 12: BEDLAM

1. Glenda Cooper, "Doctors Get Right to Force-Feed Anorexic Patients," *Independent*, August 6, 1997.

CHAPTER 13: GERALDINE'S STORY

1. Rachel Williams, "NHS Manager Preyed on Clinic's Patients, Inquiry Finds," *Guardian*, July 17, 2008.

CHAPTER 16: HOME AND BOARDING SCHOOL

1. Lisa R. Lilenfeld and Walter H. Kaye, "The Link Between Alcoholism and Eating Disorders," *Alcohol Health and Research World* 20, no. 2 (January 1996): 94–99.

CHAPTER 17: UNIVERSITY

1. "Thinking About the Body," Gender Identity Development Service," https://gids.nhs.uk/puberty-and-physical-intervention.

2. Polly Carmichael et al., "Short-Term Outcomes of Pubertal Suppression in a Selected Cohort of 12 to 15 Year Old Young

People with Persistent Gender Dysphoria in the UK," *PLOS One* 16, no. 2 (February 2, 2021): e0243894.

3. Guido Giovanardi, "Buying Time or Arresting Development? The Dilemma of Administering Hormone Blockers in Trans Children and Adolescents," *Porto Biomedical Journal* 2, no. 5 (September–October 2017): 153–56.

CHAPTER 18: FASHION

1. Lydia Spencer-Elliott, "Victoria Beckham Leaves Fans in Disbelief as She Reveals Her Favorite Meal Is SALT on Whole Grain Toast," *Daily Mail*, September 29, 2021.

CHAPTER 19: AMANDA'S STORY

1. Ängla Mantel et al., "Analysis of Neurodevelopmental Disorders in Offspring of Mothers with Eating Disorders in Sweden," *JAMA Network Open* 5, no. 1 (January 2022): e2143947.

About the Author

Hadley Freeman is a columnist and features writer for the *Sunday Times* in London. Before that, she spent twenty-two years at the *Guardian*, where she won several awards, including, most recently, Best Columnist. Her previous book, *House of Glass*, was a best seller and has been published in multiple countries. She was born in New York City, and she lives in London with her partner and their three children.